Contents

Foreword

I can think of no more suitable expert to write a book covering this area of gymnastics, than Anton Gajdos - International Gymnast, Coach and young academic when the then 'Czechoslovakia' was one of the greatest gymnastic nations of the World.

At that time contributions made by the great gymnasts - Vera Cáslavská, Jaroslav Statsny; coaches - Vladimir Prorok, Ladislav Pazdera; scientist - Gustav Hruby, to name but a few, were not only prolific, but of such value that they influenced both the author and the development of new schools of gymnastics throughout the World.

During the last decades, there has been no 'letting-up' in the research and interest of Anton.

Anton Gajdos has become a most respected and much translated writer on the techniques and development of gymnastics.

This, his latest book, is a *must* for gymnast, coach and lovers and followers of this beautiful sport.

John Atkinson MBE FNASC
Technical Director, British Gymnastics

Acknowledgements

The British Gymnastics Association and the authors would like to acknowledge financial support from:

    The United Kingdom Sports Council
    The Sports Science Support Programme of the National Coaching Foundation

and the help and cooperation of the following people and organisations in the production of this book:

    The Fédération Internationale de Gymnastique
    Dr David Kerwin, SSSP Project Director, Loughborough University
    Mark Brewin, SSSP Project Assistant, Loughborough University
    Loughborough University Audio Visual Services
    Mr John Atkinson MBE FNASC, Technical Director, British Gymnastics

Comments and correspondence relating to this book should be addressed to:

    Professor Dr Anton Gajdos
    c/o Trevor Low
    Main Street
    Bruntingthorpe
    Leicestershire
    LE17 5QF
    ENGLAND.

The Authors

Professor Dr Anton Gajdos: Author

I was born on June 1, 1940. I actively went in for gymnastics since my childhood. I used to compete in gymnastic events at school. I won the school Championship and junior competitions in the district I was living. I won the title of the Absolute Champion of Slovakia in the year 1960. In that time, I was the trainer of young gymnasts in the University sport club, SLAVIA Bratislava, which was one of the best teams not only in Slovakia, but in Czechoslovakia as well.

After graduation I became a member of our best sports club, DUKLA Prague, and for two years I participated in many top class competitions. Between the years 1964-1991 I was working as an assistant lecturer and Associate Professor in the Faculty of Physical Education and Sport at Comenius University in Bratislava. There I was lecturing on the theory and practice of gymnastics at the Department of Theory and Methodology of Gymnastics.

I led the training of our university gymnastic team, Slavia UK. This team was one of the best in our country and has won many successes. A member of my team was selected into the CSSR gymnastic team for the 1968 Olympic Games in Mexico. He was the Czechoslovakian Champion on floor exercise. Two others were members of the Czechoslovak 'B' team. Having been invited by the Belgian Royal Gymnastic Federation I trained the top Belgian male and female gymnasts before World Championships in Ljubljana, 1970. At 1971-72 I was working as an assistant lecturer at the Faculty of Physical Education and Sport in Baghdad, Iraq. From 1962 to 1989 I was a special observer and gymnastic commentator during World Championships and Olympic Games for the Czechoslovakian TV.

I performed the duties of the member of Technical Committee for men's gymnastics, the trainer of the University team, and the trainer of the Slovak national team. I have been the chief of Scientific-Methodical Section of the Czechoslovakian Gymnastic Federation in the Technical Committee for many years. I was a member of the editorial staff of the Czechoslovak professional gymnastic journal 'Sportovni a Moderni Gymnastika' (Artistic and Rhythmic Gymnastics) as well as the professional sport journal 'Tréner' (The Trainer).

I was an international judge in the 1970s. In addition to the pedagogical work at the Faculty, I lectured at various classes for the trainers of gymnastics. I studied for the Doctor of Philosophy in 1969. My thesis, 'The Theory of Teaching the Physical Training', dealt with the questions of sport preparation in top gymnasts. I obtained the title 'Candidate of Science' (C.Sc.). The topic of this dissertation work was the 'Evaluation of training load and its impact on the performance of the 11-18 year old gymnasts'. That was in 1978.

Professor Dr Anton Gajdos: Author.

In 1990 I obtained the title 'Associate Professor' (Dozent) and the topic of the work was the 'The evolution tendencies of the training load in men's and women's artistic gymnastics'.

I have written a number of professional and popular essays and articles published in home and foreign journals. I lectured the system of preparation in artistic gymnastics at the World Congress in Montreal in 1985. I have been the member of the state research team on the topics of the training system in artistic gymnastics. My practical experiences and results of the research work I summarized in my 300 page book, 'The training in artistic gymnastics', that has been published in Slovak language in 1980 and translated into French and German languages. I am engaged in the research of efficiency of sport preparation and prognosis of exercise content for all groups of performance, from beginners up to the top gymnasts.

From August 1990 until June 1991, I was an Associate Professor in the Physical Education Department at Slippery Rock University in Pennsylvania, USA where I also taught artistic gymnastics to both male and female students. From September 1991 until December 1991, I was as Associate Professor in the Jyvaskyla University, Finland.

In December 1992 I lectured at the Universities of Lisbon, Vila Real, as well as to trainers for the whole of Portugal. Mainly, I lectured about the systems of sport preparation in artistic gymnastics. In November 1993 I lectured for the specialists students of the

Hungarian University of Physical Education in Budapest.

Until 1994 I summarized the topic: 'Prognosis of the capacity of the sport preparation of the top gymnasts' and I taught as an Associate Professor at the University of Nitra, Department of Physical Education.

On March 14th, 1996 I finished my dissertation under the title: Research Aspects of Improvement of Contents and Prognosis of the World Artistic Gymnastics. I defended my research work in front of the research committee of the Academy of Physical Education and Sport in St. Petersburg, Russia. I received the highest research title, Doctor of Science.

At the present time I am General Director of the Institute for Language and Academic Preparation for Foreign Students at Comenius University, Bratislava.

Trevor Low: Editor & Co-Author

As a gymnast and coach I spent many frustrating hours searching through libraries to find useful and technical information on the sport of gymnastics. With a successful club of gymnasts to cater for I realised the need to have at hand the latest research and a selective bookshelf of practical material. This led in 1982 to the publication of GRASP, the Technical Journal for People which has, through 10 volumes, given coaches a "hands on" manual of skill progressions and tested theories for teaching and coaching gymnastics. In 1984 I became editor of The Gymnast, the official magazine of the British Gymnastics Association. I am still, after many many years of attending local, national and international tournaments, an addicted "gymnastics watcher".

I am organising the building of a second training hall for Hinckley Gymnastics Club, where I remain at the sharp end of the sport, coaching members of the Great Britain, England, Scotland and Wales men's and junior teams around a timetable of pre-school, recreational and club gymnasts.

One Hundred Years of Gymnastics at the Olympic Games

By Professor Dr Anton Gajdos
Olympic Games in Athens, 1896

The entire Greek nation welcomed the news of the continuation of the Olympic Games and Athens became the organiser with great enthusiasm despite the fact that there was not an ideal atmosphere in the country at the time. It is true that the government under the leadership of Prime Minister Trikupis stood in opposition to the Games. Prince Constantin of Greece became the President of the Organising Committee and at the initial meeting on November 12th 1894, they decided on the period from April 5th to 15th 1896 to hold the Games. Preparatory work for the Games started but internal intrigues plagued the effort. Ferenc Kemeny, a Hungarian member of the International Olympic Committee, officially announced that the Olympic Games should take place in Budapest as a part of the 1000 year celebrations of the foundation of the national state.

The Greek Prince Constantin, however, insisted that the Games take place in Athens. Money for the organisation of the Games was obtained through a request for public donations and special commemorative stamps were printed and sold. The most wealthy Greek banker, Jorge Averoff, heard of this and offered the financial support for the reconstruction of the Olympic Stadium.

The gymnastic competition took place in the open air Olympic Stadium. Seventy five gymnasts competed in the Games. The parallel bars and high bar competitions were quite interesting. For the six individual apparatus: high bar, parallel bars, pommel horse, rings, vault and rope-climbing, only gold and silver medals were awarded.

The winner of the rings was the Greek Ioannis Mitropulos. Also in this particular competition, the German Weingartner completed the difficult element known as the Cross. The German team was very talented and consisted of ten gymnasts. The captain of the team, Fritz Hoffman, finished second in the 100 m (100 yards) sprint, in a time of 12.2 seconds, to the American winner Burke. Hoffman also finished third in the 400 m (440 yards) with a time of 55.6 seconds and fourth in the high jump with a height of 170 cm. Carl Schumann won four medals and was the most successful athlete of these Games. He took his fourth medal in open-style wrestling, when he beat the Greek giant George Tsitasa, who stood a full head taller than Schuhmann. The brothers Alfred and Gustav Flatow of the German team competed with Alfred taking gold medal on the parallel bars. Interestingly, these brothers would leave Germany for Holland thirty-five years later during the Fascist period. The Gestapo found them and Gustav died in a concentration camp in Terezin on 29th January 1945, while Alfred was lucky enough to survive. For these first Games compulsory routines were not required.

Olympic Games in Paris, 1900

Pierre de Coubertin conceived that the second Olympic Games should take place in Paris at the site of the World Exhibition. Coubertin was not enthusiastic, however, after speaking to the Director of the World Exhibition, Alfred Picard. Picard promised his complete support but lacked the desire to support the Olympic Spirit. He imagined that the Olympic Games would involve fishing, three-legged races and billiards. Picard changed the rowing competition into lifeboat exercises. Due to the protests of the International Sports Federations and Coubertin, the French Sports Federation rejected these changes and turned its back on Picard. For every activity of the World Exhibition awards were given but the winners of Olympic Games competitions only received token gifts.

The programme of the Olympic Games lasted many months but the main goal of Picard was the advertisement of the World Exhibition. The Games started on 20th May 1900 with sailing competitions in Maulan and ended on 28th October with a rugby match between France and Great Britain in Paris.

134 gymnasts took part in gymnastic competition: 112 French, 9 Germans, 5 British, 3 Belgians, 2 Swiss, one Italian, one Hungarian and one Czech. There was no team competition because each country wanted to compete in their own system. Therefore, gymnasts competed only in individual events: high bar, parallel bars, vault, pommel horse, floor exercise, long jump, rope climbing, long and high jump, pole vault, and 50 kg weight lifting. The judges were able to award a maximum of 20 points and the gymnasts could gain a total of 320 points. Hugo Peitsch, a German from Berlin, finished with the best score for a foreigner while coming 29th overall. Peitsch completed his high bar routine with a double somersault and he received the maximum 20 points.

The following events were compulsory during these Games:

Pommel horse:
From a parallel stand, grasping pommels, jump to one and one half circle to right to rear support, single leg cut with left to rear, scissor backward to right, scissor backward to left, single leg cut with right to rear, three double leg circles clockwise, double rear from pommel to end of horse, rear dismount.

Rings:
From a front hang pike hang, backward swing, Felge upward swing to handstand, lower to free support scale, hold, slowly lower to hanging front scale, hold, backswing, inlocate to pike hang, kip uprise to 'L' support, straddle dismount.

Parallel bars:

Cross stand at end of bars facing inward, jump, straddle cut mount to 'L' support, hold, double leg circle clockwise over right bar to front support, backswing, through bent arm support, jump to straight arm 'L' support, hold, press with bent arms and straight body to handstand, hold, lower to shoulder stand, hold, lower to pike underarm support, kip uprise to support, backswing, straddle cut to 'L' support, hold, backswing to underarm support, back shoulder roll to support, drop to pike hang, kip uprise to support, backswing, double rear dismount.

Horizontal bar:

From hang frontway with overgrip, Stemme backward to support, flank cut to rear support, drop to rear and underswing forward, Stemme backward to free support scale with bent arms, hold, back hip circle, lower to hanging scale frontway, hold, hang, pull uprise to support, press with bent arms and straight body to handstand, squat dismount.

Olympic Games in St. Louis, 1904

Despite the adventures in Paris there was still a strong Olympic movement which led to discussion of the location for the next Olympic Games. Everyone thought that the next Games would take place in the United States and Coubertin believed that this would spread the Olympic movement worldwide.

In Paris on 21st May 1901, the International Olympic Committee decided that the third Olympic Games would occur in Chicago in 1904. U.S. President William McKinley became the honorary head of these Games, but soon after he was assassinated, and the new President, Theodore Roosevelt, was very pleased that the Games would take place in the United States. The preparation for the Games, however, experienced some difficulties. In 1903 to celebrate the inclusion of Louisiana in the United States the World Exhibition was planned to occur in St. Louis. Preparation was delayed and the start of the celebration was put back to 1904.

Through the order of the President these events were scheduled to take place together in St. Louis. By a unanimous vote by the members of the Olympic committee the location of St. Louis was established.

The situation was different than it had been in Paris. The President of the World Exhibition also served as the leader of the organization of the Olympic Games but the control of each competition was left in the hands of specialists. The programme followed the pattern of Paris by taking several months to complete. The Games began on 1st July with the gymnastic competition and finished on 23rd November with the football tournament. The organization of the Games was better than it had been in Paris but the second combination of the Olympic Games and the World Exhibition did not bring a strong Olympic spirit.

The gymnastic competition was divided into two parts, there were great differences in the final list of results. European gymnasts who had come to live in America: Germans, Norwegians and Austrians, still lacked U.S. passports but competed for minority clubs. For example, Germans claimed that gymnasts such as the Swiss Adolf Spinnler, winner of the 9 discipline competition, represented Germany because he had come to the United States with the German team. Spinnler stayed in America and returned to Switzerland after 30 years, dying in Zurich in 1951 after becoming a famous singer. There was also curiosity for the Austrian Julius Lenhart, who was at the time of the Olympics on foreign work duty in the USA. He won the 6 event individual competition as a member of the Philadelphia team, Turnverein, as well as a gold medal in the team competition. The greatest medal winner was the American Anton Heida, with possible Czech ancestry, who took gold in the team competition while winning in the pommel horse, high bar, vault and in the 7 event competition.

The gymnastic competition had a few interesting elements. For example Edward Henning took gold in baton twirling. Teams of four gymnasts had to do exercises simultaneously on four parallel and high bars. Everyone had to do two compulsory routines and one optional routine on the parallel and high bars, one compulsory vault and one compulsory and optional routine on the pommel horse.

There were nine events in all. Gymnasts could attain a maximum total 45 points with 5 points for each event. Every gymnast had to compete in three track and field events as well: shot put, long jump and the 100-yard sprint. Another Olympic Gymnastic Championship competition consisted of seven disciplines: pommel horse, vault, parallel and high bars, rings, rope climbing, and swimming. Only ten Americans competed in these events. An unbelievable feat occurred when George Eyser, who had a wooden leg, took second place to Heida. He competed in three events: shot put, long jump and finished the 100-yard dash in 15.4 seconds. Interestingly, the winner of these three events was Max Emmerich, who had the following results: 10.6 seconds in the 100-yards, 655 cm. in the long jump and 9.8 m. in the shot put.

The following events were compulsory during these Games:

Pommel horse:

From parallel stand, left hand on neck, right on left pommel with reverse grip, jump to simple Swiss to rear support on pommels, double rear from pommel to end of horse in rear support, circle clockwise, double rear to rear support on pommels, double leg circle, single leg circle with left and 180° turn to front support on pommels, double leg circle with 270° turn to left dismount.

Parallel bars:

Two routines.

Routine 1. From run, jump to centre, kip uprise to support, backswing, handstand, hold, off swing to underarm support, back shoulder roll with release to shoulderstand, hold, through bent arm support, frontswing, scissors forward to straddle sit in front of hands, hold, regrasp to rear, off swing in front, backswing, handstand, hold, frontswing, Stützkehre to support, drop to pike underarm support, kip uprise to support, backswing, handstand, hold, forward swing, rear dismount with 180° turn.

Routine 2. Cross stand at end of bars facing inward, kip uprise to 'L' support, hold, 360° turn to right over right bar, 360° turn to left over left bar to 'L' support, hold, press with straight arms and bent body to handstand, hold, through free support scale, shoulder stand, hold roll forward piked to 'L' support, hold, press to right elbow support scale, hold, slowly 90° turn to left to side scale, hold, left elbow support scale, hold, slowly 90° turn to left to side scale, hold, left elbow support scale, hold, return to front, slowly 90° turn to side scale, hold, return to front to 'L' support, hold, backswing single rear over right bar with 90° turn to left to support lying parallel on bars, straddle dismount over both bars.

Horizontal bar:

Two routines.

Routine 1. From hang front way with overgrip, frontswing, kip uprise to support, cast, back giant, back giant, at end of giant 180° to hang, stoop under bar and uprise to rear support, drop to rear, disengage bar, kip uprise to support, swing to handstand, squat dismount.

Routine 2. From hang frontway with overgrip, pull to hanging front scale, pause, pull through pike hang to back hanging scale, hold, flag scale on left, hold, flag scale on right, hold, pull uprise with turn to support, front hip circle, lower forward to inverted hang, lower to hang, dismount.

Olympic Games in London, 1908

Pierre de Coubertin looked for support for the fourth Olympic Games in Europe and found it in Rome. Support for the next Games came from Pope Pius X as well as from members of International Olympic Committees who believed that Rome should be the site of the renaissance of the Olympic spirit. Meanwhile, Coubertin conceived that Greece should be the permanent organizer of future Olympic Games and the Greeks proposed the organization of an extra Olympic Games to be held in 1906 for the 10th anniversary of the Olympic Games held in Greece in 1896. 900 athletes from 20 countries competed in these Games as members of the International Olympic Committee agreed on London as the location of the next set of Games. No one was surprised except for Coubertin. At this time there was an economic crisis occurring in Italy. London only had two years to prepare for the games. Despite the short period of time the construction of a stadium, which could hold 100,000 spectators, was completed and the rest of the planning was finished.

In the gymnastic competition, there were 106 gymnasts from 12 countries and 254 gymnasts from 8 countries in the team competition. The winning team from Sweden had 33 gymnasts while the fifth place team from France had 40 participants. In the individual competition the best gymnast was Alberto Braglia of Italy, the best overall gymnast during this period. It was interesting that the gymnastic competition took place while it was raining in the Olympic Stadium. This weather made it quite difficult for gymnasts to complete their routines. The rules for these Games were more strict but there still was not an established set of guidelines for competition. Also, at this time, the gymnastic specialists proposed that in each discipline medals should be awarded. It was conceived at this time that routines should be evaluated by difficulty and the quality of execution. This development represents a more progressive approach to gymnastics. For the London Olympic Games compulsory routines were not required.

Olympic Games in Stockholm, 1912

At the meeting of the International Olympic Committee from 27th May to the 2nd June 1909, the members decided that the fifth Olympic Games would take place in Stockholm, Sweden. On July 6th, the Olympic Games began with opening ceremonies. Sweden had prepared well for the Games by building a new Olympic Stadium which included a gymnasium for gymnastic competition.

In the gymnastic competitions, the participating countries lacked a consistent set of guidelines and so three separate categories were used: a Swedish system, a combined system and an optional system of routines and events. At the start there were 267 athletes from 12 countries. The winner of the gymnastic competition was Alberto Braglia, the famous Italian, who attained 135 points out of a maximum of 144. In the team competition, operating under the Swedish system, there were three teams consisting of 74 gymnasts. A member of the Swedish team, Claes Wersall, had five brothers in the organizing committee and so a special honorary gold medal was given to their mother. In the team competition using the combined system, five different countries took part. During 60 minutes these teams executed floor exercises or routines on different apparatus, such as running and walking. Each team could field between 16 and 40 gymnasts. Evaluation for this competition was very simple. For example, if a team of 30 gymnasts received 1,800 points and executed 6 disciplines, they would get a final score of 1,800 divided by 180 (6 disciples multiplied by 30 gymnasts) equalling 10.0 points. For the Olympic Games in Stockholm, compulsory routines were not required.

Olympic Games in Antwerp, 1920

The International Olympic Committee decided in 1911 in Budapest that the next Olympic Games would take place in Berlin in 1916. Germany showed great interest in this event and on 8th June 1913 Kaiser Wilhelm opened a new, gigantic Olympic Stadium in Berlin which could hold 60,000 spectators. Four days after the Olympic Congress took place in Paris on 28th June 1914, where several members demanded that the Games should not occur in Berlin as events occurred in Sarajevo which signalled the start of World War I. The Paris Congress was the first place where the political positions of the members encouraged a stance of political neutrality. Members of this Congress spoke with their German counterparts and believed that the Games could take place in Berlin without difficulties. It was at this time that the German army occupied Belgium. The only positive act achieved by the International Olympic Committee was the move of the centre of the International Olympic Committee to Lausanne. It was only a formality, however, because during World War I the International Olympic Committee did not meet. Despite German expectations, the War did not come to a quick end and most of the European youth were not in Olympic competitions and training but instead in trench warfare. Many famous athletes died during the course of the war. The first World War was not short as Coubertin and many others had imagined but rather it was an event which changed world history.

The meeting of the International Olympic Committee in Lausanne in 1919 was led by Swiss President, Gustav Ador, who decided that the seventh Olympic Games would take place in Antwerp. Belgium was given the location of the Olympic Games in order to boost the morale of the Belgians who had suffered the first invasion of the German army. The organisers, however, had only one year to prepare for the Games and had to construct a new stadium and other facilities. Despite the time constraint, Belgium was able to complete preparations in time for the start of the Games. Invitations were not sent to Austria, Germany, Hungary, Bulgaria and Turkey.

On 14th August 1920, the Olympic flag containing five connected rings was brandished for the first time in the Olympic Stadium. The International Gymnastic Federation was not satisfied with the programme of these Olympic Games, however, the President of the Fédération Internationale de Gymnastique (F.I.G.) was a Belgian named Cuperus. The precise guidelines for the gymnastic competition remained unsettled and the style of competition remained haphazard. The programme contained four systems: the European system of team competition, the Swedish system for team competition, the optional form of team competition and the individual form of competition. For example, in the European system of competition, the Czechoslovak team consisted of 18 members who took fourth place among the five teams competing. Part of these competitions consisted of the 110 m hurdles. The evaluation of the judges was poor during these Games. The winning team from Italy and the second place team from Belgium consisted of 28 gymnasts. There were not a great number of spectators for the gymnastic competitions because of rain and bad weather conditions.

The following events were compulsory during these Games:

Pommel horse:

From cross stand, left hand on neck, right on left pommel in reverse grip, circle of the left leg under the left and right hand with half turn to the left to side stand forwards, left hand on pommel with elgrip, right hand on the end of horse, the same exercise with right leg to the rightside, squat to 'L', rear support, single leg circle with left to rear, upswing double leg to left, single leg cut with left to rear, single leg cut with right to rear, single leg fake with left to left, single leg cut with right to right, single leg cut with right to rear, single rear dismount to the left side of the horse.

Parallel bars:

Diagonal stand in centre of bars, jump with single leg cut over back bar, backswing and scissors backward to straddle seat, off swing to front, through bent arm support, backswing, Stützkehre backward to support, 'L', hold, backswing, through bent arm support, backswing to left elbow support scale, hold, press to shoulder stand, hold, forward shoulder roll, Stemme backward to support, frontswing, backswing, through handstand front dismount, right arm on bar, left arm to the side.

Horizontal bar:

From hand front way with overgrip, 'L' hang, hold, through pike hang, pull uprise to rear support, hold, regrasp to undergrip, front hip circle in rear support, regrasp to overgrip, lower to rear to hanging rear scale, hold, pull through squat to pull over to support, drop to rear, underswing forward, backswing, frontswing with 180° turn, kip to support, drop to rear, underswing forward, backswing with 180° turn to hand in undergrip, kip uprise to support, swing to handstand, front dismount.

Olympic Games in Paris, 1924

There were several candidates applying for the position of host for the eighth Olympic Games. Among these cities were Amsterdam, Los Angeles, Rome, Barcelona and Prague. At the twelfth meeting of the Czechoslovak Olympic Committee on 19th April 1920, Dr Jiri Guth announced that the Czechoslovak government agreed that Prague could be the organizer of the next Olympic Games but there was a fear that there would not be enough money to host the Games. Los Angeles and Amsterdam were in the best positions to get the Games. It came as a great surprise when the President of the International Olympic Committee, Coubertin, announced that after the 1924 Olympic Games he would leave his position with the International Olympic Committee and that he supported Paris as the next host of the Olympic Games. The United States and Italy did not agree with this proposal but other members of International Olympic Committee respected this plan. Thus, the opening ceremonies took place on 5th July 1924, in the new stadium in the part of Paris known as Columbes. The organisers prepared the first small village near the Olympic Stadium.

There were nine teams in the gymnastic competition in Paris. Good news came from USA when it became known that three Czechs, three Germans, one Swiss and one American would compete for the USA. It was through this that Frank Kriz, 30, would be the best in the competition and he in fact won the vault with a score of 9.98. He was followed closely by Koutny with a score of 9.97. The Czechoslovak team had difficulty on the third apparatus when Indruch hurt himself and a reserve gymnast was not allowed to compete in his place. Due to this setback the Czechoslovak team had to stop competing in these Games. They only continued competing in individual events. It turned out well for the Czechoslovak team because the six members of the team took a total of nine medals during these Games. Bedrich Supcik won the first gold for Czechoslovakia in rope climbing, with a height of 9 m and a time of 7.2 seconds, at the time an unofficial world record. It was surprising when the Yugoslav Leon Stukelj, among the 72 gymnasts, won a gold medal just in front of Prazak and Supcik, both of Czechoslovakia. The Swiss gymnasts were by far the best in the pommel horse competition, taking the first four places. On the rings, the Italian Francesco Martino was the best, while the Czechs Prazak was second, Vacha was third and Supcik finished fifth. Italy won the team competition, with the Italian Mandrini coming in fourth place in the individual competition. Stukelj won the high bar with a routine that started with a uprise backward to free scale support.

The following events were compulsory during these Games:

Pommel horse:
From parallel stand left hand on right pommel, right on croup, jump to Kehre to rear

support on pommels, single leg circle with left to rear, single leg circle with right to left, two double leg circles anticlockwise, single leg cut with left to rear, upswing to right, scissors forward to left, scissors forward to right, scissors forward to left, single leg circle with left to right to front support, single leg circle with right to left, double leg circle travel down, double leg circle on end, Kehre in to rear support, single leg circle with left to right, half double leg circle clockwise to front support, double leg circle counter clockwise with 180° turn on left arm dismount, right arm on neck, stand back to horse.

Still rings:
From front hang, pull to pike hang, backswing, Stemme backward to support, Felge backward stretched to handstand, hold, lower to free support scale, hold, cross, hold, hanging scale frontway, hold, backswing, inlocate to rear hanging scale, hold, Stemme "flag" to 'L' support, hold, press with bent arms and straight body to handstand, hold, lower with bent arms to inverted hang, backswing, inlocate to pike, straddle dismount.

Parallel bars:
Cross stand at end of bars, jump, straddle cut mount to 'L' support, hold, backswing, double leg cut to left to support, backswing, double leg cut to right to support, backswing, handstand, pirouette forward, offswing to underarm support, shoulder roll backward, shoulder roll backward to bent arm support, frontswing, Stützkehre to support, 'L', hold, press to free support scale, hold, drop to pike hang, basket to underarm support, pike underarm support, backswing, forward shoulder roll, Stemme backward to support, frontswing, double rear dismount.

Horizontal bar:
From hang frontway with overgrip, frontswing, Stemme backward with double leg cut to rear support, rear hip circle in support, drop to rear, disengage feet, kip to free support scale, hold, drop to rear, underswing forward with 180° turn to mixed grip, Stemme backward to right elbow support scale, hold, 180° turn in scale, lower forward to hanging front scale, hold, squat under bar to hanging rear scale, hold, flag uprise to rear support, regrasp to undergrip, cast forward to hang, backswing with 180° turn and regrasp to overgrip, kip uprise to support, free support to handstand, back giant, cross change to two front giants, front giant, at end of giant, front dismount.

Olympic Games in Amsterdam, 1928

Coubertin, the leader of the International Olympic Committee since its beginning in 1896, left his position as President despite the concerns of the other members. On 28th May 1925, the Belgian Henri de Baillet-Latour was elected as the second President of the International Olympic Committee.

As a new Olympic Stadium in Amsterdam was being constructed, problems arose. Finally, the Olympic Stadium was completed with a capacity of 60,000 spectators. Only one Olympic athlete won more than two gold medals, the 23 year old Swiss gymnast Georges Miez who took three golds medals and one silver. The most successful part of the Czechoslovak delegation was the gymnastic team which consisted of eight members: Vacha, Loffler, Gajdos, Effenberger, Supcik, Vesely, Koutny and Tikal. These gymnasts won one gold, three silver and two bronze medals. Ladislav Vacha took the gold medal on the parallel bars. His routine was one of the most difficult. In the middle of his routine Vacha executed a salto rearward to underarm support and finished with a cartwheel. The Italian Romeo Neri also did an interesting routine on the parallel bars which included a salto rearward to support connected with another salto to underarm support. The Swiss, Eugene Mack, performed an original dismount on the parallel bars which involved a backswing to a handstand with a quarter turn, a one-handed handstand and a straddle dismount. On the high bar, Loffler executed his routine with a dismount which included a one-handed handstand and a straddle at the end. In the team competition, there was a strong struggle between the Swiss and Czechoslovak gymnastic teams. The Italian team, which had won in Stockholm, Antwerp and Paris only took sixth place in Amsterdam. In the floor exercise, the Czechoslovakian team performed a very exquisite and polished programme. In the individual competition, the Swiss, Miez won in front of his fellow countryman Hanggi and the 30 year old Stukelj of Yugoslavia. In fourth place was a rising Olympic talent, the Italian Romeo Neri. In sixth place was the 20 year old Finn Heikki Savolanen, a medical student at the time, who would participate in the fifteenth Olympic Games in Helsinki twenty-four years later, in 1952.

The Olympic Games in Amsterdam also witnessed the first women's gymnastic competition. Among the five 12 member teams, Holland was the winning team followed by Italy and Great Britain.

The following events were compulsory during these Games:

Pommel horse:
From cross stand, left hand on right pommel, right on croup, wendeswing with 90° turn to right to front support on pommels, one and one half double leg circles to rear support, single leg cut with right to left, scissor forward to right, single leg cut with left to

front, single leg cut with left to right, scissor forward to left, single leg cut with right to front , double leg circle anticlockwise, single leg cut with right to left, upswing to right, scissors backward to left, single leg cut with right to rear, double leg circle travel down, Kehre in, rear dismount with 90° turn, right sidearm.

Still rings:

From front hang, pull with straight body Felge upward to 'L' support, press straight body and bent arms to handstand, hold, lower to free support scale, hold, lower to hanging scale rearway, hold, pull to inverted hang, lower to hanging scale frontway, backswing, inlocate to pike hang, backswing, frontswing, Felge upward swing to handstand, hold, with insteps against straps, lower through inverted cross to inverted hang, close legs, pike hang, backswing, inlocate to pike hang, straddle dismount.

Parallel bars:

From cross stand at end of bars facing outward, grasp in outer grip, jump, basket to handstand, through bent arm support, frontswing, Stützkehre to support, drop to pike hang, kip uprise to support, backswing, handstand, hold, lower to shoulder stand, forward shoulder roll to Stemme backward with straddle cut forward to support, offswing to underarm support, back shoulder roll to shoulder stand, hold, press with bent arms and straight body to handstand, hold, salto rearward to underarm support, Stemme forward to support, rear vault with 90° turn to 'L' hang on one bar, pull uprise support, regrasp left to undergrip and press with straight arms and bent body to handstand, half pirouette forward to handstand on both bars, cartwheel dismount.

Horizontal bar:

From hang frontway with overgrip, frontswing, Stemme backward to Stalder support, drop terror, disengage legs and kip uprise, backswing to handstand, back giant, cross change on second giant to undergrip, front giant, at end of second giant, squat through to rear support, front seat circle, eagle swing forward, Stemme backward with change to overgrip, back hip circle in free support, underswing, Stemme backward, flank dismount.

Olympic Games in Los Angeles, 1932

The Americans made excellent preparations for their second Olympic Games with the hope of improving the impression left by the less than ideal conditions of the Olympic Games in St. Louis. Over the course of two years an Olympic Stadium, named the Colliseum, was constructed which could hold 105,000 spectators. A novelty of these Games was the Olympic Village which consisted of 500 Swedish cottages located about 20 km outside Los Angeles in Baldwin Hill. For the first time at the Olympics the national anthems of winners were played. Due to an economic crisis brought by the Great Depression, President Hoover was not able to come to officially open the Games. Travel across the Atlantic Ocean was very expensive for Europeans and so many countries only sent one athlete as a symbol of their nations. This was the case for Czechoslovakia, who only sent seven athletes and no gymnasts, despite the fact that in the past and at the time Czechoslovakia had the best gymnastic team.

The gymnastic competition included 46 gymnasts from 7 countries. In the team competition there were only five teams but each team only had four members. Italy had a prime opportunity to do well in the gymnastic competition because athletes from Switzerland, Czechoslovakia and Yugoslavia were not present to compete. Romeo Neri won the individual competition including the gold medal in the parallel bars. The Hungarian Istvan Pelle won two gold and two silver medals. These Games also included the first participation of Japan, who learned quite a bit about gymnastic techniques and competitions. In the individual competition, Georges Miez of Switzerland, upon learning that his score on the floor exercise was only good enough for the silver medal, protested by not taking part in the rest of the Olympics. It was a great surprise when the American Dallas Bixler was victorious in the high bar competition. The Finnish Savolainen and Terasvorta finished with the same score of 54.2 in the high bar and were told that they must repeat their routine. Terasvirta, however, refused to repeat the event and so the silver medal went to nine year older Savolainen. The Twenty year old Italian Guglielmetti surprised everyone by winning the vault competition. The gymnastic competition in Los Angeles was not ideal because many of the best European Gymnasts did not take part in the games.

The following events were compulsory during these Games:

Pommel horse:

From parallel stand, left hand on neck, right on left pommel, jump to Kehre in to rear support on pommels, double leg circle clockwise, Kehre out to rear support on neck, one and one half double leg circle clockwise on neck to front support, single leg circle with right to left, Kehre in to rear support on pommels, single leg circle with left to right, single leg cut with right to rear, single leg cut with left to front, scissor forward to right, scissor forward to left, single leg cut with right to front, single leg circle with right to left, three double leg circles counter clockwise, single leg cut with left to rear, single leg cut with right to rear, three double leg circles clockwise, Kehre out to rear support on neck, Schwaben flank dismount, back to horse.

Parallel bars:

From parallel stand at centre facing bars, in undergrip, jump to support and press with straight arms and bent body straddle to handstand on one bar, close legs and half pirouette to handstand, hold, lower to free support scale, hold, swing to 'L', drop rearward to basket to underarm support, frontswing to piked underarm support, backswing, Stemme backward with 180° turn, backswing to handstand, hold, frontswing through bent arm support and hop with 90° turn to outside of bars to front hanging scale, hold, through 'L' hang, pull uprise to support, backswing with half pirouette to handstand on both bars, hold, lower to shoulder stand and roll forward to Stemme backward to handstand, offswing to underarm support, frontswing to piked underarm support, backswing, Stemme backward to free scale support, pause, with 90° turn, straddle dismount over left bar, back to bar.

Still rings:

From front hang, pull to hanging scale frontway, hold, pull to inverted hang, hold, pike hang, stretch forward to hanging scale frontway, lower to hang, pull through cross to support, drop rearward to pike hang, back kip to handstand, hold, lower to free support scale, hold, lower to hanging scale rearway, hold, dislocate rearward, frontswing, Felge swing upward to 'L' support, press with straight arms and bent body to handstand, hold, fall forward with bent arms to backswing, Stemme backward to support, lower through cross to hanging scale frontway, hold, backswing, inlocate, straddle dismount.

Horizontal bar:

From hang frontway with mix grip, left under, frontswing, Stemme backward, Kehre in to rear support, back seat circle, drop to rear, disengage legs, kip uprise, forward hip circle, change to undergrip, two front giants, at end of second, stoop to support standing on bar, front sole circle, swing to handstand, two front giants, at end of second giant, change to overgrip in support, underswing with 180° turn to mixed grip, high frontswing with 180° turn, two back giants, cross change to handstand in undergrip, two front giants, at end of second giant, straddle dismount.

Olympic Games in Berlin, 1936

In Barcelona in 1931, it was decided that the eleventh Olympic Games would take place in Berlin. While the Nazi party was at first against the Olympic Games, Hitler soon changed their feelings upon taking power. Hitler believed that the Olympic Games was an opportunity for him to push forward his ideology and regime. At the meeting of the International Olympic Committee in Vienna in 1933, many members questioned whether Jewish athletes would be permitted to compete in the Games. The German member Theodor Lewald assured everyone that the Berlin Olympics would take place with the principle of equal participation and with the absence of discrimination. While the members of the International Olympic Committee were satisfied at the time with the situation, 1933 saw Germany expel all Jewish athletes from the German Sports Federations. Important people from cultural and sports fields were very upset with these developments and suggested that the Games take place in another country. Despite the strong opposition to the Olympic preparations in Berlin, the President of the International Olympic Committee, Baillet-Latour, shocked everyone by announcing a personal meeting with Hitler where Latour said, "I have the honour to inform you that I had a meeting with the German Chancellor and he promised me that he would guarantee that the Games would take place following the spirit and intent of the Olympic Charter. There is no support among the membership of the International Olympic Committee for a boycott of these Games.". The leadership of the Games was under the control of the army and secret police, who took steps to stop any opposition within Germany. While preparations took place in Berlin with some degree of optimism, there was also a strong sense of danger and doubt about the Games.

In the gymnastic competition there were fourteen teams and 111 individual gymnasts. The German gymnasts experienced the most success and benefited from being at home. The hero of the Games was Goerges Miez, who managed to take the gold in the floor exercise after 12 years of competing. He said, "We had minimal time for learning the difficult elements of the routines. From Monday through Saturday, I worked as a teacher. At one o'clock, I would go by train from Chiasse to Zurich, which lasted six hours, and then I would train until ten o'clock at night, sleep there, train the next day again and return to Chiasse that night. My team mate Edi Steinemann also trained in this fashion, working all week as a blacksmith and only training at the weekend.".

Alois Hudec, winner of the gold on the rings, recalls his experience in Berlin, "The judges were terrible. Most of them were Germans and they favoured the home gymnasts. This situation did not help us in our efforts to reach the finals of the competition. Our scores were between 8 and 9 points even though we performed very good routines. When I executed my routine on the rings, I received 9.4 and wished to repeat my routine because I did not feel that that score would be good enough for a medal. Everyone was surprised at my request but I received a 9.663 on my second effort. From the second discipline, I stayed in first place until the final event, the vault. At this point, the judges were not satisfied with my position and I soon dropped to third place. I was most successful on the rings. When I started my routine, all 20,000 spectators became silent. When I jumped to the rings, I hung there for a few moments. I increased the pause in the difficult crossing technique from three to six seconds in order to impress the judges. When I finished my routine everyone applauded. I got a score of 9.8 on the optional ring routine, which was combined with the compulsory routine, for a total score of 19.433. This was good enough for the gold medal. I received a special award, the book entitled 'Olympia'."

During this time the newspapers wrote that Hudec was not only the best on the rings, but also on the parallel bars, as well as being a gymnast of the highest ability and skills. "We finished second and took the silver medal in the team competition," said Marie Vetrovska Siroka, a member of Czechoslovak team, "....even though most experts knew that we were the best!" The atmosphere in Berlin was not ideal for the foreign athletes. Due to the favouritism of the judges the German team finished first at the Berlin Games.

The following events were compulsory during these Games:

Pommel horse:
From parallel stand, grasp pommels, jump and single leg cut with right to left, scissor backward to right, single leg cut with left to rear, travel down to rear support on end, single leg cut with right to left, Kehre in to rear support on pommels, one half double leg circle, single leg cut with right to front, scissor forward to left, single leg cut with left to right. one and one half double leg circles clockwise, single leg cut with right to rear, scissor backward to left, scissor backward to right, single leg cut with left to rear, two double leg circles anticlockwise, Kehre out, Deutsch to flank dismount.

Still rings:
From front hang, pull with straight body to inverted hang, back kip to 'L' support, hold, press with bent body and straight arms to handstand, hold, lower to free support scale, hold, cross, hold, lower to hanging scale frontway, pause, backswing inlocate with straight body, backswing, Stemme backward to support, Felge swing upward to handstand, hold, lower through free support scale to 'L' support, offswing, frontswing, dislocate rearward, straddle dismount.

Parallel bars:
From parallel stand at side of bars with mixed grips, jump, front vault with 90° turn to right to support, drop to rear, basket to hang, glide kip to 'L' support, hold, press with

bent arms and straight body to handstand, hold, reverse pirouette, frontswing, drop to rear, cast to underarm support, Stemme backward with half turn to support, backswing, handstand with quarter turn to handstand on one bar, straddle dismount.

Horizontal bar:

From hang frontway with undergrip, frontswing, Stemme backward with pirouette to handstand, drop to rear, disengage legs, stoop through the rear uprise to rear support, flank to rear to support, underswing with 180° turn to mixed grip, frontswing to handstand, two front giants, early pirouette, two front giants, at end of second giant, stoop through, front seat circle, dismount forward.

Olympic Games in London, 1948

At the closing ceremonies of the Berlin Olympics, the President of the International Olympic Committee, Baillet-Latour, thanked the organizers of the Games and invited all athletes and coaches to meet at the 1940 Olympic Games in Tokyo and Sapporo, not aware that there would not be a meeting until twelve years later. Following these Games, Hitler started to occupy neighbouring countries and the Second World War began on 1st September 1939, after the German invasion of Poland. The greatest war in history followed with over 50 million deaths and with around 12 million people dying in concentration camps.

Among the many victims of the war were some of the world's greatest gymnasts. For example, Frantisek Pechacek and Ladislav Vacha of Czechoslovakia died while Jan Gajdos suffered through his experience in a concentration camp and died soon after the war. Twice Olympic Champion Viktor Cukarin of the USSR spent many years in concentration camps but went on to compete in future Olympic Games. These are only a few examples of gymnasts who suffered and perished during the Second World War.

The Games scheduled for 1944 in London were also postponed due to the war. In 1945 the new President of the International Olympic Committee, Edstrom, and the other members of this Committee decided to hold the fourteenth Olympic Games in London. The bad economic situation and other postwar problems prevented a smooth preparation for the up coming Games. The organizers did not have time to build a new Olympic Stadium or an Olympic Village to house athletes. The main activities of these games took place at the Empire Stadium in Wembley and in other locations which were far away from each other.

The gymnastic competitions in London took place later because heavy rain forced the events indoors, where they took place in Empress Hall, remembered afterwards by Miloslava Misakova-Camkova, a member of the Czechoslovakian gold winning team. As she recalls, "Three days after arriving in London my younger sister Eliska became ill with an increasing temperature. An English doctor informed us that she must go immediately to the hospital in Uxbridge. Tests and examinations revealed the worst news, she had children's polio. At this time there was no cure for this problem. Still we had to try to compete in this gymnastic competition. Meanwhile, Dr. Hornof gave Eliska his blood with the hopes of improving her condition. At eight o'clock in the morning we began competing with the Belgian team. At ten o'clock the beam competition took place and after the first event the Czechoslovakian team was in fourth place. At this moment the Czechoslovakian team agreed to compete in the name of Eliska and achieve the best results possible. They scored three scores of 9.0 points on the beam which was better than any other team. When we competed on the rings even the typically quiet English spectators applauded. Then there was a minor tragedy! The scores of the last gymnasts were not calculated with the other scores for all of the teams. The Hungarians had a weak score while we had a high score. The final medal standing depended on the scores of the last discipline, the group exercise. Despite the fact that there were few spectators, our team did a baton twirling routine as if it was a concert performance. There was no mention of our excellent all round effort at the time."

At the same instant that Czechoslovakia learned that they had won the gold medal they also heard the tragic news that Eliska Misakova had passed away. Their joy turned into sadness. On Saturday morning, when the results were announced, Eliska was on their minds. The International Olympic Committee awarded her a special gold medal in memoriam.

In the men's gymnastic competition, Finland had unexpectedly good results when they beat the Swiss team. Both teams were far better than the other competing teams. Heikki Savolainen and Allen Terasvirta, gymnasts from the Olympic Games in 1928 and 1936, once again competed for the Finnish team. The Swiss Michael Reusch won the gold medal on the parallel bars with the same routine that he executed during the 1936 Games in Berlin. The organization of the gymnastic competition was good but the men and women competed together, filling the stadium with so much apparatus that it resembled a labyrinth.

Olympic Games in Helsinki, 1952

At the second round of the meeting of the International Olympic Committee in Stockholm in 1947, Helsinki, the capital city of Finland, was given the organization of the fifteenth Olympic Games. The number of athletes participating in these games set a new record. There were over 5,000 athletes from 69 countries at the Games. The first appearance of the USSR in the Olympic Games was a very important event. Of the Soviet athletes at the Games, the members of the gymnastic teams were the best. The gymnastic competition took place in two halls, in Messuhalli near the Olympic Stadium and in a smaller location in Kisahalli. During the first training session, the specialists saw that the Soviet team would produce good results during the competition. Over the course of two weeks the Soviet national anthem could be heard often in tribute to the victories of the Soviet gymnasts. They won nine out of fifteen gold medals. 185 men from 29 countries participated in the gymnastic competition while 134 women from 18 countries competed. The most successful gymnast of these Games was the 31 year old Soviet Viktor Cukarin.

The teams consisted of eight members but only the top five scores were calculated toward the results. Japan only brought five gymnasts to the Games and so it was not an advantage for them. After the compulsory exercises Stalder from Switzerland was in first place in front of the Soviets, Shaginjan and Mouratov. Cukarin was in fourth place at this point. In the optional programme, however, the Soviets improved their positions. For example, Shaginjan scored the highest score of the competition on the rings with a 9.95. In the women's individual competition the best gymnast was Maria Gorochovskaya.

Olympic Games in Melbourne, 1956

During the third round of voting at the 1949 meeting of the International Olympic Committee in Rome it was decided that Melbourne would be the site of the sixteenth Olympic Games. Members of the committee were concerned that this location might be a problem because the Games would take place in December. The great geographical distance of the Australian continent was also a concern of the Committee at this time. The organizers renovated the Cricket Ground to serve as the main Olympic Stadium and gymnasts had their competition in the hall of West Melbourne Stadium.

There were 128 gymnasts from 21 countries taking part in the gymnastic competition. A large struggle began in Melbourne between the Soviet Union and Japan in the men's competition. At the centre of the Soviet team was the 35 year old Viktor Cukarin who had won the Olympic gold medal two times in the past. The Japanese team was led by the 36 year old Takasi Ono. The victory of the Soviet team did not come easily because the Japanese performed very well in the optional routines. During this competition even the well experienced Boris Sachlin was very nervous due to the sense of competition between the teams. Cukarin, the captain of the Soviet team, performed quite well and set the tone for the rest of the team. He won the individual all around competition followed by the Japanese Ono who was only 0.05 points behind. The Czechoslovak team vied with the Finnish team for the bronze medal. At the end of the competition Finland managed to edge out the Czechoslovaks. The Australian team only participated to learn from the more experienced teams. There was a new evaluation of the gymnastic routines in the team competition. Instead of eight gymnasts on each team there were only six. The best five scores were used to calculate the final results.

In the women's competition, there was the start of a new era of gymnastic excellence by Larissa Latynina of the Soviet Union. At these Games she won four gold medals and one silver. The 35 year old Hungarian Agnes Keleti was the second most successful as she won three gold medals and two silver. In the team competition gymnasts competed in four disciplines as well as rhythmic gymnastic routines. There were mostly static elements in the women's competition. Only the Japanese included more dynamic elements in their routines, handsprings and pirouettes. Eva Bosakova from Czechoslovakia performed a very interesting routine on the balance beam. She died in 1991 in Prague at the age of sixty.

Cukarin recalls his preparation for the 1956 games in Melbourne, "We executed all six disciplines in two days and on the third day we rested. It was important that we practised during one training session both compulsory and optional routines. The most important thing for gymnasts hoping to achieve their best in the Games is to love the sport and do everything possible to make this come true."

Figure 1.1. Yuri Titov (URS).

Olympic Games in Rome, 1960

Preparations for the seventeenth Olympic Games in Rome, the "Eternal City", went very well. The gymnastic competition took place in the well known spa, Caracallo. In the men's team competition gymnasts from twenty countries participated. The high point of the struggle between the Soviet and Japanese teams came when Japan won the gold in the team competition and began an era of dominance which would last until 1979. A strong fight between the Czechoslovaks and the Italians, who had the famous Swiss coach Jack Gunthard, occurred with the Italian team taking the bronze medal.

In the individual all-round competition there were 130 gymnasts from 28 countries. Chakhlin of the Soviet Union was the overall winner with Ono coming in second. Yuri Titov of the Soviet Union took the bronze medal and later became President of the F.I.G.. For the first time medal winners were required to perform a second optional exercise in addition to the routines presented in the all-round competition, winning three gold medals as well as the all-round competition.

In the women's competition, there were seventeen teams with a total of 124 gymnasts from a record 27 countries. The Soviet team was again the strongest in the team competition while the Czechoslovak team improved and took the silver medal in Rome. In the finals three gymnasts from Czechoslovakia competed for medals: Bosakova on the beam and floor exercise, Cáslavská on the beam and Tacova on the vault. Bosakova performed an excellent routine which gave her the gold medal. Nikolaeva was the winner in the vault competition executing a new element. Latynina won her second all-round gold medal followed by three Soviet team mates. The evaluation system during these Games involved three judges.

The Soviet Union took fifteen out of a possible eighteen medals. Boris Chakhlin was a great innovator in gymnastic training. He executed many routines during short periods of time. This intensification in his preparation brought him excellent results in the competitions. When Chakhlin finished competing in gymnastics in 1966 he went on to become a long time member of the Technical Committee of the F.I.G..

Olympic Games in Tokyo, 1964

At the meeting of the International Olympic Committee in Munich in 1959, Tokyo was chosen as the site of the eighteenth Olympic Games. The gymnastic competition was held in the Metropolitan Gymnasium with a capacity of 6,500. This hall was full during the entire gymnastic competition. There was great interest in the women's gymnastic competition. There were 10 women's teams with 23 individual gymnasts representing 24 countries. It was the first Olympic Games where gymnasts from every continent participated.

There was tough competition between the Soviet and Czechoslovak women's teams. Larissa Latynina, 29 years old at this time, was the most impressive gymnast of the Soviet team. She took the silver medal in the all-round but the overall winner was Vera Cáslavská of Czechoslovakia. Cáslavská became a favourite of the Japanese before the Games and remained popular after her victory. She won gold medals on the vault and on the beam. Cáslavská also executed difficult and original elements on the uneven bars including a backswing with a full pirouette. On the vault she performed a Yamashita piked, which was new at the time. The 19 year old Radochla of East Germany surprised many people when she won a silver medal on the vault.

In the team competition the Soviets were again the best. The team consisted of Latynina, Astakhova, Volceckaya, Zamotajlova-Ljuchina, Gromova and Manina. The team from Czechoslovakia took the silver medal by finishing only 0.901 points behind the Soviets. In the optional programme Czechoslovakia beat the Soviets by 0.132 points. The home team, Japan, won the bronze medal in the women's team competition.

In the men's competition the Japanese continued to be the best in gymnastics. Yukio Endo took the gold medal in the all-round individual competition. In an unusual case three gymnasts shared the silver medal: Chakhlin, Lishitski and Tsurumi. It was a great surprise in the finals when Menichelli of Italy performed his own original routines in the floor exercise and took the gold medal. Yamashita also won the vault competition with some difficult elements, including a Yamashita piked with a full twist.

Vera Cáslavská, at present a member of the International Olympic Committee, said the following about her training, "I always tried to find out about what could help me develop my gymnastic ability more efficiently. I was not a robot and didn't follow my trainer's commands without questioning things. I was interested in developing my gymnastic talent on my own whenever I could. I asked myself how many elements and to what degree of proficiency I should include in my training sessions. For example, I told myself before that I must execute my routines on each apparatus with a goal of 9.8 and with a minimum score of 9.5. I trained as if I was in actual competition. This was an effective system for me and contributed to my success."

Olympic Games in Mexico City, 1968

At the meeting of the International Olympic Committee in 1963 it was determined that the nineteenth Olympic Games would take place in Mexico City. The organizing committee and the Mexican government put forth great efforts to prepare a new Olympic Stadium and a brand new stadium for the gymnastic competition, the Auditorio National. The gymnastic competition was very popular among the Mexican people and there was great anticipation before the Games.

In the men's gymnastic competition there were 16 teams consisting of 95 gymnasts with 12 countries participating in the individual competition. Once again the main competition was between Japan and the Soviet Union. The Japanese team won and was led by Sawao Kato who won the overall all-round individual competition. The Soviet team came in second place and was led by Mikhail Voronin who took second behind Sawao Kato by only 0.05 points. There was a great struggle for the bronze between the East Germans and the team from Czechoslovakia. In the end the East Germans were victorious by a mere 0.05 points.

In the women's gymnastic competition, there were a total of 101 gymnasts from 30 countries and 14 teams. In the team competition Czechoslovakia and the Soviet Union were the strongest. After the compulsory exercises the Soviet team were in first place by 0.95 points. The Czechoslovak team won the optional programme by 0.3 points. This drama concluded with the Soviet team in first place followed by Czechoslovakia, East Germany led by Erika Zuchold with Japan coming in fourth.

In the women's all-round individual competition there was a strong struggle between Vera Cáslavská of Czechoslovakia and Natalia Kuchinskaya of the Soviet Union. Kuchinskaya, however, did poorly in the uneven bars and only scored 8.45 points. Due to this she only took a bronze medal while Sinaida Voronina received the silver medal. The fourth place position was vied for by Erika Zuchold and Larissa Petrik who eventually finished in a tie. Cáslavská, who had prepared very well for these Games, took the gold medal in the overall as well as the gold in the vault, uneven bars and the floor exercise.

Vera Cáslavská recalls the Games in Mexico City, "Our trainer Slavka Matlochova had a very simple regime. Do routines carefully and with ease during the Games because you have already prepared thoroughly and you don't need to be nervous and doubtful when you compete. When I had finished my routine on the beam I only received 9.60 points and all of the spectators were unsatisfied. My coach protested the score and after a short time the judges decided to increase my score to 9.80. On the floor exercise I competed with a Mexican temperament and scored 9.85. Once again a protest to the judges took place but this time they chose not to change the first score. By the time I came to the vault event I was tired and could not concentrate. On the uneven bars, I did not try any risky elements and only did those things which I knew very well."

During these Games, for the first time, gymnasts competed who were quite young. For example, the average age of the Soviet women's gymnasts was eighteen years old. Also at this time the degree of difficulty of the optional routines increased too.

Figure 1.2. Ludmila Turisheva (URS).

Olympic Games in Munich, 1972

The Munich organizers promised the rest of the world that the twentieth Olympic Games would include an appropriate celebration of this anniversary and preparations for the Games were excellent. In the men's gymnastic competition there were 113 gymnasts. For the first time in the Olympic Games a second exercise was performed by the best 36 gymnasts from the team competition. In the team competition the traditional rivalry between Japan and the Soviet Union for the gold medal continued. Japan again finished first followed by the Soviets. Third place was taken by the East German team and the Polish team, led by the three Kubica brothers, came in fourth.

In the individual all-round competition the Japanese Sawao Kato again took the gold medal with his team mates Kenmotsu winning the silver and Nakayama the bronze. The debut of the nineteen year old Soviet Andrianov, who would later become a great Champion, occurred at these Games. He took fourth place and won the floor exercise. At the present time Andrianov is a coach in Japan.

After these Games the Japanese coach Yukio Endo said, "We won the team competition but in the individual competition we did not win many medals because we included several original elements which involved some risks.". Interestingly these Games were the last in which one country could win all three medals in individual gymnastic competition. Following the Munich Games the F.I.G. decided that only two gymnasts from one country could participate in the finals.

In the women's gymnastic competition, there were 118 competitors who prepared for an extravaganza with many original elements. The Soviet team was able to take the gold without any major competition from the other teams. Olga Korbut of the Soviet Union emerged as a great gymnastic star while her team mate Ludmilla Turishcheva won the overall gold medal. East Germany finished second to the Soviets and was led by Karin Janz who was second in the overall individual competition. The bronze medal was taken by the team from Hungary. The Romanian team was only in sixth place during these Games but would later become consistently the world's best. The Soviet team consisted of the following gymnasts: Turishcheva, Korbut, Lazakovich, Burda, Saadi and Koshel. The average age of the members of this team was 18.7 years while Erika Zuchold of East Germany was the oldest competitor at age 25.

Olympic Games in Montreal, 1976

In May 1970 the International Olympic Committee chose Montreal as the site of the twenty-first Olympic Games. The gymnastic competition took place in the Forum, the location of Canadian ice hockey games. Every one of the 16,000 seats of the stadium was full during the competition. Only twelve men's and women's teams were permitted to take part in the gymnastic competition because the International Olympic Committee decided to limit the size of the tournament.

There were 90 male gymnasts from 20 countries in these Games. Once again the focus was on the competition between Japan and the Soviet Union. Members of the Japanese team were experienced and averaged 26.3 years old while the Soviets were an average of 19.8 years old. In the end the Japanese team was victorious by a slim margin of 0.4 points. The 29 year old Sawao Kato vied with the 24 year old Soviet Andrianov for the gold medal. The Soviet coach, Nikolai Tolkacev, had done an excellent job preparing Andrianov for these Games and this led to four medals, making him the most successful athlete at the Montreal Games. Sawao Kato took the silver medal with a final score which was a full 1.0 point lower than Andrianov. The bronze medal was won by the 29 year old Tsukahara of Japan.

In the team competition East Germany and Hungary fought for the bronze medal. In the end the East Germans managed to beat the Hungarians by 0.2 points. Fifth place was taken by West Germany and sixth place was filled out by Romania.

In the women's competition there were 86 gymnasts. These Games witnessed the beginning of the long rivalry between the Soviet Union and Romania. The Romanian team averaged 15.8 years of age while the young Champion Nadia Comaneci was only 14 years old. The Soviet team, meanwhile, averaged a much higher 19.8 years of age. Comaneci and Kim raised the level of gymnastic competition by receiving perfect 10.0 points. The Soviet team was the overall winner by 3.2 points over the Romanian team. Third place was taken by East Germany.

In the individual women's all-round competition Comaneci was the gold medal winner followed by Kim and Turishcheva, both of the Soviet Union. The Montreal Games was the final Olympics for Ludmilla Turishcheva. Today she is the President of the Ukrainian Gymnastic Federation. In the final competition Comaneci finished with the maximum score of 20.0 points on the uneven bars and also won the beam. Kim was the winner of the vault and the floor exercise. Comaneci, however, was by far the best gymnast in Montreal, getting the top mark an unprecedented seven times.

The trainer for Ludmilla Turishcheva and many other top gymnasts such as Shaposhnikova and Yurchenko, Vladislav Rastorockij, commented on the world of training:

1. Don't work with stupid gymnasts! You must find clever gymnasts. Gymnasts are

not robots but rather they must be able to communicate with the trainer.

2. Teach gymnasts so that they understand what is expected. Gymnasts should be able to think for themselves.

3. Gymnasts must like training and the trainer must try to build this feeling in the gymnasts. Gymnasts must feel as though they are learning something new and improving every day.

4. Teach gymnasts that they must try to achieve the highest score every time they compete and if they do this they will become excellent athletes. Turishcheva was not only a strong gymnast but also was a very good student.

5. Trainers must explain what they want very clearly. Trainers must learn things themselves and continue to read and to think about what they have read.

6. Trainers must want their gymnasts to execute each element with high quality so that in competition their gymnasts can do well.

7. Young gymnasts must learn to have passion for their sport. It is necessary to make two hours of training feel like only two minutes.

8. Trainers must always be honest with their gymnasts. Gymnasts must trust and respect their trainers demands and instructions. Only with this relationship can a trainer help develop an excellent gymnast.

Olympic Games in Moscow, 1980

The organizers of the twenty second Olympic Games in Moscow made excellent preparations including world class stadia. There was a great tragedy when Western countries, led by the United States of America, decided to boycott these Games in protest of the Soviet troops' presence in Afghanistan. Due to this boycott many strong gymnastic teams and individuals did not take part in the Moscow Olympics. On 19th July opening ceremonies took place in the main Olympic stadium with 5,333 athletes from 81 countries and included an Olympic speech by Nikolai Andrianov.

In the men's competition there were 65 gymnasts from eight countries. The greatest progress was seen in the Cuban team. The Soviet team was by far the best and finished ahead of the second place East German team by more than eight points. The following gymnasts made up the victorious Soviet team: Ditiatin, Andrianov, Tkatchev, Makuts, Markelov and Asaryan.

In the individual all-round competition the main rivalry was between the Soviets Ditiatin and Andrianov. In the end Ditiatin was the winner over his team mate.

In the women's gymnastic competition the Soviets were again the best followed by Romania. The winning team from the Soviet Union had the following members: Davidova, Filatovova, Kim, Shaposhnikova, Naymushinova and Zacharovova. In the all-round individual competition, the Soviet Davidova was the gold medal winner followed by the Romanian Comaneci who was tied with the East German Gnauck. Today Davidova is a coach in Canada after finishing studies at the Faculty of Physical Education and Sport in Leningrad. Comaneci emigrated to the United States of America and currently lives there. She continues to support Romanian gymnastics and is a promoter of artistic gymnastics around the world. Interestingly, the Moscow Congress of the F.I.G. decided at this time to prohibit girls under age 14 from taking part in official gymnastic competitions.

Figure 1.3. Natalia Shaposhnikova (URS).

Figure 1.4. Stoian Delchev (BUL).

Olympic Games in Los Angeles, 1984

The Olympic Games in Los Angeles suffered as much as the Moscow Games had due to a boycott. Socialist countries, led by the Soviet Union, decided not to participate in these Games, the only exceptions were a male gymnast and a female gymnast from Romania. The gymnastic competition took place in the Pauley Pavilion.

In the men's competition the most important rivalry was between the USA and Chinese teams because the form of the Japanese was not so good at this time. The USA team surprised everyone by defeating the 1983 World Champion team from China. After the compulsory programme the USA led by less than one point over China. Everyone assumed the Chinese team would be able to overtake the USA squad in the optional part of the competition. The USA however, led by Bart Conner and Peter Vidmar, did very well and for the first time in history the USA were the best gymnastic team in the Olympics. In the individual all-round competition the Japanese Gushiken was the gold medal winner in front of the American Vidmar by only 0.025.

In the women's team competition the Romanian team was the best followed by the USA who were 1.15 points behind. In the all-around individual competition many experts thought that the seventeen year old Szabo would by the winner. The American Mary Lou Retton, however, surprised these experts and managed to take the gold. Retton was coached by the Romanian Bela Karoly who had emigrated to the United States of America and was instrumental in preparing her for these Games.

Figure 1.5. Bart Conner (USA).

Olympic Games in Seoul, 1988

The capital of South Korea, Seoul, was chosen to host the twenty-forth Olympic Games by the 84th session of the International Olympic Committee in Baden-Baden on September 30th 1981. Gymnastic competitions took place in a hall which was an attraction of the Olympic Park, located 14 kilometres of the city of Seoul. The hall, with a capacity of 15,000 spectators, was sold out during all gymnastic competitions.

Both the men's and women's field was composed of 12 full teams and a number of individual gymnasts. Participants in the men's team competition were: China, Soviet Union, Italy, USA, Bulgaria, Hungary, France, Japan, FRG, GDR, Canada, Romania. Individual competitors were from: Australia, Sweden, Austria, Brazil, Switzerland, Great Britain, South Korea, Spain, Czechoslovakia, Mexico, Portugal, Yugoslavia, Israel and Taiwan.

In the men's team competition it was obvious from the first apparatus that the USSR team was unrivalled. They were the best prepared. In the compulsory programme they had a much higher score, 295.70 points, and in the optional programme they received even more, 297.65 points. The USSR team consisted of these gymnasts: Artemov, Lukin, Bilozerchev, Kharkov, Gogoladze and Novikov. They achieved the best score in the history of the Olympic Games. From a total of 600 points they got 593.35 points. The gymnasts from China, however, did not show their true abilities and their best gymnast Li Ning in compulsory and optional programmes made several mistakes and didn't manage to compete in the final, competition two, which was a big surprise. Good results were achieved by Wang Chongshang who took 6th place and Lou Yun who took 12th place. In the team competition China took only 4th place. Owing to the poor achievements of the Chinese team 2nd and 3rd places were given to the teams of GDR and Japan. In the team of GDR the best gymnast, S. Kroll, did not compete as well as he could, especially on the high bar, and therefore the whole load resided on the young gymnast S. Tippelt. He took the 4th place behind the Soviets: Artemov, Lukin and Bilozerchev.

The Japanese gymnasts did a good job on the last apparatus and took the 3rd place. When receiving the medals all of them cried, they could not believe their wonderful success after such a long time. The last places in the team competition were France (10th), USA (11th), and FRG (12th).

In the finals competition on the floor exercise came the 18 year old Kharkov (USSR), who at the beginning of his routine performed a double salto stretched with full twist. On the pommel horse three gymnasts took the gold: Bilozerchev, Borkai and Geraskov. The all around Olympic winner was Artemov who also became the most successful gymnast at these Olympic Games and received four gold medals. This successful gymnast, after his active career in 1989, went to the USA and at the present time he works as a trainer.

In the women's competitions were teams from the following countries: Japan, Canada, Romania, Bulgaria, South Korea, Czechoslovakia, Soviet Union, Spain, Hungary, USA and China. Individual competitors also were from: Sweden, Belgium, Greece, Portugal, Guatemala, Austria, Switzerland, France, Brazil, Italy, Great Britain, Australia, FRG and Israel.

In the team competition we saw a great fight between the teams from USSR and Romania. The team from USSR consisted of Baitova, Shevchenko, Shushunova, Laschenova, Strascheva and Boginskaya. The best from this team was Shushunova. The team from Romania consisted of Silivas, Popa, Voina, Potorac, Dobre and Golija. The best was Silivas. The Soviets were leading after the compulsory programme with not even a point before the Romanian gymnasts. But the Romanians did not give up in the optional programme and were behind the Soviets by only 0.45 points. The final victory was achieved by the Soviets with 1.35 points ahead of Romania. An unbelievable fight came between the teams from GDR and USA for the 3rd place and went on to the last apparatus. The gymnasts from GDR achieved on the uneven bars a high score of 49.325 points and took the third place. The USA team stayed behind with only 0.30 points in fourth place. The last places took the teams from Canada (11th) and Japan (12th), who in the optional programme only achieved 190.95 points.

In the individual all around competition we saw a breathtaking fight between Shushunova and Silivas. This fight lasted to the last apparatus when Shushunova scored on the vault full 10.00 points and this determined her final victory. In the apparatus finals Silivas did an excellent job and took three gold medals: on uneven bars, beam and floor exercises and one bronze medal on vault. In third place was Boginskaya who on the floor and on the beam received 9.90 points.

E. Shushunova, after graduation from the Faculty of Physical Education and Sport, started working as a coach in St. Petersburg. S. Boginskaya prepared in Houston, USA, under the leadership of B. Karolyi for the Olympic Games in Atlanta in 1996.

Olympic Games in Barcelona, 1992

The twenty-fifth Olympic Games in Barcelona were among the largest and most successful Olympic Games in history. The gymnasts contributed to this terrific success with their difficult performances. The competition was held from July 26th to August 2nd in the newly built marvellous Sports Palau Sun Jordi.

In the men's team competition were these teams: the Unified Team, China, Japan, Germany, Italy, USA, Romania, Korea, Hungary, Bulgaria, Switzerland and Great Britain. Best prepared were the gymnasts from the former Soviet Union, who competed together for the last time. They were: Scherbo, Belenki, Misutin, Sharipov, Voropajev and Korobchinski. Already after the compulsory exercises they were two points ahead of the Chinese. This 2.0 points difference was increased to five after the optional exercises. An excellent performance was given by the Japanese who finally took the bronze. In 11th place was the Swiss and in the last 12th place was the team from Great Britain, behind the Unified Team by more than 27 points.

In the all around individual competition, competition II, Vitaly Scherbo was the best and performed his life time best. He managed to get 59.025 points, just over the magic 59 point line. In 2nd and 3rd place were his teammates Misutin and Belenki. Fourth place was taken by Andreas Wecker from Germany. Between first placed V. Scherbo and last placed Curtis from Canada was a difference of nearly 5 points.

The apparatus finals again starred V. Scherbo who won on four apparatus: pommel horse, rings, vault and bars, and became the most successful sportsman at the Olympic Games in Barcelona. The floor was won by Li Xiaoshuang, China, who was the only performer to complete the triple salto backward. The gold medal on the pommel horse was shared by V. Scherbo and Pal Gil-Su (PRK) who performed a long and very difficult routine.

However, the biggest surprise was the performance of T. Dimas from the USA who won the high bar competition in front of A. Wecker and Misutin.

In the women's team competition were these teams: the Unified Team, Romania, USA, China, Spain, Hungary, Australia, France, Germany, Canada, Peoples' Republic of Korea and Bulgaria. These were the final standings in the team competition.

In the Unified Team the best was Boginskaya, for whom in the compulsory exercises the lowest scores were on vault (9.890 points) and on uneven bars (9.875 points). Also on the uneven bars in the optional exercises she received only 9.862 points. Boginskaya finally received in the team competition the second highest score 79.287 points. The best gymnast from the Romanian team was C H. Bontas who received the lowest score on the compulsory exercise on vault (9.812 point) and in the optional exercise on beam (9.862 points) and finally received the third highest score, 79.211 points, that meant third place. The best USA gymnast was Shannon Miller who received the highest score in the women's team competition, 79.311 points. Big surprise was the bad performance of T. Gutsu from CEI on beam where she received only 9.425 points.

In the individual all around competition big fighting was between Gutsu, Miller, Milosovici, Bontas and Boginskaya. Best performance was shown by Gutsu who had the lowest scores on beam and floor exercises. However, the score on vault and bars, 9.950 point, made with the total score of 39.737 points the final victory possible. More than 2.1 points were between the first and the last: K. Shadbolt (AUS).

On apparatus finals on vault seven or eight gymnasts performed Yurchenko with full twist. The first place took H. Onodi and L. Milosovici. On the uneven bars an excellent performance was from Lu Li from China, who included in her routine: Jaeger salto, Tkatchev and ended with straight double salto backward and received the highest possible score 10.0 points. On the beam T. Lisenko performed her routine without any mistakes and was awarded with the gold medal. On the floor exercises Milosovici won with the highest score of 10.0 points.

Figure 1.6. Alexei Voropaev (EUN).

Figure 1.7. Svetlana Boginskaya (EUN).

Olympic Games in Atlanta, 1996
By Trevor Low

The first and the last. The first Olympic Games with the Soviet block competing as separate nations and the last Olympic Games with set exercises. There was much at stake and with typical USA hype the biggest most commercial Games ever was a fantastic sporting success. There were many practical problems in the organisation of the 1996 Olympic Games but each sporting event was perfectly run. Many will remember the Atlanta Games for that one solitary moment of tragedy when a bomb exploded in Centennial square but we must recognise the enormous strides forward that sport made in Atlanta, new records, new elements, new faces, new Champions. For many years the F.I.G. had been trying to address the problem of 'little girls' dominating the gymnastic events and at last we saw in Atlanta a return to the mature grace and beauty of women in sport. Dominique Moceanu almost stood alone as the token elfin, fantastic in gymnastics but overshadowed by the beauty of her peers.

The Romanian women arrived with a weakened team and their dream of a grand slam slipped away. By the end of the set exercises Russia was ahead of the USA by less than a mark with Romania in third position.

With the voluntary routines the event was even tighter but with Russia faltering at beam the USA caught up and made a one point lead of their own. No one was left feeling disappointed in the 32,000 seater Georgia Dome Stadium: it had been an amazing match and the best had won. Romania took bronze with China once again showing great gymnastics with at times costly errors. The most feared result of an ex-Soviet 1, 2 and 3 did not materialise as the Ukraine finished in 5th place and Belarus 6th. The playing field was much more level than had been imagined.

The men's team competition put Leonid Arkaev in the ranks of 'legend'. Here was a man who had a passion for gymnastics that was to bring Russia the Olympic Team title. Romania died, Germany fell all over the pommel horse and China, so close all the time, could not find that extra stability when it counted. Russia won both set and voluntary routines and were clear winners. China took silver and the Ukraine took the bronze medals.

The Men's All Around Competition

Even with the difficulty required in the code, the opening round of the men's individual Olympic competition produced 16 scores over 9.6 points. Amid unreal support, almost manic in ferocity, the USA's Blaine Wilson opened with 9.373 on rings for an early second place, just behind Nemov of Russia. Even though successive rounds saw him fall from second to fourth to thirteenth the support did not falter and doubled as he climbed back to eleventh, ninth and finished tenth. For McCready and Roethlisberger the US crowd gave the same home nation blitz encouragement and earned from all the sports in every arena of Atlanta a rather poor reputation for drowning out every other competitor. But this is the USA and of course 32,000 people calling for their heroes will be loud, that is the nature of the home advantage. Let it be said the fun loving audience in Georgia Dome sung and mimed YMCA with even greater excitement to whip themselves into a sporting party mood.

Scherbo and Li Xiaoshuang seemed to be miles behind Nemov but in fact only two tenths separated the top 16 players with Alexei opening on pommels with his best score of the day with stock Magyar Shivado passes then milling his way through a flared spindle Magyar sequence in and around the handles in all manner of possible hand placements. Vitaly Scherbo was already a little rattled by his placing with shoulder shrugs and eyes lifted to heaven pleading for enlightenment and there were times during this Games that I thought that Vitaly was hard done by. There was a comment passed that, 'Scherbo had had his day', but he is after all the gymnasts' gymnast, one of the most complete examples of all the qualities of gymnastics known in one person.

But with round two the weakness of Scherbo's rings, 9.537 (relative weakness) was to prevent him rising any further than bronze. With a shoulder injury to train with Vitaly had not been able to prepare rings well and with slightly high cross positions his gold ambitions were lost. The Chinese Li and Zhang came through with pommels, of course, with certainly the best shape and line in the world for this apparatus. Andreas Wecker could still smile after trashing pommels again. Pommels seem to come back to Andreas like elephant jokes, he smiles because it is a joke, not because it is funny. Nemov held on to first place with a piked to straight Guczoghy on rings and Voropaev swung into fourth at bar, Kovacs and Kovacs to hop pirouette with double double straight to dismount. Christian Leric of France dismounted bar with a double double tucked over the top, a double twisting Straumann.

Nemov's vault is enormous but not the most perfect style and his 9.7 against Li's 9.775 at rings reversed their standing in round three. Voropaev's floor was excellent and for a while it looked like he could hold onto bronze place. Zhang, and I also think Li, held too many strength parts high with Zhang paying a higher price. Shen, the third Chinese finalist, had his moment in round four with a short stay in the bronze house, while for Voropaev it was the dog house, pommels, not so much a flop combination as a flopped routine, 8.4.

The fifth round and high bar put Nemov back on top. Gienger from Kovacs and double double straight for 9.8. Li's parallel bars was a touch scrappy but double pike back in the bars never looks to make a good swing connection. And there was no questioning the look of the dismount, double pike to a scrambled landing, held, but only just.

Scherbo at last climbed into the medal places, but two tenths adrift he had to wait for

Nemov or Li to make an error to pass any higher.

Nemov's floor, like his vault is never faultless even when the tumbling is accurate and 9.687, for Nemov at least, is not so high a score. At bar Li held on to a yesterday combination of hop full to one arm Tkatchev repeated for start value and double straight dismount, 9.787, just enough. China had her first all around Olympic medal. And with three gymnasts in the top five the Chinese machine could not be ignored. And also look at the 'oldies', Belenki 6th, Korobchinski, 15th and Chechi 17th (hanging in there for the rings final and a place in history).

The Women's All Around Competition

Never was a competition more charged with expectation. Of the 32,000 members of the audience 30,000 began the chant U-S-A, U-S-A, U-S-A. The noise was together inspiring, awesome and intimidating. The other 2000 people had to join in the hysteria. Dawes, Miller and Morceanu were but part of this flow of energy which made the table and chair vibrate. It was that loud. This was a great competition.

Rosa Galieva opened on beam with 9.825 to lead the first round, a beautiful exercise with full twisting Korbut flip in classic choreography. Chorkina was a little less steady on beam with 9.787 which allowed Mo and Dawes to take third and second places with vault and bars. Dawes is a supreme bar worker although I worry that the continuity of the routine is lost in places with simple upstart cast parts to hold the great difficulties together. Miller was good enough on bars but 9.75 was only worth eighth place, such was the level of performance. Svetlana Boginskaya closed the first round with her new floor routine, just what everyone wanted and needed to see. Svetlana has not lost her character. But 9.6 rewarded some quick thinking landings with headspring full twisting front punch birani punch looking a bit add-on-ish.

Svetlana Chorkina never really looked settled and her floor with 9.7 was still not worrying the top places. Lilia Podkopayeva also started her competition looking like she did not want to win, 9.781 on vault. With bars she woke up a little and with a big leg bend on her Shaposhnikova made 9.8! Mo with a first round bar score of 9.8 and now 9.799 at vault had no defence against Shannon Miller on beam, perhaps the best I have seen her perform, 9.862, quality and accuracy for third place. The design of the routine from the back roll sequence shows the hand of a master. Dina Kotchetkova hit 9.825 on beam and she found herself in the silver medal position. But no mistaking the effect of an 9.825 for Dominique Dawes on beam. Flip to two feet flip to two feet full in back out. The audience flipped and for a while went wildly out of their skulls as the name DAWES USA arrived at the top of the leader board. Even though only 38 thousandths of a mark separated the first four places it was the all important NUMBER ONE USA which started the riot. With

Miller and Dawes on their way to floor and vault there was more than a hint of 'it's in the bag' around the Georgia Dome.

Mo opened the third round on the beam with a one arm lift and with round-off to two feet layout to two feet, she hit 9.8. Moceanu was chirpy on floor but really lacked the heavy armament of powerful tumbles to reach the top of the scoreboard. Not that 9.687 is at all bad but I think that the day of the gym slip Champions has all but gone, the public and the judges' eye has mellowed. Shannon Miller hammered in a swift double straight, 2½ twist punch front and .... went out of the floor area. She was visibly surprised and lost for a moment that cool composure for which she is known. It was all gone ... and she knew it. Years of training and the prize had gone. The full in back out dismount scarcely held the tears at bay. 32,000 people flood the Dome. Then the USA bounced back as 'our Dominique' took to the floor. USA USA USA ALL THE WAY. All of the way out of the area and down on her rear end. Miss Dawes could not help but cry, 2½ twists to the carpet, the cheers cut short. 32,000 people flooded the Dome. Only a brave lifeboat could rescue a medal for the USA. And now a dramatic change in the top places. Gogean of Romania, floor, 9.8 for powerful accurate tumbling up to fourth, Milosovici, beam 9.775, not awe inspiring with flip quarter turn twice, flip layout and double tuck but near faultless, fifth place. Mo and Kotchetkova were tied in first place, and Podkopayeva with a neat beam hung on to third. In some way I can not see over balletic style looking absolutely right on beam. I can read it all right on floor but on beam it is just a little bit of 'look I can do the ballet up here as well', know what I mean? I like to see beam flow along a bit with a language of its own. Svetlana Chorkina was just at the edge of being out of it but with bars to go this World Champion was capable of anything.

Had all this been worked out beforehand? It was too exciting to be a coincidence. Dina Kotchetkova came into the final round on her worst event, vault, and try as she might her feet would not stick to the floor, 9.581 was good enough for sixth place only. Gina Gogean had her best event to finish on, vault, and with 9.775 was right on the button for 39.075 and the silver medal. Simona Amanar also drew vault last and in Romanian style with double twisting Yurchenko made 9.843 to pull in to third place. On floor Lavinia Milosovici did everything she knew and with more experience than most of the other competitors put together she held double straight, three whips to double twist punch front and full in back out for 9.812 to share third place and the bronze with Svetlana Chorkina, how could she? With her new element Shaposhnikova half turn ... no catch .. down and out of the running.

Gold was down to Lilia Podkopayeva or Mo Hulian. Lilia up first on floor was able to bring the 32,000 crowd out of their depression with a fabulous routine where her dance was at one with incredible tumbling. Handspring flyspring double front half twist for openers! 9.887 left Mo needing 9.9 from somewhere. Already there was celebrating going on, quietly, but celebrating it was. Mo is good but 9.9 good? With double straight the quiet celebrating was interrupted, with front full twist punch front it stopped. The Georgia Dome was fixed on Mo. Then 12 square metres was just a bit too small for Miss Mo, 2½ twist punch front out of bounds and into the bushes. And she still had the spirit for a wry smile as if she had played the last card knowingly. For Lilia Podkopayeva Olympic gold. For Romania silver and bronze. For Octavian Belu the quiet respect of his peers with three of the world's greatest gymnasts on the Olympic podium.

Figure 1.8. Simona Amanar (ROM).

The Men's Finals

Floor exercise for men is one of the favourite events for the USA audience and with so many superstars in the finals there was always going to be a sensational battle for gold. Podgorni of Russia was first up with a massive triple which ended with a walk out of the area, not a good gold medal habit. The Ukraine's Grigori Mitsutin jumped full in back out straight for an opener then trashed a hollow front full twist. With Vitaly Scherbo chasing his dream of an Atlanta gold his double double straight looked to be a bit dodgy. Then his his double twist to punch front one and a quarter ended up with Vitaly looking punched, absolutely lost in space, gone, gone, gone. Alexei Nemov steadied the nerve but lacked a defined cleanness of style, 9.8. Ioannis Melissanidis had the advantage of being the innovator of the whip entry tumbling and although his exercise is relatively bare of linking interest he gives very little away. Whip double straight punch front, whip double twist, hollow front full twist and double straight punch front gave almost no grounds for deduction. The man with a mission scored 9.85. Aymes of France did not have the fire to carry higher than 9.75 and Ivanov who had double straight to punch one and a quarter front fell short with 9.75. Li Xiaoshuang was last up and was faultless, double double straight, hollow front hollow front hollow front full twist, hollow front full twist, a wide flared circle through handstand and double straight to end. It was a close call but probably this time I was with the judges. Li maybe lacked a little passion and Ioannis had more invention in his tumbling and the judges should always state the winner. Li with 9.837 just shrugged his shoulders and stood happily to the right of Melissanidis. Greece had its first gold medal.

Pommel horse was an interesting final, more technical in its faults. For me Huang Huadong had the most interesting routine construction but he spilled forward at the dismount, 9.712. Hatakeda, Japan, Korolev to handstand with a hop half turn. Fan Bin, China, went on and on and on and then tried to use his face to dismount with. Nemov was brilliant but plays the code a little and 9.787 was top bats for what he did, enough for bronze. Marius Urzica and Li Donghua were in all respects way out in front. Both had European and World Championship reputations, both had the cutting edge. Li had the better line, Marius the more risk possibly. But Li finishes with a low value element in a high value routine, a deduction? Should be. Marius changed his routine mid swing, but only on show to those in the know. For the judges it was Li by a short head, 9.875 to 9.825, Olympic Champion by five hundredths of a point. Switzerland did well to adopt this pommel horse supremo.

Rings, rings, rings. Speak only one name. Yuri Chechi. Never has one man so dominated an event. His rivals, even in the final could not match his precision, his determination or his strength. At twenty minutes past midnight Yuri Chechi added the Olympic gold to his collection. If the American women's win was the most screamed about result, this gold medal was a moment in sporting history which needed no cheering or applauding or stamping of feet. A single silent 'yes' was all that was needed to honour the inevitability of this feat, Yuri Chechi, Olympic Champion, rings.

Vault was Scherbo's next best chance of a win. Korobchinski was first up and proved that time matures gymnastics with a handspring double front but like Voropaev it lacked that little bit extra. From Korea Yeo Hong Chul launched handspring front 1½ and 2½ twists, tricky vaults with quite unsteady landings but 9.756 was questionably a medal winning score. He seemed more unhappy with his own staggering around than with the score. Nemov and Scherbo choose Yurchenko entries. Both used Yurchenko half on and front half off, Nemov beyond the bonus grid, Scherbo in the middle. Scherbo was very tight on style and landing but those two tenths bonus for distance gave the gold to Alexei. The distance rule was always going to be contentious and in fact is removed from the next code, not before time. Scherbo was the best vaulter but the rules defeated him. Vitaly bronze, Yeo silver and for Alexei his Olympic gold.

At parallel bars, for Scherbo again disappointment. For my money it should have been Vitaly Scherbo's gold but the judges saw him as bronze medallist, an even more disappointed Jair Lynch of the USA with silver and Rustam Sharipov of the Ukraine with gold. Rustam's routine was terrific, very accurate with doubles with Healy combinations well executed, but was it any better than Scherbo? Vitaly opened Moy to double front piked, flying back to one bar, Stutz to one bar, Healy top hop three quarters and float hop half turn then double pike out. I would have had it just ahead. It seemed that Scherbo had no friends amongst the judges in Atlanta.

High bar provided the last thrills for the 32,000 Georgia Dome fanatics and a result which by mathematics may have been right but which rewarded the most outrageous routine with bronze. Nemov with Kovacs piked to immediate Gienger and double double straight dismount only made bronze, jointly with Scherbo and Fan Bin. Andreas Wecker with Kovacs tucked into back giants, again Kovacs tucked into back giants and then single twisting double straight dismount was awarded gold, relatively faultless I accept, but showing Nemov to be well undervalued. The silver went to Krasimir Dounev of Bulgaria, absolutely correct. So the men's apparatus finals brought gold to the historic giants of gymnastics, Switzerland, Italy, Russia, Ukraine and Germany with a Centennial gold for Greece. And it is no surprise that like the record books the memory quickly fails to remember who was second and third.

The Women's Finals

The women's finals started with Svetlana Boginskaya vaulting in probably her last Olympic event. The fact that she is good enough to compete in this Olympics and challenge the rest of the world says everything that should be said about this remarkable gymnast. Svetlana had been seen for the first time in her long career with problems rehearsing skills and landings but on demand for the judges 9.712 and fifth place. There was in my mind only one winner, Simona Amanar of Romania with Yurchenko double twist and Yurchenko half in straight front with just a short step out. Mo Hulian made the same Yurchenko double twist with a handspring front piked half out, very clean but not monumental enough to shift Simona. With Gina Gogean in bronze Romania were again showing their class with at last the precious gold in their hands.

Bars proved to be tricky for at least the audience to understand and it must have been influenced by opinion and preference when there were so many good routines with so little faults to separate the scoring, with Dominique Dawes as the crowd favourite. The American dream can come alive for US winners at the Olympic Games. A PR company had pre-rated all the USA gymnasts on their 'earning potential' taking into considering their past record, marketability and ... their 1996 Olympic result. Dominique was in third place with the condition that she must win an Olympic gold medal. Without it her earning capacity was near the bottom of the list. And we are not talking a few dollars here, think in millions of dollars difference and a life income for gold against a four year rush. Kerri Strug had landed one bad leg on a fortune, would Dominique Dawes get there? Not this time. A great bars, big skills but 9.8 was under the mark. Under the mark, under marked this time was Podkopayeva, tight form and the best Gienger of the Olympics with 9.787, nowhere. Amy Chow is unique amongst the US women as she has opened up new technical ground and found a swing vocabulary of her own, a joint silver medal does not begin to reward this routine where only the double double dismount has an obvious deduction (it could be a tighter shape). Bi Wenjing shared that silver medal and might have been gold had she been a bit taller. Quite clearly there was nothing between Bi's routine and Svetlana Chorkina's but the Russian looks so good in those long elegant turns and changes. Svetlana also has the advantage of a more complete design and construction, the exercise is a 'whole'. A tearful Svetlana was embraced by Leonard Arkaev who had nursed this great gymnast from 'potential' to Olympic Champion. I have to end the bars story with another Russian performance which did not win a medal. Dina Kotchetkova, joint fifth, 9.787. Giant full to Tkatchev up inside the bars and immediate Pac somersault, Shaposhnikova to back uprise clear circle to handstand with double straight dismount. Dina is a gymnast's gymnast. She has everything and needs only for the light to shine on her.

Beam: Shannon Miller, end of story. It was as simple as that, Shannon is unique on this event. Flic layout to layout back, the Miller and full in back out perfectly set in choreography like a diamond in platinum. The separation between gold, 9.862 and silver, 9.825, may have just been that over elaborate balletic style of Podkopayeva's. With 9.787

Gina Gogean erred in the opposite direction, great tumbling, flip to one flip to two feet double tuck dismount, but a little under presented. Interestingly Marinescu came off with full twisting tuck back and Morceanu fell (spectacularly but safe) on the beam. If we needed to confirm that the day of the gymslip gymnast was over we had it here. Shannon Miller is one of the world's most acclaimed gymnasts and must stand next to Carl Lewis as America's most rewarded sports achiever.

Floor was Dominique Dawes' last chance to strike gold and she made no errors this time in her punch front combination. It was a medal routine but only bronze. Once again the judges were placed in an impossible position of using a technically engineered code to separate Lilia Podkopayeva and Simona Amanar. The tumbling of Simona was so good. Double straight, whip to 2½ twist punch front, triple twist and full in back out, all high clean and nailed. Lilia had the grand opening, handspring flyspring double front half turn and the pretty lyrical choreography to entertain. And surely here is the difference that must be explained. Skating at least is honest in awarding 'artistic merit' marks even if at times they have a bizarre idea of beauty. They at least recognise in the adjudication process the art or entertainment value. Oh dear, now I've done it. Entertainment is the popular and public enjoyment of culture and art. It's the common man's way of appreciating Picasso. And that is why Lilia won the gold medal. Send your hate mail to me please ...

Gymnastics Results from the Olympic Games: 1896-1996

Men's Gymnastics: Team Competitions

1904

Gold	USA/AUT	370.13	**Silver**	USA	356.37	**Bronze**	USA	352.69

John Grieb	Emil Beyer	John Duha
Anton Heida	John Bissinger	Charles Krause
Max Heiss	Arther Rosenkampff	George Mayer
Phillip Kassell	Julian Schmitz	Robert Maysack
Julius Lenhart	Otto Steffen	Philip Schuster
Ernst Reckeweg	Max Wolf	Edward Siegler

1908

Gold	SWE	438	**Silver**	NOR	425	**Bronze**	FIN	405

Gösta Åsbrink	Arther Amundsen	Eino Forsström
Per Bertilsson	Carl Albert Anderson	Otto Granström
Hjalmar Cedercona	Otto Authén	Johan Kemp
Andreas Cervin	Hermann Bohne	Livan Kyykoski
Rudolf Degermark	Trygve Böysen	Heikki Lehmusto
Carl Folcker	Oskar Bye	Johan Lindroth
Sven Forssman	Conrad Carlsrud	Yrjö Linko
Eric Granfelt	Sverre Gröner	Edvard Linna
Carl Hårlemann	Harald Halvorsen	Martti Markanen
Nils Hellsten	Peter Hol	Kaarlo Mikkolainen
Arvid Holmberg	Eugene Ingebretsen	Veli Niëminen
Carl Holmberg	Ole Iverson	Kaarlo Kustaa Paasia
Osvald Holmberg	Per Mathias Jespersen	Arvo Pohjanpää
Gunnar Höjer	Sigurd Johannessen	Eino Railio
Hugo Jahnke	Nicolai Kiaer	Keikki Riipinen
John Jarlén	Carl Klaeth	Arno Saarinen
Gustaf Johnsson	Thor Larsen	Einar Sahlsten
Rolf Jonsson	Rolf Lefdahl	Arne Salovaara
Sven Landberg	Anders Moen	Viktor Smeds
Olle Lanner	Frithjof Olsen	Kaarlo Soinio
Axel Ljung	Carl Pedersen	Kurt Enoch Stenberg
Osvald Moberg	Paul Pedersen	Väino Töri
Carl Norberg	Sigvard Sivertsen	Karl Magnus Wegelins
Thomas Norberg	John Skrataas	
Thor Norberg	Harald Smedvik	
Axel Norling	Andreas Strand	
Daniel Norling	Olaf Syvertsen	
Gustaf Olsen		
Leonard Peterson		
Sven Rosén		
Gustaf Rosenquist		
Carl Sifverstrand		
Axel Sjöblom		
Birger Sörvik		

Haakon Sörvik
Karl Johan Svensson-Sarland
Karl-Gustaf Vingquist
Nils Widforss

1912

Gold	ITA	265.75	**Silver**	HUN	227.25	**Bronze**	GBR	184.5

Pietro Bianchi	Lajos Aradi	Albert Betts
Guido Boni	József Berkes	William Cowhig
Alberto Braglia	Imre Erdõdy	Sydney Cross
Giuseppe Domenichelli	Samu Fóti	Harry Dickason
Carlo Fregosi	Imre Gellért	Herbert Drury
Alfredo Gollini	Gyõzõ Halmos	Bernard Franklin
Francesco Loy	Ottó Hellmich	Leonard Hanson
Giovanni Mangiante	István Herczeg	Samuel Hodgetts
Lorenzo Mangiante	József Keresztsei	Charles Luck
Serafino Marrarochi	János Korponai	William MacKune
Guido Romano	Elemér Pászty	Ronald McLean
Paolo Salvi	Árpád Pétery	Alfred Messenger
Luciano Savorini	Jenõ Réti	Henry Oberholzer
Adolfo Tunesi	Ferenc Szücs	Edward Pepper
Giorgio Zampori	Õdõn Téry	Edward Potts
Angelo Zorzi	Géza Tuli	Reginald Potts
Arnaldo Andreoli		George Ross
Ettore Bellotto		Charles Simmons
		Arther Southern
		William Titt
		Charles Vigurs
		Samuel Walker
		John Whitaker

1920

Gold	ITA	359.885	**Silver**	BEL	346.785	**Bronze**	FRA	340.1

Pietro Bianchi	Eugéne Auwerkerken	Georges Berger
Fernando Bonatti	Théophile Bauer	Emile Bouchés
Luigi Cambiaso	François Classens	René Boulanger
Luigi Contessi	Augustus Cootmans	Alfred Buyenne
Carlo Costigliolo	François Gibens	Eugène Cordonnier
Luigi Costigliolo	Jean van Guysse	Léon Delsarte
Giuseppe Domenichelli	Albert Haepers	George Lucien Démanet
Roberto Ferrari	Dominique Jacobs	Paul Joseph Durin
Carlo Fregosi	Félicien kempeneers	Georges Duvant
Romualdo Ghiglione	Jules Labéeu	Fernand Fauconnier
Ambrogio	Hubert Lafortune	Arthur Hermann
Francesco Loy	Auguste Landrieu	Albert Hersoy
Vittorio Lucchetti	Charles Lannie	André Higelin
Luigi Maiocco	Constant Loriot	Auguste Hoël
Ferdinando Mandrini	Ferinand Minnaert	Louis Kempe
Giovanni Mangiante	Nicolas Maerloos	George Lagouge
Lorenzo Mangiante	Louis Stoop	Paulin Alexandre Lemaire

Antonio Marovelli	Alphonse van Mele	Ernest Lespinasse
Michele Mastromarino	François Verboven	Emile Martel
Giuseppe Paris	Jean Verboven	Jules Pirard
Manlio Pastorini	Julien Verdonck	Eugéne Pollet
Ezio Roselli	Joseph Verstraeten	George Thurnherr
Paolo Salvi	Georges Vivex	Julien Wartelle
Giovanni Battista Tubino	Julianus Wagemans	Paul Wartelle
Giorgio Zampori		
Angelo Zorzi		

1924

Gold	ITA	839.058	**Silver**	FRA	820.528	**Bronze**	SUI	816.661

Luigi Cambiasi	Eugène Cordonnier	Hans Grieder
Mario Lertoara	Léon Delsarte	August Güttinger
Vittorio Lucchetti	François Gangloff	Jean Gutweniger
Luigi Maiocco	Jean Gounot	Georges Miez
Fernando Mandrini	Arthur Hermann	Otto Pfister
Francesco Martino	André Higelin	Antoine Rebetez
Giuseppe Paris	Joseph Huber	Carl Widmer
Giorgio Zampori	Albert Séguin	Josef Wilhelm

1928

Gold	SUI	1718.63	**Silver**	TCH	1712.25	**Bronze**	YUG	1648.75

Hans Grieder	Josef Effenberger	Eduard Antosijevic
August Güttinger	Jan Gajdos	Dragutin Ciotti
Hermann Hänggi	Jan Koutny	Stane Derganc
Eugen Mack	Emanuel Löffer	Boris Gregorka
Georges Miez	Bedrich Supcik	Antun Malej
Otto Pister	Ladislav Tikal	Ivan Porenta
Eduard Steinemann	Ladislav Vácha	Josip Primozic
Melchoir Wetzel	Vaclav Vesely	Leon Stukelj

1932

Gold	ITA	541.85	**Silver**	USA	522.275	**Bronze**	FIN	509.995

Oreste Capuzzo	Frank Cumiskey	Mauri Noroma
Savino Guglielmetti	Frank Haubold	Veikko Pakarinen
Alfred Schwarzmann	Eugen Mack	Aleksanteri Saarvala
Willi Stadel	Georges Miez	Heikki Savolainen
Walter Steffens	Michael Reusch	Esa Seeste
Matthias Volz	Eduard Steinemann	Martti Uosikkinen

1936

Gold	GER	657.43	**Silver**	SUI	654.802	**Bronze**	FIN	638.468

Franz Beckert	Walter Bach	Mauri Noroma
Konrad Frey	Albert Bachmann	Veikko Pakarinen
Alfred Schwarzmann	Eugen Mack	Aleksanteri Saarvala
Willi Stadel	Georges Miez	Heikki Savolainen
Walter Steffens	Michael Reusch	Esa Seeste
Matthias Volz	Eduard Steinemann	Martti Uosikkinen

1948

Gold	FIN	1358.3	**Silver**	SUI	1356.7	**Bronze**	HUN	1330.85

Paavo Aaltonen	Christian Kipfer	László Baranyai
Veikko Huhtanen	Walter Lehmann	János Mogyorósi-Klencs
Kalevi Laitinen	Robert Lucy	Ferenc Pataki
Olavi Rove	Michael Reusch	Lajos Sántha
Heikki Savolainen	Josef Stalder	Lajos Tóth
Einari Teräsvirta	Emil Studer	Ferenc Várkõi

1952

Gold	URS	574.4	**Silver**	SUI	567.5	**Bronze**	FIN	564.2

Vladimir Beljakov	Hans Eugster	Paavo Aaltonen
Josif Berdijev	Ernst Fivian	Kalevi Laitinen
Evgeni Koroljkov	Ernst Gebendinger	Onni Lappalainen
Dmitri Leonkin	Jack Günthard	Kaino Lempinen
Valentin Mouratov	Hans Schwarzentruber	Berndt Lindfors
Mikhail Pereljman	Josef Stalder	Olavi Rove
Grant Shaginjan	Melchoir Thälmann	Heikki Savolainen
Viktor Tchoukarine	Jean Tschabold	Kalevi Viskari

1956

Gold	URS	568.25	**Silver**	JPN	566.4	**Bronze**	FIN	555.95

Albert Asaryan	Nobuyuki Aihara	Raimo Heinonen
Valentin Mouratov	Akira Kono	Onni Lappalainen
Boris Shakhlin	Masami Kubota	Olavi Leimuvirta
Pavel Stolbov	Takashi Ono	Berndt Lindfors
Viktor Tchoukarine	Masao Takemoto	Martti Mansikka
Yuri Titov	Shinsaku Tsukawaki	Kalevi Suoniemi

1960

Gold	JPN	575.2	**Silver**	URS	572.7	**Bronze**	ITA	559.05

Nobuyuki Aihara	Albert Asaryan	Giovanni Carminucci
Yukis Endo	Valeri Kerdemilidi	Pasquale Carminucci
Takashi Mitsukuri	Nikolai Miligulo	Gianfranco Marzolla
Takashi Ono	Vladimir Portnoi	Franco Menichelli
Masao Takemoto	Boris Shakhlin	Orlando Polmonari
Shuji Tsurumi	Yuri Titov	Angelo Vicardi

1964

Gold	JPN	577.95	Silver	URS	575.45	Bronze	GER	559.05

Yukio Endo	Sergei Diomidov	Siegfried Fülle
Takuji Hayata	Viktor Leontyev	Philipp Fürst
Takashi Mitsukuri	Viktor Lisitsky	Erwin Koppe
Takashi Ono	Boris Shakhlin	Klaus Köste
Shuji Tsurumi	Yuri Tsapenko	Günter Lyhs
Haruhiro Yamashita	Yuri Titov	Peter Weber

1968

Gold	JPN	575.9	Silver	URS	571.1	Bronze	GDR	557.15

Yukio Endo	Sergei Diomidov	Günter Beier
Sawao Kato	Valeri Lljinykh	Matthias Brehme
Takeshi Kato	Valeri Karasev	Gerhard Dietrich
Eizo Kenmotsu	Vladimir Klimenko	Siegfried Fülle
Akinori Nakayama	Viktor Lisitsky	Klaus Köste
Mitsuo Tsukahara	Mikhail Voronin	Peter Weber

1972

Gold	JPN	571.25	Silver	URS	564.05	Bronze	GDR	559.7

Shigeru Kasamatsu	Nikolai Andrianov	Matthias Brehme
Sawao Kato	Viktor Klimenko	Wolfgang Klotz
Eizo Kenmotsu	Alexander Maleev	Klaus Köste
Akinori Nakayama	Edvard Mikaelian	Jürgen Paeke
Teruichi Okamura	Vladimir Shukin	Reinhard Rychly
Mitsuo Tsukahara	Mikhail Voronin	Wolfgang Thüne

1976

Gold	JPN	576.85	Silver	URS	576.45	Bronze	GDR	564.65

Shun Fujimoto	Nikolai Andrianov	Roland Brückner
Hisato Igarashi	Alexander Ditiatin	Rainer Hanschke
Hiroshi Kajiyama	Gennadi Kryssin	Bernd Jaeger
Sawao Kato	Vladimir Marchenko	Wolfgang Klotz
Eizo Kemmotsu	Vladimir Markelov	Lutz Mack
Mitsuo Tsukahara	Vladimir Tikhonov	Michael Nikolai

1980

Gold	URS	589.6	Silver	GDR	581.15	Bronze	HUN	575.0

Nikolai Andrianov	Andreas Bronst	Ferenc Donáth
Eduard Azarian	Roland Brückner	György Guczoghy
Alexander Ditiatin	Ralf-Peter Hemmann	Zoltán Kelemen
Bogdan Makuts	Lutz Hoffman	Petér Kovács
Vladimir Markelov	Lutz Mack	Zoltán Magyar
Alexander Tkatchev	Michael Nikolay	István Vámos

1984

Gold	USA	591.4	Silver	CHN	590.8	Bronze	JPN	586.7

Bart Conner	Li Xiaoping	Koji Gushiken
Timothy Daggett	Li Ning	Noritoshi Hirata
Mitchell Gaylord	Li Yuejiu	Nobuyuki Kajitani
James Hartung	Lou Yun	Shinji Morisue
Scott Johnson	Tong Fei	Koji Sotomura
Peter Vidmar	Xu Zhiqiang	Kyoji Yamawaki

1988

Gold	URS	593.35	Silver	GDR	588.45	Bronze	JPN	585.6

Vladimir Artemov	Holger Behrendt	Yukio Iketani
Dmitri Bilozertchev	Ralf Büchner	Hiroyuki Konishi
Vladimir Gogoladze	Ulf Hoffmann	Koichi Mizushima
Sergei Kharkov	Silvio Kroll	Daisuke Nishikawa
Valeri Lioukine	Sven Tippelt	Toshiharu Sato
Vladimir Nouvikov	Andreas Wecker	Takahiro Yamada

1992

Gold	EUN	585.45	Silver	CHN	580.375	Bronze	JPN	578.25

Valeri Belenki	Guo Linyao	Yataka
Roustam Charipov	Li Chunyang	Takashi Chinen
Vitaly Scherbo	Li Dashuang	Yoshiaki Hatakeda
Igor Korobtchinski	Li Ge	Yukio Iketani
Grigori Mitsuitin	Li Jing	Masayuki Matsunaga
Alexei Voropaev	Li Xiaozhuang	Daisuke Nishikawa

1996

Gold	RUS	576.778	Silver	CHN	575.539	Bronze	UKR	571.541

Sergei Charkov	Zhuang Jinjuig	Igor Korobchinski
Nikolay Kurkov	Fan Bin	Oleg Kosiak
Alexei Nemov	Shen Jian	Grigori Mitsuitin
Evgeny Podgorni	Fan Hongbin	Vladimir Shanenko
Dmitriy Trush	Li Xiaozhuang	Rustam Sharipov
Dmitri Vasilenko	Huang Huadong	Alexandre Svetlichnyi

Men's Gymnastics: Individual All Round Competition

1900

Gold	Gustave Sandras	FRA	302
Silver	Nöel Bas	FRA	295
Bronze	Lucien Demanet	FRA	293

1904

Gold	Anton Heida	USA	161
Silver	George Eyser	USA	152
Bronze	William Merz	USA	135

1908

Gold	Alberto Braglia	ITA	317
Silver	Stanley Walter Tysal	GBR	312
Bronze	Louis Segurra	FRA	297

1912

Gold	Alberto Braglia	ITA	135
Silver	Louis Ségura	FRA	132.5
Bronze	Adolfo Tunesi	ITA	131.5

1920

Gold	Giogio Zampori	ITA	88.35
Silver	Marco Torrès	FRA	87.62
Bronze	Jean Gounot	FRA	87.45

1924

Gold	Leon Stukelj	YUG	110.34
Silver	Robert Prazák	TCH	110.323
Bronze	Bedfich Supcik	TCH	106.93

1928

Gold	Georges Miez	SUI	247.5
Silver	Hermann Hänggi	SUI	246.625
Bronze	Leon Stukelj	YUG	244.875

1932

Gold	Romeo Neri	ITA	140.625
Silver	István Pelle	HUN	134.925
Bronze	Heikki Savolainen	FIN	134.575

1936

Gold	Alfred Schwarzmann	GER	113.1
Silver	Eugen Mack	SUI	112.334
Bronze	Konrad Frey	GER	111.532

1948

Gold	Veikko Huhtanen	FIN	229.7
Silver	Walter Lehmann	SUI	229
Bronze	Paavo Aaltonen	FIN	228.8

1952

Gold	Viktor Tchoukarine	URS	115.7
Silver	Grant Shaginjan	URS	114.95
Bronze	Josef Stalder	SUI	114.75

1956

Gold	Viktor Tchoukarine	URS	114.25
Silver	Takashi Ono	JPN	114.2
Bronze	Yuri Titov	URS	113.8

1960

Gold	Boris Shakhlin	URS	115.95
Silver	Takashi Ono	JPN	115.9
Bronze	Yuri Titov	URS	115.6

1964

Gold	Yukio Endo	JPN	115.95
Silver	Shuji Tsurumi	JPN	115.4
	Boris Shakhlin	URS	
	Viktor Lisitsky	URS	

1968

Gold	Sawao Kato	JPN	115.9
Silver	Mikhail Voronin	URS	115.85
Bronze	Akinori Nakayama	JPN	115.65

1972

Gold	Sawao Kato	JPN	114.65
Silver	Eizo Kenmotsu	JPN	114.575
Bronze	Akinori Nakayama	JPN	114.325

1976				*1980*			
Gold	Nikolai Andrianov	URS	116.65	**Gold**	Alexander Ditiatin	URS	118.65
Silver	Sawao Kato	JPN	115.65	**Silver**	Nikolai Andrianov	URS	118.225
Bronze	Mitsuo Tsukahara	JPN	115.575	**Bronze**	Stoian Delchev	BUL	118

1984				*1988*			
Gold	Koji Gushiken	JPN	118.7	**Gold**	Vladimir Artemov	URS	119.125
Silver	Peter Vidmar	USA	118.675	**Silver**	Valeri Lioukine	URS	119.025
Bronze	Li Ning	CHN	118.575	**Bronze**	Dmitri Bilozertchev	URS	118.975

1992				*1996*			
Gold	Vitaly Scherbo	EUN	59.025	**Gold**	Xiaoshuang Li	CHN	58.423
Silver	Grigori Misioutine	EUN	58.925	**Silver**	Alexei Nemov	RUS	58.374
Bronze	Valeri Belenki	EUN	58.625	**Bronze**	Vitaly Scherbo	BLR	58.197

Men's Floor Exercise

1932				1936			
Gold	István Pelle	HUN	28.8	**Gold**	Georges Miez	SUI	18.666
Silver	Georges Miez	SUI	28.3	**Silver**	Josef Walter	SUI	18.5
Bronze	Mario Lertora	ITA	27.7	**Bronze**	Eugen Mack	SUI	18.466
					Konrad Frey	GER	

1948				1952			
Gold	Ferenc Pataki	HUN	19.35	**Gold**	William Thoresson	SWE	19.25
Silver	János Mogyorósiklencs	HUN	19.2	**Silver**	Tadao Uesako	JPN	19.15
Bronze	Zdenek Ruzicka	TCH	19.05		Jerzy Jokiel	POL	

1956				1960			
Gold	Valentin Mouratov	URS	19.2	**Gold**	Nobuyuki Aihara	JPN	19.45
Silver	Nobuyuki Aihara	JPN	19.1	**Silver**	Yuri Titov	URS	19.325
	William Thoresson	SWE		**Bronze**	Franco Menichelli	ITA	19.275
	Viktor Tchoukarine	URS					

1964				1968			
Gold	Franco Menichelli	ITA	19.45	**Gold**	Sawao Kato	JPN	19.475
Silver	Viktor Lisitsky	URS	19.35	**Silver**	Akinori Nakayama	JPN	19.4
Bronze	Yukio Endo	JPN	19.35	**Bronze**	Takeshi Kato	JPN	19.275

1972				1976			
Gold	Nikolai Andrianov	URS	19.175	**Gold**	Nikolai Andrianov	URS	19.45
Silver	Akinori Nakayama	JPN	19.125	**Silver**	Vladimir Marchenko	URS	19.425
Bronze	Shigeru Kasamatsu	JPN	19.025	**Bronze**	Peter Kormann	USA	19.3

1980				1984			
Gold	Roland Brückner	GDR	19.75	**Gold**	Li Ning	CHN	19.925
Silver	Nikolai Andrianov	URS	19.725	**Silver**	Lou Yun	CHN	19.775
Bronze	Alexander Ditiatin	URS	19.7	**Bronze**	Koji Sotomura	JPN	19.7
					Philippe Vatuone	FRA	

1988				1992			
Gold	Sergei Kharikov	URS	19.925	**Gold**	Li Xiaozhuang	CHN	9.925
Silver	Vladimir Artemov	URS	19.9	**Silver**	Grigori Misioutine	EUN	9.787
Bronze	Lou Yun	CHN	19.85		Yukio Iketani	JPN	

1996

Gold	Ioannis Melissanidis	GRE	9.850
Silver	Xiaoshuang Li	CHN	9.837
Bronze	Alexei Nemov	RUS	9.800

Men's Pommel Horse

1896					*1904*			
Gold	Louis Zutter	SUI			**Gold**	Anton Heida	USA	42
Silver	Hermann Weingartner	GER			**Silver**	George Eyser	USA	33
Bronze	Gyula Kakas	HUN			**Bronze**	William Merz	USA	29

1924					*1928*			
Gold	Josef Wilhelm	SUI	21.23		**Gold**	Hermann Hänggi	SUI	19.75
Silver	Jean Gutweninger	SUI	21.13		**Silver**	Georges Miez	SUI	19.25
Bronze	Antoine Rebetez	SUI	20.73		**Bronze**	Heikki Savoiainen	FIN	18.83

1932					*1936*			
Gold	István Pelle	HUN	19.07		**Gold**	Konrad Frey	GER	19.333
Silver	Omero Bonoli	ITA	18.87		**Silver**	Eugen Mack	SUI	19.167
Bronze	Frank Haubold	USA	18.57		**Bronze**	Albert Bachmann	SUI	19.067

1948					*1952*			
Gold	Veikko Huhtanen	FIN	19.35		**Gold**	Viktor Tchoukarine	URS	19.5
	Heike Savolainen	FIN			**Silver**	Grant Shaginjan	URS	19.4
	Paavo Aaltonen	FIN				Evgeni Koroljkov	URS	

1956					*1960*			
Gold	Boris Shakhlin	URS	19.25		**Gold**	Eugen Ekman	FIN	19.375
Silver	Takashi Oni	JPN	19.2		**Silver**	Boris Shakhlin	URS	19.375
Bronze	Viktor Tchoukarine	URS	19.1		**Bronze**	Shuji Tsumuri	JPN	19.15

1964					*1968*			
Gold	Miroslav Cerar	YUG	19.525		**Gold**	Miroslav Cerar	YUG	19.325
Silver	Shuji Tsurumi	JPN	19.325		**Silver**	Oll Laiho	FIN	19.225
Bronze	Yuri Tsapenko	URS	19.2		**Bronze**	Mikhail Voronin	URS	19.2

1972				**1976**			
Gold	Viktor Klimenko	URS	19.125	**Gold**	Zoltán Magyar	HUN	19.7
Silver	Sawao Kato	JPN	19.00	**Silver**	Eizo Kemmotsu	JPN	19.575
Bronze	Eizo Kemmotsu	JPN	18.95	**Bronze**	Nikolai Andrianov	URS	19.525
					Michael Nikolay	GDR	

1980				**1984**			
Gold	Zoltán Magyar	HUN	19.925	**Gold**	Li Ning	CHN	19.95
Silver	Alexander Ditiatin	URS	19.8		Peter Vidmar	USA	
Bronze	Michael Nikolay	GDR	19.775	**Bronze**	Timothy Daggett	USA	19.825

1988				**1992**			
Gold	Lyubomir Gueraskov	BUL	19.95	**Gold**	Vitaly Scherbo	EUN	9.925
	Zsolt Borkai	HUN			Pae Gil-su	PRK	
	Dmitri Bilozertchev	URS		**Bronze**	Andreas Wecker	GER	9.887

1996			
Gold	Donghua Li	SUI	9.875
Silver	Marius Urzica	ROM	9.825
Bronze	Alexei Nemov	RUS	9.787

Men's Rings

1896				**1904**			
Gold	Ioannis Mitropoulos	GRE		**Gold**	Herman Glass	USA	45
Silver	Hermann Weingärtner	GER		**Silver**	William Merz	USA	35
Bronze	Petros Persakis	GRE		**Bronze**	Emil Voigt	USA	32

1924				**1928**			
Gold	Francesco Martino	ITA	21.553	**Gold**	Leon Stukelj	YUG	19.25
Silver	Robert Prazák	TCH	21.483	**Silver**	Ladislav Vácha	TCH	19.17
Bronze	Ladislav Vácha	TCH	21.43	**Bronze**	Emanuel Löffler	TCH	18.83

1932				**1936**			
Gold	George Gulack	USA	18.97	**Gold**	Alois Hudec	TCH	19.433
Silver	William Denton	USA	18.6	**Silver**	Leon Stukelj	YUG	18.867
Bronze	Giovanni Lattuada	ITA	18.5	**Bronze**	Matthias Volz	GER	18.667

1948			
Gold	Karl Frei	SUI	19.8
Silver	Michael Reusch	SUI	19.55
Bronze	Zdenek Ruzicka	TCH	19.25

1952			
Gold	Grant Shaginjan	URS	19.75
Silver	Viktor Tchoukarine	URS	19.55
Bronze	Dimitri Leonkin	URS	19.4
	Hans Eugster	SUI	

1956			
Gold	Albert Azaryan	URS	19.35
Silver	Valentin Mouratov	URS	19.15
Bronze	Masao Takemoto	JPN	19.1
	Masami Kubota	JPN	

1960			
Gold	Albert Azaryan	URS	19.725
Silver	Boris Shakhlin	URS	19.5
Bronze	Takashi Ono	JPN	19.425

1964			
Gold	Takuji Hayata	JPN	19.475
Silver	Franco Menichelli	ITA	19.425
Bronze	Boris Shakhlin	URS	19.4

1968			
Gold	Akinori Nakayama	JPN	19.45
Silver	Mikhail Voronin	URS	19.325
Bronze	Sawao Kato	JPN	19.225

1972			
Gold	Akinori Kakayama	JPN	19.35
Silver	Mikhail Voronin	URS	19.275
Bronze	Mitsuo Tsukahara	JPN	19.225

1976			
Gold	Nikolai Andrianov	URS	19.65
Silver	Alexander Ditiatin	URS	19.55
Bronze	Danut Grecu	ROM	19.5

1980			
Gold	Alexander Ditiatin	URS	19.875
Silver	Alexander Tkatchev	URS	19.725
Bronze	Jiri Tabák	TCH	19.6

1984			
Gold	Koji Gushiken	JPN	19.85
	Li Ning	CHN	
Bronze	Mitchell Gaylord	USA	19.825

1988			
Gold	Holger Behrendt	GDR	19.925
	Dmitri Bilozertchev	URS	
Bronze	Sven Tippelt	GDR	19.875

1992			
Gold	Vitaly Scherbo	EUN	9.937
Silver	Li Jing	CHN	9.875
Bronze	Li Xiaozhuang	CHN	9.862
	Andreas Wecker	FRG	

1996			
Gold	Yuri Chechi	ITA	9.887
Silver	Szilveszter Csollany	HUN	9.812
	Dan Burinca	ROM	9.812

Men's Vault

1896

Gold	Karl Schuhmann	GER	
Silver	Louis Zutter	SUI	
Bronze	Hermann Weingäartner	GER	

1904

Gold	Anton Heida	USA	36
	George Eyser	USA	
Bronze	William Merz	USA	31

1924

Gold	Frank Kriz	USA	9.98
Silver	Jan Koutny	TCH	9.97
Bronze	Bohumil Morkovsky	TCH	9.93

1928

Gold	Eugen Mack	SUI	28.75
Silver	Emanuel Löffler	TCH	28.5
Bronze	Stane Derganc	YUG	28.375

1932

Gold	Savino Guglielmetti	ITA	54.1
Silver	Alfred Joachim	USA	53.3
Bronze	Edward Carmichael	USA	52.6

1936

Gold	Alfred Schwarzmann	GER	19.2
Silver	Eugen Mack	SUI	18.967
Bronze	Matthias Volz	GER	18.467

1948

Gold	Paavo Aaltonen	FIN	19.55
Silver	Olavi Rove	FIN	19.5
Bronze	Ferenc Pataki	HUN	19.25
	János Mogroyósiklencs	HUN	
	Leo Sotornik	TCH	

1952

Gold	Viktor Tchoukarine	URS	19.2
Silver	Masao Takimoto	JPN	19.15
Bronze	Takashi Ono	JPN	19.1
	Tadeo Uesako	JPN	

1956

Gold	Helmuth Bantz	GER	18.85
	Valentin Mouratov	URS	
Bronze	Yuri Titov	URS	18.75

1960

Gold	Boris Shakhlin	URS	19.35
Silver	Takashi Ono	JPN	19.35
Bronze	Vladimar Portnoi	URS	19.225

1964

Gold	Haruhiro Yamashita	JPN	19.6
Silver	Viktor Lisitski	URS	19.325
Bronze	Hannu Rantakari	FIN	19.3

1968

Gold	Mikhail Voronin	URS	19
Silver	Yukio Endo	JPN	18.95
Bronze	Sergei Diomidov	URS	18.925

1972

Gold	Klaus Köste	GDR	18.85
Silver	Viktor Klimenko	URS	18.825
Bronze	Kikolai Andrianov	URS	18.8

1976

Gold	Nikolai Andrianov	URS	19.45
Silver	Mitsuo Tsukahara	JPN	19.375
Bronze	Hiroshi Kajiyama	JPN	19.275

1980				1984			
Gold	Nikolai Andrianov	URS	19.825	**Gold**	Lou Yun	CHN	19.95
Silver	Alexander Ditiatin	URS	19.8	**Silver**	Li Ning	CHN	19.825
Bronze	Roland Brückner	GDR	19.775	**Bronze**	Koji Gushiken	JPN	
					Mitchell Gaylord	USA	
					Shinji Morisue	JPN	

1988				1992			
Gold	Lou Yun	CHN	19.875	**Gold**	Vitaly Scherbo	EUN	9.856
Silver	Sylvio Kroll	GDR	19.862	**Silver**	Grigori Misioutine	EUN	9.781
Bronze	Park Jong Hoon	KOR	19.775	**Bronze**	Yoo Ok Ryul	KOR	9.762

1996			
Gold	Alexei Nemov	RUS	9.878
Silver	Hong-Chul Yeo	KOR	9.756
Bronze	Vitaly Scherbo	BLR	9.724

Men's Parallel Bars

1896				1904			
Gold	Alfred Flatow	GER		**Gold**	George Eyser	USA	44
Silver	Louis Zutter	SUI		**Silver**	Anton Heida	USA	43
Bronze	Hermann Weingartner	GER		**Bronze**	John Duha	USA	40

1924				1928			
Gold	August Güttinger	SUI	21.63	**Gold**	Ladislav Vácha	TCH	18.83
Silver	Robert Prazák	TCH	21.61	**Silver**	Josep Primozic	YUG	18.5
Bronze	Giorgio Zampori	ITA	21.45	**Bronze**	Hermann Hänggi	SUI	18.08

1932				1936			
Gold	Romeo Neri	ITA	18.97	**Gold**	Konrad Frey	GER	19.067
Silver	István Pelle	HUN	18.6	**Silver**	Michael Reusch	SUI	19.034
Bronze	Heikki Savolainen	FIN	18.27	**Bronze**	Alfred Schwarzmann	GER	18.967

1948					**1952**			
Gold	Michael Reusch	SUI	19.75		**Gold**	Hans Eugster	SUI	19.65
Silver	Veikko Huhtanen	FIN	19.65		**Silver**	Viktor Tchoukarine	URS	19.6
Bronze	Josef Stalder	SUI	19.55		**Bronze**	Josef Stalder	SUI	19.5
	Christian Kipfer	SUI						

1956					**1960**			
Gold	Viktor Tchoukarine	URS	19.2		**Gold**	Boris Shakhlin	URS	19.4
Silver	Masami Kubota	JPN	19.15		**Silver**	Giovanni Carminucci	ITA	19.375
Bronze	Takashi Ono	JPN	19.1		**Bronze**	Takashi Ono	JPN	19.35
	Masao Takemoto	JPN						

1964					**1968**			
Gold	Yukio Endo	JPN	19.675		**Gold**	Akinori Nakayama	JPN	19.475
Silver	Shuji Tsurumi	JPN	19.45		**Silver**	Mikhail Voronin	URS	19.425
Bronze	Franco Menichelli	ITA	19.35		**Bronze**	Vladimir Klimenko	URS	19.225

1972					**1976**			
Gold	Sawao Kato	JPN	19.475		**Gold**	Sawao Kato	JPN	19.675
Silver	Shigeru Kasamatsu	JPN	19.375		**Silver**	Nikolai Andrianov	URS	19.5
Bronze	Eizo Kenmotsu	JPN	19.25		**Bronze**	Mitsuo Tsukahara	JPN	19.475

1980					**1984**			
Gold	Alexander Tkatchev	URS	19.775		**Gold**	Bart Conner	USA	19.95
Silver	Alexander Ditiatin	URS	19.75		**Silver**	Nobuyuki Kajitani	JPN	19.925
Bronze	Roland Brückner	GDR	19.65		**Bronze**	Mitchell Gaylord	USA	19.85

1988					**1992**			
Gold	Vladimir Artemov	URS	19.925		**Gold**	Vitaly Scherbo	EUN	9.9
Silver	Valeri Lioukine	URS	19.9		**Silver**	Li Jing	CHN	9.812
Bronze	Sven Tippelt	GDR	19.75		**Bronze**	Guo Linyao	CHN	9.8
						Igor Korobtchinski	EUN	
						Masayuki Matsunaga	JPN	

1996			
Gold	Rustam Sharipov	UKR	9.837
Silver	Jair Lynch	USA	9.825
Bronze	Vitaly Scherbo	BLR	9.800

Men's High Bar

1896			
Gold	Hermann Weingärtner	GER	
Silver	Alfred Flatow	GER	
Bronze	Aristovophoulos Petmetsas	GRE	

1904			
Gold	Anton Heida	USA	40
	Edward Hennig	USA	
Bronze	George Eyser	USA	39

1924			
Gold	Leon Stukelj	YUG	19.73
Silver	Jean Gutweninger	SUI	19.236
Bronze	André Higelin	FRA	19.163

1928			
Gold	Georges Miez	SUI	19.17
Silver	Romeo Neri	ITA	19
Bronze	Eugen Mack	SUI	18.92

1932			
Gold	Dallas Bixler	USA	18.33
Silver	Heikki Savolainen	FIN	18.07
Bronze	Einer Teräsvirta	FIN	18.07

1936			
Gold	Aleksanteri Saarvala	FIN	19.367
Silver	Konrad Frey	GER	19.267
Bronze	Alfred Schwarzmann	GER	19.233

1948			
Gold	Josef Stalder	SUI	19.85
Silver	Walter Lehmann	SUI	19.7
Bronze	Veikko Huhtanen	FIN	19.6

1952			
Gold	Jack Günthard	SUI	19.55
Silver	Josef Stalder	SUI	19.5
Bronze	Alfred Schwarzmann	GER	19,5

1956			
Gold	Takashi Ono	JPN	19.6
Silver	Yuri Titov	URS	19.4
Bronze	Masao Takemoto	JPN	19.3

1960			
Gold	Takashi Ono	JPN	19.6
Silver	Masao Takemoto	JPN	19.525
Bronze	Boris Shakhlin	URS	19.475

1964			
Gold	Boris Shakhlin	URS	19.625
Silver	Yuri Titov	URS	19.55
Bronze	Miroslav Cerar	YUG	19.5

1968			
Gold	Mikhail Voronin	URS	19.55
	Akinori Nakayama	JPN	
Bronze	Elzo Kenmotsu	JPN	19.375

1972			
Gold	Mitsuo Tsukahara	JPN	19.725
Silver	Sawao Kato	JPN	19.525
Bronze	Shigeru Kasamatsu	JPN	19.45

1976			
Gold	Mitsuo Tsukahara	JPN	19.675
Silver	Eizo Kemmotsu	JPN	19.5
Bronze	Eberhard Gienger	GER	19.475
	Henri Boerio	FRA	

1980					1984			
Gold	Stoian Delchev	BUL	19.825		**Gold**	Shinji Morisue	JPN	20
Silver	Alexander Ditiatin	URS	19.75		**Silver**	Tong Fei	CHN	19.975
Bronze	Nikolai Andrianov	URS	19.675		**Bronze**	Koji Gushiken	JPN	19.95

1988					1992			
Gold	Vladimir Artemov	URS	19.9		**Gold**	Trent Dimas	USA	9.875
	Valeri Lioukine	URS			**Silver**	Grigori Misioutine	EUN	9.837
Bronze	Holger Behrendt	GDR	19.8			Andreas Wecker	GER	

1996			
Gold	Andreas Wecker	GER	9.850
Silver	Krasimir Dounev	BUL	9.825
Bronze	Vitaly Scherbo	BLR	9.800

Women's Gymnastics: Team Competitions

1928

Gold	NED	316.75	**Silver**	ITA	289.00	**Bronze**	GBR	258.25

Estella Agstteribbe	Bianca Ambrosetti	Anne Broadbent
Petronella Burgerhof	Lavinia Gianoni	Lucille Desmond
Elka de Levie	Luigina Giavotti	Margaret Hartley
Helena Nordheim	Virginia Giorgi	Amy Jagger
Annie Polak	Germana Malabarba	Isobel Judd
Jud Simons	Clara Marangoni	Jessica Kite
Jacoba Stelma	Luigina Perversi	Madge Moreman
Jacomina van den Berg	Diana Pizzavini	Edith Pickles
Alida van den Bos	Anna Tanzini	Ethel Seymour
Anna van der Vegt	Carolina Tronconi	Ada Smith
Petronella van Randwijk	Ines Vercesi	Hilda Smith
Hendrika van Rumt	Rita Vittadini	Doris Woods

1936

Gold	GER	506.5	**Silver**	TCH	503.6	**Bronze**	HUN	499.00

Trudi Meyer	Marie Bajerová	Margit Csillik
Erna Bürger	Vlasta Dekanova	Margit Kalocsai
Käthe Sohnemann	Bozena Dobesová	Iiona Madary
Isolde Frölian	Vlasta Foltova	Gabriella Mészáros
Anita Bärwirth	Anna Hrebrinová	Margit Sándor-Nagy
Paula Pöhlsen	Matylda Pálfyová	Olga Törös
Friedel Iby	Zdenka Vermirovská	Judit Tóth
Julie Smith	Marie Vetrovská	Eszter Voit

1948

Gold	TCH	445.45	**Silver**	HUN	440.55	**Bronze**	USA	422.6

Zdenka Honsová	Anna Fehér	Ladislava Bakanic
Marie Kovárová	Erzsébet Gulyás	Marian Barone
Miloslava Misáková	Irén Karcsics	Dorothy Dalton
Milena Müllerová	Mária Kõvi	Meta Elste
Vera Ruzicková	Margit Sándor	Helen Schifano
Olga Silhánová	Erzsébet Sarkany	Clara Schroth
Bozena Srncová	Olga Tass	Anita Simonis
Zdenka Vermirovská	Edit Vásárhelyi	

1952

Gold	URS	527.03	**Silver**	HUN	520.96	**Bronze**	TCH	503.32

Nina Botscharova	Andrea Bodó	Hana Bobková
Pelageja Danilova	Erzsébet Gulyás	Alena Chadimová
Marja Gorokhovskaya	Irén Karcsics-Daruházi	Jana Rabasová
Ekaterina Kalintshuk	Ágnes Keleti	Alena Reichová
Galina Minaitscheva	Margit Korondi	Matylda Sinová
Galina Shamrai	Károlyne Perényi	Bozena Srncová
Galina Urbanovitsh	Olga Tass	Vera Vancurová-Rylichová
	Mária Zalai	Eva Vechtová

1956

Gold	URS	444.8	**Silver**	HUN	443.5	**Bronze**	ROM	438.2

Polina Astakhova	Andrea Bodó	Gheorgheta Hurmuzachi
Ludmila Egorova	Erzsébet Gulyás	Sonia Iovan
Lidia Kalinina	Ágnes Keleti	Elena Leusteanu
Larissa Latynina	Aliz Kertész	Elena Margarit
Tamara Manina	Margit Korondi	Elena Sacalici
Sofia Mouratova	Olga Tass	Emilia Vatasoiu

1960

Gold	URS	382.32	**Silver**	TCH	373.323	**Bronze**	ROM	372.053

Polina Astakhova	Eva Vechtová- Bosáková	Sonia Iovan
Lidia Kalinina Ivanova	Vera Cáslavská	Atanasia Ionescu
Larissa Latynina	Matylda Sinová-Matousková	Elena Leusteanu
Tamara Lyukhina	Hana Ruzicková	Emilia Lita
Sofia Muratova	Ludmila Svédová	Elena Niculesc
Margarita Nikolaeva	Adolfina Tacová	Uta Poreceanu

1964

Gold	URS	380.89	Silver	TCH	379.989	Bronze	JPN	377.889

Polina Astakhova	Vera Cáslavská	Toshiko Aihara
Ludmila Gromova	Mariana Krajcirová-Némethová	Ginko Chiba
Larissa Latynina	Jana Posnerová	Keiko Ikeda
Tamara Manina	Hana Ruzicková	Taniko Nakamura
Elena Volchetskaya	Jaroslava Sedlacková	Kiyoko Ono
Tamara Zamotailova	Adolfina Tkaciková	Hiroko Tsuji

1968

Gold	URS	382.85	Silver	TCH	382.2	Bronze	GDR	379.1

Liubov Burda	Vera Cáslavská	Maritta Bauerschmidt
Olga Kareseva	Mariana Krajcirová-Némethová	Karin Janz
Natalia Kuchinskaya	Jana Posnerova-Kubicková	Marianne Noack
Larissa Petrik	Hana Lisková	Magdalena Schmidt
Ludmila Turischeva	Bohumila Rimnácová	Ute Starke
Zinaida Voronina	Miroslava Sklenicková	Erika Zuchold

1972

Gold	URS	380.5	Silver	GDR	376.55	Bronze	HUN	368.25

Liubov Burda	Irene Abel	Ilona Békési
Olga Korbut	Angelika Hellmann	Mónika Császár
Antonina Koshel	Karin Janz	Márta Kelemen
Tamara Lazakovitch	Richarda Schmeisser	Anikó Kéry
Elvira Saadi	Christine Schmitt	Krisztina Medveczky
Ludmila Turischeva	Erika Zuchold	Zsuzsan Nagy

1976

Gold	URS	390.35	Silver	ROM	387.15	Bronze	GDR	385.1

Maria Filatova	Nadia Comaneci	Carola Dombeck
Svetlana Grozdona	Mariana Constantin	Gitta Escher
Nelli Kim	Georgeta Gabor	Kerstin Gerschau
Olga Korbut	Anca Grigoras	Angelika Hellmann
Elvira Saadi	Gabriela Trusca	Marion Kische
Ludmila Turischeva	Teodora Ungureanu	Steffi Kräker

1980

Gold	URS	394.9	Silver	ROM	393.5	Bronze	GDR	392.55

Elena Davydova	Nadia Comaneci	Maxi Gnauck
Maria Filatova	Rodica Dunka	Silvia Hindorff
Nelli Kim	Emilia Eberle	Steffi Kräker
Elena Naimushina	Cristina Elena Grigoras	Katharina Rensch
Natalia Shaposhnikova	Melita Rühn	Karola Sube
Stella Zakharova	Dumitrita Turner	Birgit Süss

1984

Gold	ROM	392.2	Silver	USA	391.2	Bronze	CHN	388.6

Lavinia Agache	Pamela Bileck	Zhou Ping
Laura Cutina	Michelle Dusserre	Wu Jiani
Cristina Grigoras	Kathy Johnson	Zhou Qiurui
Simona Pauca	Julianne McNamara	Huang Qun
Mihaela Stanulet	Mary Lou Retton	Ma Yanhong
Ecaterina Szabó	Tracee Talavera	Chen Yongyan

1988

Gold	URS	395.475	Silver	ROM	394.125	Bronze	GDR	390.875

Svetlana Baitova	Aurelia Dobre	Gabriele Fähnrich
Svetlana Boginskaya	Eugenia Golea	Martina Jentsch
Elena Chevtchenko	Celestina Popa	Dagmar Kersten
Elena Chouchounova	Gabriela Potorac	Ulrike Klotz
Natalia Lachtchenova	Daniela Silivas	Betti Schieferdecker
Olga Strajeva	Camelia Voinea	Dörte Thümmler

1992

Gold	EUN	395.666	Silver	ROM	395.079	Bronze	USA	394.704

Svetlana Boginskaya	Cristina Bontas	Wendy Bruce
Roza Galieva	Gina Gogean	Dominique Dawes
Tatiana Goutsou	Vanda Hadarean	Shannon Miller
Elena Groudneva	Lavinia Milosovici	Elizabeth Okino
Tatiana Lyssenko	Maria Neculita	Kerri Strug
Oxana Tchoussovitina	Mirela Pasca	Kim Zmeskal

1996

Gold	USA	389.225	Silver	RUS	388.404	Bronze	ROM	388.246

Amanda Borden	Svetlana Chorkina	Simona Amanar
Amy Chow	Elena Dolgopolova	Gina Gogean
Dominique Dawes	Rozalia Galiyeva	Ionela Loaies
Shannon Miller	Elena Grosheva	Alexandra Marinescu
Dominique Moceanu	Dina Kochetkova	Lavinia Milosovici
Jayce Phelps	Eugenia Kuznetsova	Mirela Tugurlan
Kerri Strug	Oksana Liapina	

Women's Gymnastics: Individual All Round Competition

1952

Gold	Marija Gorokhovskaya	URS	76.78
Silver	Nina Botsharova	URS	75.94
Bronze	Margit Korondi	HUN	75.82

1956

Gold	Larissa Latynina	URS	74.933
Silver	Ágnes Keleti	HUN	74.633
Bronze	Sofia Mouratova	URS	74.466

1960

Gold	Larissa Latynina	URS	77.031
Silver	Sofia Muratova	URS	76.696
Bronze	Polina Astakhova	URS	76.164

1964

Gold	Vera Cáslavská	TCH	77.564
Silver	Larissa Latynina	URS	76.998
Bronze	Polina Astakhova	URS	76.965

1968

Gold	Vera Cáslavská	TCH	78.25
Silver	Zinaida Voronina	URS	76.85
Bronze	Natalia Kuchinskaya	URS	76.75

1972

Gold	Ludmila Turischeva	URS	77.025
Silver	Karin Janz	GDR	76.875
Bronze	Tamara Lazakovitch	URS	76.85

1976

Gold	Nadia Comaneci	ROM	79.275
Silver	Nelli Kim	URS	78.675
Bronze	Ludmila Turischeva	URS	78.625

1980

Gold	Elena Davydova	URS	79.15
Silver	Maxi Gnauck	GDR	79.075
Bronze	Nadia Comaneci	ROM	79.075

1984

Gold	Mary Lou Retton	USA	79.175
Silver	Ecaterina Szabó	ROM	79.125
Bronze	Simona Pauca	ROM	78.675

1988

Gold	Elena Chouchounova	URS	79.662
Silver	Daniela Silivas	ROM	79.637
Bronze	Svetlana Boginskaya	URS	79.4

1992

Gold	Tatiana Goutsou	EUN	39.737
Silver	Shannon Miller	USA	39.725
Bronze	Lavinia Milosovici	ROM	39.687

1996

Gold	Lilia Podkopayeva	UKR	39.225
Silver	Gina Gogean	ROM	39.075
Bronze	Simonia Amanar	ROM	39.067

Women's Vault

	1952		
Gold	Ekaterina Kalintshuk	URS	19.2
Silver	Marija Gorokhovskaya	URS	19.19
Bronze	Galina Minaitsheva	URS	19.16

	1956		
Gold	Larissa Latynina	URS	18.833
Silver	Tamara Manina	URS	18.8
Bronze	Olga Tass	HUN	18.733
	Ann-Sofi Colling	SWE	

	1960		
Gold	Margarita Nikolaeva	URS	19.316
Silver	Sofia Muratova	URS	19.049
Bronze	Larissa Latynina	URS	19.016

	1964		
Gold	Vara Cáslavská	TCH	19.483
Silver	Larissa Latynina	URS	19.283
Bronze	Birgit Radochla	GER	19.283

	1968		
Gold	Vera Cáslavská	TCH	19.775
Silver	Erika Zuchold	GDR	19.625
Bronze	Zinaida Voronina	URS	19.5

	1972		
Gold	Karin Janz	GDR	19.525
Silver	Erika Zuchold	GDR	19.275
Bronze	Ludmila Turischeva	URS	19.25

	1976		
Gold	Nelli Kim	URS	19.8
Silver	Ludmila Turischeva	URS	19.65
	Carola Dombeck	GDR	

	1980		
Gold	Natalia Shaposhnikova	URS	19.725
Silver	Steffi Kräker	GDR	19.675
Bronze	Melita Rühn	ROM	19.65

	1984		
Gold	Ecaterina Szabó	ROM	19.875
Silver	Mary Lou Retton	USA	19.85
Bronze	Lavinia Agache	ROM	19.75

	1988		
Gold	Svetlana Boginskaya	URS	19.905
Silver	Gabriela Potorac	ROM	19.83
Bronze	Daniela Silivas	ROM	19.818

	1992		
Gold	Henrietta Ónodi	HUN	9.925
	Lavinia Milosovici	ROM	
Bronze	Tatiana Lyssenko	EUN	9.912

	1996		
Gold	Simona Amanar	ROM	9.825
Silver	Huilan Mo	CHN	9.768
Bronze	Gina Gogean	ROM	9.750

Women's Asymmetric Bars

1952			
Gold	Margit Korondi	HUN	19.4
Silver	Marija Gorokhovskaya	URS	19.26
Bronze	Ágnes Keleti	HUN	19.16

1956			
Gold	Ágnes Keleti	HUN	18.966
Silver	Larissa Latynina	URS	18.833
Bronze	Sofia Mouratova	URS	18.8

1960			
Gold	Polina Astakhova	URS	19.616
Silver	Larissa Latynina	URS	19.416
Bronze	Tamara Ljukhina	URS	19.399

1964			
Gold	Polina Astakhova	URS	19.332
Silver	Katalin Makray	HUN	19.216
Bronze	Larissa Latynina	URS	19.199

1968			
Gold	Vera Cáslavská	TCH	19.65
Silver	Karin Janz	GDR	19.5
Bronze	Zinaida Voronina	URS	19.42

1972			
Gold	Karin Janz	GDR	19.675
Silver	Olga Korbut	URS	19.45
	Erika Zuchold	GDR	

1976			
Gold	Nadia Comaneci	ROM	20
Silver	Teodora Ungureanu	ROM	19.8
Bronze	Márta Egerváry	HUN	19.775

1980			
Gold	Maxi Gnauck	GDR	19.875
Silver	Emilie Eberle	ROM	19.85
Bronze	Steffi Kräker	GDR	19.775

1984			
Gold	Ma Yanhong	CHN	19.95
	Julianne McNamara	USA	
Bronze	Mary Lou Retton	USA	19.8

1988			
Gold	Daniela Silivas	ROM	20
Silver	Dagmar Kersten	GDR	19.987
Bronze	Elena Chouchounova	URS	19.962

1992			
Gold	Li Lu	CHN	10
Silver	Tatiana Goutsou	EUN	9.975
Bronze	Shannon Miller	USA	9.962

1996			
Gold	Svetlana Chorkina	RUS	9.850
Silver	Wenjiing Bi	CHN	9.837
Bronze	Amy Chow	USA	9.837

Women's Beam

	1952				1956			
Gold	Nina Botsharova	URS	19.22	**Gold**	Ágnes Keleti	HUN	18.8
Silver	Marija Gorokhovskaya	URS	19.13	**Silver**	Eva Bosáková	TCH	18.633
Bronze	Margit Korondi	HUN	19.02		Tamara Manina	URS	

	1960				1964			
Gold	Eva Bosáková	TCH	19.283	**Gold**	Vera Cáslavská	TCH	19.449
Silver	Larissa Latynina	URS	19.233	**Silver**	Tamara Manina	URS	19.399
Bronze	Sofia Muratova	URS	19.232	**Bronze**	Larissa Latynina	URS	19.382

	1968				1972			
Gold	Natalia Kuchinskaya	URS	19.65	**Gold**	Olga Korbut	URS	19.4
Silver	Vera Cáslavská	TCH	19.575	**Silver**	Tamara Lazakovitch	URS	19.375
Bronze	Larissa Petrik	URS	19.25	**Bronze**	Karin Janz	GDR	18.975

	1976				1980			
Gold	Nadia Comaneci	ROM	19.95	**Gold**	Nadia Comaneci	ROM	19.8
Silver	Olga Korbut	URS	19.725	**Silver**	Elena Davydova	URS	19.75
Bronze	Teodora Ungureanu	ROM	19.7	**Bronze**	Natalia Shaposhnikova	URS	19.725

	1984				1988			
Gold	Simona Pauca	ROM	19.8	**Gold**	Daniela Silivas	ROM	19.924
	Ecaterina Szabó	ROM		**Silver**	Elena Chouchounova	URS	19.875
Bronze	Kathy Johnson	USA	19.65	**Bronze**	Gabriela Potorac	ROM	19.837

	1992				1996			
Gold	Tatiana Lyssenko	EUN	9.975	**Gold**	Shannon Miller	USA	9.862
Silver	Li Lu	CHN	9.912	**Silver**	Lilia Podkopayeva	UKR	9.825
Bronze	Shannon Miller	USA		**Bronze**	Gina Gogean	ROM	9.787

Women's Floor Exercise

1952			
Gold	Ágnes Keleti	HUN	19.36
Silver	Marija Gorokhovskaya	URS	19.2
Bronze	Margit Korondi	HUN	19

1956			
Gold	Ágnes Keleti	HUN	18.733
	Larissa Latynina	URS	
Bronze	Elena Leustean	ROM	18.7

1960			
Gold	Larissa Latynina	URS	19.583
Silver	Polina Astakhova	URS	19.532
Bronze	Tamara Ljukhina	URS	19.499

1964			
Gold	Larissa Latynina	URS	19.599
Silver	Polina Astakhova	URS	19.5
Bronze	Anikó Ducza	HUN	19.3

1968			
Gold	Larisa Petrik	URS	19.675
	Vera Cáslavská	TCH	
Bronze	Natalia Kuchinskaya	URS	19.65

1972			
Gold	Olga Korbut	URS	19.575
Silver	Ludmila Turischeva	URS	19.55
Bronze	Tamara Lazakovitch	URS	19.45

1976			
Gold	Nelli Kim	URS	19.85
Silver	Ludmila Turischeva	URS	19.825
Bronze	Nadia Comaneci	ROM	19.75

1980			
Gold	Nelli Kim	URS	19.875
	Nadia Comaneci	ROM	
Bronze	Natalia Shaposhnikova	URS	19.825

1984			
Gold	Ecaterina Szabó	ROM	19.975
Silver	Julianne McNamara	USA	19.95
Bronze	Mary Lou Retton	USA	19.775

1988			
Gold	Daniela Silivas	ROM	19.937
Silver	Svetlana Boginskaya	URS	19.887
Bronze	Diana Doudeva	BUL	19.85

1992			
Gold	Lavinia Milosovici	ROM	10
Silver	Henrietta Ónodi	HUN	9.95
Bronze	Tatiana Goutsou	EUN	9.912
	Shannon Miller	USA	
	Christina Bontas	ROM	

1996			
Gold	Lilia Podkopayeva	UKR	9.887
Silver	Simona Amanar	ROM	9.850
Bronze	Dominique Dawes	USA	9.837

The Development of Difficulty in Men's Floor Exercise

The historical roots of acrobatic exercises can be found in folk games and dances delivered from the desire of common people to express the pleasure of motion. At the beginning, the elements from dance and acrobatics were merged and it was very difficult to differentiate between them. This connection is still preserved in contemporary folk dances, e.g. in Moravian shepherd games or forest robber dances. From that time on, original dance movements began to separate. The name of acrobatics has its origin in the Greek word "akrobates" - rising up. Acrobatic exercises were known to ancient Egyptians and Greeks, in Italy and Scandinavia as early as two thousand years B.C.. Acrobatic exercises are painted on the walls of Knoss palace (158-140 B.C.) as well as on various relics of those times (urns, goblets, frescos). There were for example backward handsprings performed by couples and handsprings over an attacking bull.

The origin of new difficult acrobatic exercises came step-by-step with people selling their abilities and skill. Touring acrobats showed their art and skill to the public at fairs as well as at the parties of the nobility and at the courts of Emperors and Kings. In the course of time, the church of some countries, such as Germany, considered acrobatics to be the devil's work. The excellent Italian acrobat Archangelo Tuccaro, (1538-1616), played an important role in the development of acrobatics at the turn of the 16th and 17th centuries. He performed his art at the court of the German Emperor Maximilian II, and later at the court of the French King Charles IX. He wrote the first school book in the history of acrobatics named "Trois Dialogues de l'Exercise de Sauter et Voltiger en l'Air" in which he described rotations, such as handsprings and saltos, (Figures 2.1 & 2.2) and also tilts according to his own experiences.

Figure 2.1.

Figure 2.2.

Physical education was penetrating step-by-step into schools during the 18th century and acrobatics was also making its way into the school drill. The greatest development of acrobatics was recorded after the delivery of German gymnastics - Vieth and Jahn brought handsprings and saltos into the physical education of their pupils. The name of floor exercises was found for the first time in the works of A. Spiess, (1810-1858) (Figure 2.3). This prominent pedagogue described the importance of acrobatics and floor exercises for school physical education. He created floor exercises which were developed into an individual event because of their rising number of elements. The name of floor exercise was chosen because elements were performed simply on the floor.

Adolf Spiess (1810–1858)

Figure 2.3.

Competitors aimed their skill firstly at the geometrical accuracy of separate elements. The motor content and composition of the floor exercises of that time were simple lines and rhythms with many mirrored movements (Figure 2.4).

Figure 2.4.

The most difficult movements were: standing forward somersault (Figure 2.5), handstand (Figure 2.6), forward handspring (Figure 2.7).

Figure 2.5.

Figure 2.6.

Figure 2.7.

Floor exercises were included into the programme of World Championships and Olympic Games as well as into the programme of other international competitions, but their content and forms of evaluation were different. The first prescribed compulsory exercises were for the II Olympic Games in Paris, 1900. It was a routine only for one gymnast! Then later a compulsory exercise for one gymnast was prescribed for the 1930 World Championships in Luxembourg. From 1900 to 1930 compulsory exercises were prescribed for all groups. For example the World Championships of 1907 in Prague had this compulsory exercise, (Figure 2.8). "Group floor exercises" of 10-12 minutes were last performed at the Olympic Games of 1928 in Amsterdam. ' 10 points were knocked off for not observing the time limitation. All groups finished their exercise before the limited time because of this possible point deduction.

Figure 2.8.

Judgement of the floor exercise was very complicated. Two judges evaluated the combination and difficulty of the floor routine. Another two judges marked the individual performances and a final judge evaluated the team work of the gymnasts. Judges of the first two groups could give 20 points, but their difference could not be greater than 1.75. These points were then added up, divided by two and multiplied by six giving a maximum of 120 points. The judge of the team work could give a maximum of 10 points with his evaluation being multiplied by six. The maximum number of points given for the team work was 60 meaning teams could receive a perfect 300 points!

At the 1930 World Championships in Luxembourg gymnasts also competed with an optional floor routine. The best was J. Primozic (YUG). At the 1932 Olympic Games in Los Angeles the best was Istvan Pelle (HUN). At the 1934 World Championships in Budapest and at the Olympic games of 1936 in Berlin the best was G. Miesz (Figure 2.9) and in Berlin the second place was J. Walter (SUI). Some elements from his optional routine are shown in Figure 2.10. In Berlin, 1936 a very difficult routine was made by E. Löffler (TCH) circling both legs twice, (Figure 2.11).

Figure 2.9.

Figure 2.10.

Figure 2.11.

The content of the floor exercise was changing up to the 1930s. Gymnasts included more acrobatic elements into their routines which were connected into units. At the World

Championships in Prague, 1938, the World Champion on the floor was J. Gajdos (TCH). His routine had 22 swing parts (dynamic), 20 elements hold parts, and 3 elements strength parts. The most difficult elements were handspring backward, round-off salto forward tucked and round-off handspring backward (Figure 2.12).

Figure 2.12.

A gymnastic carpet with a degree of springiness was first used at the 1936 Olympic Games in Berlin. Carpet was first mentioned in 1927: Hacker, the Munich teacher of physical education, used it for the first time. In the course of time the quality of the carpet rose and in 1963, two experts, Reuther and Spieth, demonstrated a double wooden construction of remarkable resilience to the F.I.G. technical committee in Esslingen. This system was then used for the first time during the gymnastics competition at the 1964 Olympic Games in Tokyo. This gymnastic carpet system is still in use today.

From 1946 on, the content of the floor exercise and acrobatics rapidly changed. The best gymnasts of the 1950s and early 1960s were Stalder (SUI), Thoresson (SWE), Muratow (USSR), Takemoto and Aihara (JAP). Todorow (BUL) was the first to perform the backward double somersault tucked in his routine at the 1956 Olympic Games in Melbourne. Figure 2.13 shows the routine of Aihara who won the 1960 Olympic Games in Rome.

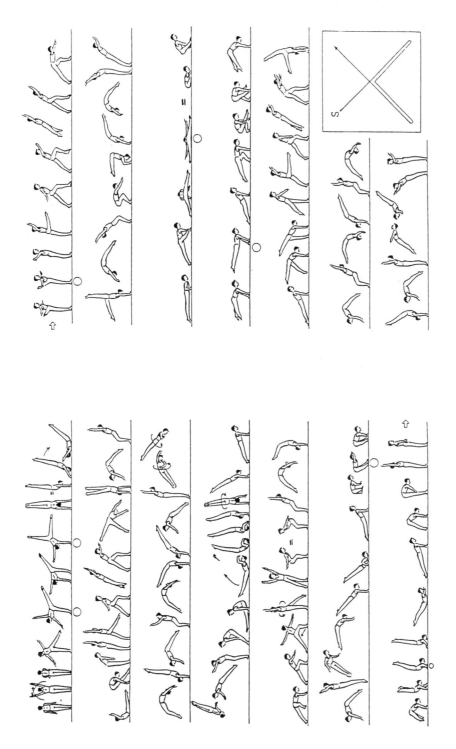

Figure 2.13.

Compulsory Routines

The following figures show the compulsory routines performed at the Olympic Games of 1936 (Figure 2.14), 1948 (Figure 2.15) and 1952 (Figure 2.16), as well as the compulsory routine performed at the 1954 World Championships (Figure 2.17).

Figure 2.14.

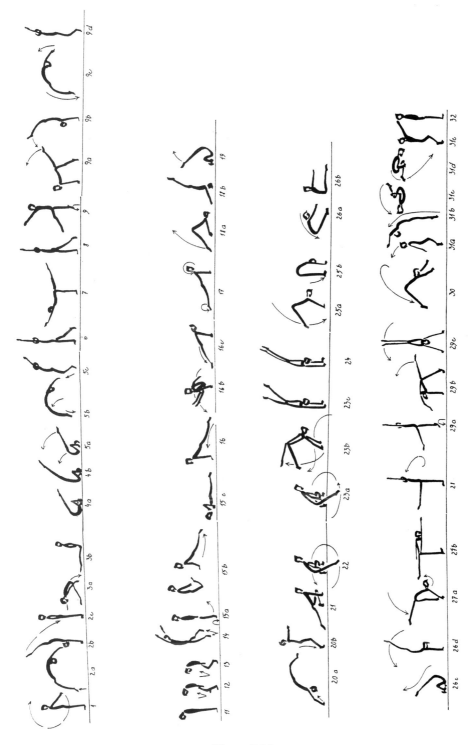

Figure 2.15.

Figure 2.16.

Figure 2.17.

Optional Difficulty

Difficulty of acrobatic elements performed in the optional routines of gymnasts at the World Championships in Prague.

2 x handspring backward, salto backward tucked	44
Round-off, stretched salto backwards	31
Round-off, salto sideways tucked	24
Round-off, handspring backwards, stretched salto backwards	22
Round-off, stretched salto backwards with ½ twist (180°)	39
Handspring backward, salto backward tucked	20
Round-off, handspring backward, salto stretched, handspring backward	19
Round-off, handspring backwards, salto backward stretched with full twist	19
Salto forward tucked, round-off, salto backward tucked	18
Round-off, salto backward stretched with $^1/_1$ twist (360°)	15

A conspicuous break in floor exercise design was seen in the routine of Franco Menichelli (ITA) at the World Championships in Prague and at the 1964 Olympic Games in Tokyo. Menichelli's routine was packed full of difficult dynamic acrobatic elements without any considerable rest or hold positions. Menichelli's floor exercise performed at the 1964 Olympic Games was a poem in motion, a demonstration of spirit and elegance with a high degree of flexibility and amplitude (Figure 2.18). Such a routine was shown at this competition for the first time. It is necessary to emphasise not only the work of Franco Menichelli himself but also the creative work of his Swiss coach Jack Günthard.

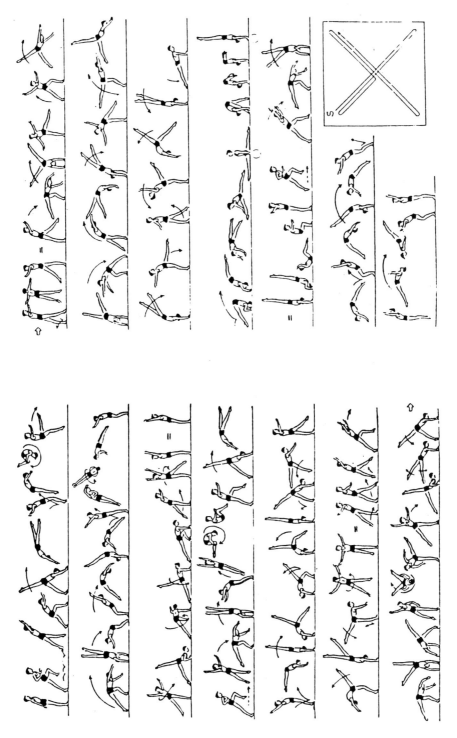

Figure 2.18.

Later on, gymnasts included more and more difficult elements into their routines by which time they were achieving higher and higher scores. The difficulty of routines performed by the finalists during the period from the 1974 World Championships to the 1981 World Championships is shown below (Table 2.1, Jordanov, 1984).

Table 2.1.

Rank	Difficulty	Vama (1974)	Montreal (1976)	Strasbourg (1978)	Fort Worth (1979)	Moscow (1980)	Moscow (1981)	Average (Av.)
1	B	3	4	4	3	1	1	2.7
	C	3	3	6	6	7	7	5.3
	B + C	6	7	10	9	8	8	8.0
2	B	3	3	5	1	4	1	2.8
	C	3	4	3	5	4	7	4.3
	B + C	6	7	8	6	8	8	7.1
3	B	5	3	4	2	3	1	3.0
	C	3	5	3	4	6	6	4.5
	B + C	8	8	7	6	9	7	7.5
4	B	3	3	5	3	1	3	3.0
	C	4	4	4	3	5	5	4.2
	B + C	7	7	9	6	6	8	7.2
5	B	3	3	3	1	4	3	2.8
	C	3	5	5	6	4	5	4.7
	B + C	6	8	8	7	8	8	7.5
6	B	5	5	3	4	5	5	4.6
	C	3	2	4	3	5	5	3.7
	B + C	8	7	7	7	10	10	8.2
7	B			4	3		1	2.7
	C			5	3		5	4.3
	B + C			9	6		6	7.0
8	B			4	3		1	2.7
	C			4	3		6	4.3
	B + C			8	6		7	7.0
Av.	B	3.7	3.5	4.0	2.5	3.0	2.0	3.1
	C	3.3	3.8	4.3	4.1	5.2	5.8	4.4
	B + C	7.0	7.3	8.3	6.6	8.2	7.8	7.5

In the 1970s many gymnasts performed very difficult elements. For example the Japanese E.Kenmocu included stretched backward salto with 3 twists at the 1970 World Championships in Ljubljana. At the 1976 Olympic Games in Montreal the floor was won by N. Andrianov (USSR) with the following routine:

Round-off, flic-flac, full in back out, extension roll to handstand with straight arm, stand. Round-off Arabian dive roll to straddle out, double leg circles to split (very clean). Another double leg circle to front support. stand. Round-off, layout step out turn, single leg circle and kick to handstand in corner, stoop down, turn. Y-scale. Round-off, flic-flac, double back (with cowboy tuck). The score was 9.80 points.

At these Olympic Games Keranow (BUL) performed a new element, the double salto sideways tucked. At the 1977 World Cup in Oviedo, N. Andrianov did for the first time on floor stretched double salto backward. A very nice routine was performed by K. Thomas (USA) at the 1978 and 1979 World Championships (Figure 2.19). Here he did a new element, jump backward with ½ turn and 1½ salto forward tucked into a roll.

In 1980 Li Yuejiu (CHI) did a double Tsukahara (Figure 2.20). At the 1981 World Championships in Moscow J. Korolev (USSR) performed a handspring double salto forward tucked (Figure 2.21). V. Ljukin (USSR), at the 1987 European Championships in Moscow, did triple salto backwards (Figure 2.22).

Figure 2.19.

Figure 2.20.

Figure 2.21.

Figure 2.22.

At the 1984 Olympic Games held in Los Angeles Li Ning won floor with this routine:

Full-in - back-out, double backward somersault, double pike backward somersault, Flair spindle, press handstand, side somersault to front scale and double tuck backward somersault.

The winner on floor at the World Championships 1987 was Lou Yun (CHN) who did this routine:

Round-off, flic-flac, side-in ¾ twisting layout, half turn Swedish fall, step lunge turn to corner. Tucked side salto, round-off, flic-flac, double tuck, half turn Swedish fall, straddle stand, piked press reverse pirouette, handspring punch front 1¼, squat up, half turn. Dive roll, scale. Round-off, flic-flac, double tuck.

At the World Championships in Rotterdam the gymnasts did these element connections in the exercises performed by the 174 gymnasts involved (V. Klimenko, 1988).

Elements	Times Performed
Round-off, flic-flac, backward double salto	180
Round-off, flic-flac, double salto with $^1/_1$ turn	94
Round-off, flic-flac, stretched double salto	40
Thomas circle with circle in opposite direction	40
Double leg flank	21
Sideways double salto	13
Stretched backward salto with $^3/_1$ twists	6
Backward double salto flic-flac forward salto	2
Stretched backward double salto, flic-flac, backward double salto	1
Stretched backward double salto with $^1/_1$ turn	1
Stretched backward double salto with $^2/_1$ turns	2
Forward handspring with forward double salto	1

At the end of the acrobatic series a forward salto was performed as a counter movement after the following elements:

Backward salto	13
Stretched backward salto with $^1/_1$ turn	34
Stretched backward salto with $^2/_1$ turns	8
Stretched backward salto with 1½ turns	6
Double backward salto	1

At the 1988 Olympic Games in Seoul the best was S. Kharkov (URS) and second was V. Artemov (URS).

At the 1989 World Championships in Stüttgart the finalists did an average on floor of 1.75 D, 3.4 C, 1.9 B elements. The winner, Korobchinski (URS) performed 2 'D' and 4 'C' elements. At the 1991 World Championships held in Indianopolis, Korobchinski (URS) won again with this acrobatic series:

Round-off, flic-flac, double layout full-out, handspring layout front, round-off Arabian 1¾, round-off, flic-flac, double layout.

From 212 routines performed in Indianopolis the following movements were most frequently performed:

D - parts

Tsukahara tucked or piked	76
Tsukahara stretched	9
Double salto backward stretched	48

C - parts

Double salto backward tucked or piked	214 (47)
Salto stretched backward with $^2/_1$ turns	56
Salto forward, salto forward	75
Thomas Flair into handstand	21
Salto forward stretched	19
1½ salto forward to roll	14
Salto backward tucked, salto forward tucked	15

In total 486 C parts were performed, of this 55 at the beginning, 177 at the end, 207 in the middle of the exercise and 29 strength parts (K. Schläger, 1992).

At the 1992 Olympic Games in Barcelona the winner was Li Xiaoshuang (CHI) with:

Round-off, flic-flac, triple back, round-off, flic-flac, double twist punch front 1¼, front, front, roll out, round-off, flic-flac, double layout.

Second was Mitsutin (UKR):

Round-off, flic-flac, double layout full-out, front, front, step out handspring layout, front, round-off Arabian dive roll, round-off, flic-flac, double layout.

In the last few years a very successful gymnast on the floor was Neil Thomas (GBR). He and his coach, Eddie Van Hoof, prepared a new and very difficult element, the straight front somersault with 720° twist (Figure 2.23 by J. Atkinson, 1993). Neil Thomas performed this element for the first time at the 1993 World Championships preliminaries in Birmingham.

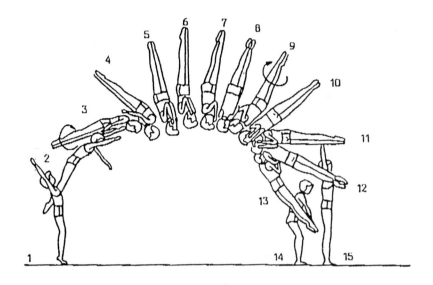

Figure 2.23.

In the finals Neil Thomas came second with:

Round-off, flic-flac, double layout full-out, flic-flac, tuck back punch front. Front handspring layout front, layout front, layout front-full, headspring, Flair handstand to split, straddle press. Handspring layout front, full headspring, side aerial, Y-scale. Round-off, flic-flac, tucked full in back out.

The 1993 the winner was G. Mitsutin (UKR) with this routine:

Round-off, flic-flac, double layout full-out, front step out handspring layout front full. Planche press out. Round-off Arabian dive roll, stag jump, front scale. Round-off, flic-flac, double layout.

The Winners on Men's Floor

1930	Primozic	(YUG)
1932	Pelle	(HUN)
1934	Miesz	(SUI)
1936	Miesz	(SUI)
1938	Gajdos	(TCH)
1948	Pataki	(HUN)
1950	Stalder	(SUI)
1952	Thoresson	(SWE)
1954	Mouratov & Takemoto	(URS) & (JAP)
1956	Mouratov	(URS)
1958	Takemoto	(JAP)
1960	Aihara	(JAP)
1962	Aihara & Endo	(JAP) & (JAP)
1964	Menichelli	(ITA)
1966	Nakayama	(JAP)
1968	Kato	(JAP)
1970	Nakayama	(JAP)
1972	Andrianov	(URS)
1974	Kasamatsu	(JAP)
1976	Andrianov	(URS)
1978	Thomas	(USA)
1979	Thomas & Bruckner	(USA) & (RDA)
1980	Bruckner	(RDA)
1981	Korolev & Yuejiu Li	(URS) & (CHN)
1983	Tong Fei	(CHN)
1984	Li Ning	(CHN)
1985	Tong Fei	(CHN)
1987	Lou Yun	(CHN)
1988	Kharkov	(URS)
1989	Korobchinski	(URS)
1991	Korobchinski	(URS)
1992	Korobchinski	(URS)
1993	Li Xiaoshuang	(CHN)
1993	Misutin	(UKR)
1994	Scherbo	(BLR)
1995	Scherbo	(BLR)
1996	Scherbo	(BLR)

The Development of Difficulty in Men's Pommel Horse Exercise

The oldest note of exercises performed on pommel horse came from the 4th century in a fragment from a Roman military report. Unknown P.V.Renatus Vegetius described the structure and equipment of a Roman legion and he also made a note of Roman warriors' drills on a wooden horse. This episode was chosen by a certain inventive artist of the 17th century who developed horse-exercises consisting mostly of jumps and vaultage.

Vaultage was included in the curriculum of academics of riding and fencing in the 18th century. One of the first reports on vaultage came from 1603 when the master of fencing Wilibald Weingarten from Weimar taught children the art of dancing, jumping and vaultage. A bushy-tailed wooden horse with a head was still in use at the end of the 17th and at the beginning of the 18th century (Figure 3.1). A horse used as an apparatus was still bushy-tailed but without a head, adjustable to an arbitrary height and fixed to the floor (Figure 3.2).

Figure 3.1.

Figure 3.2.

In the second half of the 19ᵗʰ century, the production of horses with a straight back began, (Figure 3.3), and later on the wooden frame was covered with linen or leather. The pommels as well as the filling were made of iron covered with leather. Development of motor content was aimed at the defensive skills drill, at the perfection of mounting a horse, and at offensive and defensive actions with arms.

Figure 3.3.

Utilization of a horse as an apparatus was shown for the first time by our American compatriots at the competition held in Cesky Brod in 1887 where they performed repeated double leg circles. Our opinion of competitive gymnastics changed under the influence of the French school where they performed longer routines and the first rules were formulated. Routines consisted of endurance and held elements such as 'L' supports, planches, handsprings and stretching exercises.

Difficulty of routines had a rising tendency and they were composed taking into consideration symmetry and uniformity.

Pommel horse was included in the programme of the Olympic Games and World Championships as well as in the programme of other international competitions, but their content and forms of evaluation were different. The first prescribed compulsory exercise was at the 1900 Olympic Games held in Paris.

This was the routine at these Olympic Games:

From stand, grasping pommels, jump to one and one half circle to right to rear support, single leg cut with left to rear scissor backward to right, scissor backward to left, single leg cut with right to rear, three double leg circles clockwise, double rear from pommel to end of horse, rear dismount.

For the 1st World Championships in Antwerp in 1903 this was the compulsory routine (Figure 3.4).

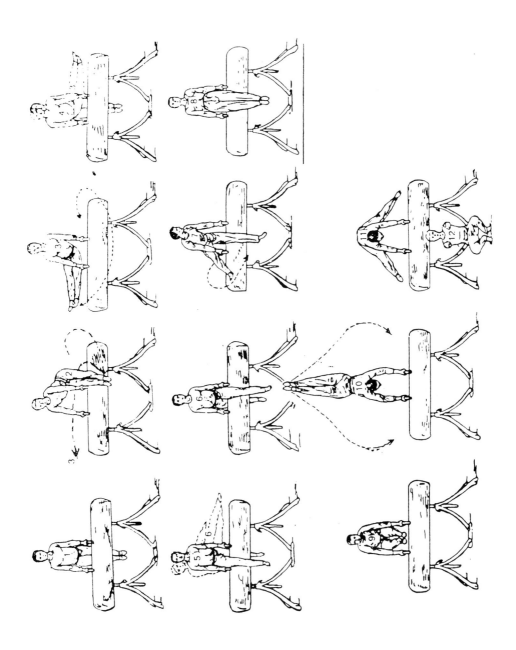

Figure 3.4.

Diplomacy played the most important role in the programme composition of top competitions right from the beginning. For example we obtained the inclusion of pommel horse exercises into the programme of the 1907 World Championships in Prague, the French obtained rings exercises in which they were the best at the 1909 World Championships in Luxembourg. Our gymnasts obtained the pommel horse exercises to be the fixed part of every competition at the 1911 World Championships in Torino. From this time pommel horse has been a part of every competition at the World Championships and at the Olympic Games.

Pommel horse reached its stable form without neck and back around 1920. It became 180 cm long and its body was of the same width with two bow-shaped wooden pommels with a metal bar inside.

In the 1920s and 1930s the Czech gymnasts ranked amongst the best gymnasts on the pommel horse. Our gymnasts shown in Figure 3.5 from left to right are: M. Klinger, the winner equal with N. Jindrich and L. Stukelj at the 1922 World Championships. After World War II he was for many years the President of the Technical Committee of the F.I.G.: J. Sládek was 3rd at the 1934 World Championships: J.Gajdos was 2nd at 1926 World Championships, 3rd at the 1930 World Championships: E. Löffler, J. Novotny: J. Tintera, A. Vechet, father of the E. Bosáková: V. Petracek, was 1st place equal with Reusch at 1938 World Championships: B. Povejsil, J. Kollinger, F. Hospodka, A. Hudec.

Figure 3.5.

Routines in the 1930s consisted mostly of one leg cuts, scissors forward and backward, double leg circles to both sides, as well as double leg circles rearways with turns and double leg circles with turns. The gymnasts ended their routines mostly with rear vault dismount, flank or float dismont after flank (German circle). The evaluation of separate judges was in most cases different, sometimes with a visible idea to derrogate the competitor. For example the difference between the Finnish and the Swiss judges' evaluation of our gymnast at the 1934 World Championships in Budapest was 2 points. When our protest against this evaluation was solved by the judges committee, earlier prepared evaluations of our gymnast were found against the Finnish judge! At the 1928 Olympic Games in Amsterdam the winner on the pommel horse was Hermann Hanggi, Switzerland (Figure 3.6). At the 1936 Olympic Games in Berlin the winner on pommel horse was Konrad Frey, Germany (Figure 3.7).

Figure 3.6.

Figure 3.7.

Expressive progress was noticed in the motor content of routines after World War II. They consisted mainly of double leg circles with turns, exercises performed on the whole body of the horse and exploitation of the far end of the horse for different modifications of rearways double leg circles. The greatest influence upon this trend were the Soviet gymnasts: Beljakov Chukarin, Lavrushtschenko and Chaguinjan as well as their follower Boris Shaklin. The difficulty and the contents of the compulsory exercises for the 1936 Olympic Games in Berlin, the 1948 Olympic Games in London, the 1952 Olympic Games in Helsinki and the 1958 World Championships in Moscow are shown in Figures 3.8, 3.9, 3.10 & 3.11. At the 1954 World Championships in Rome the pommel horse Champion was G. Chaguinjan with the routine shown in Figure 3.12.

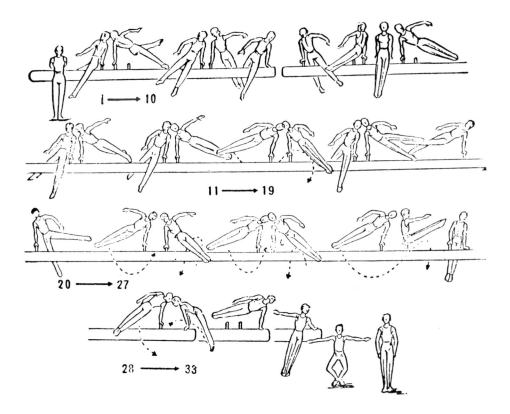

Figure 3.8.

Figure 3.9.

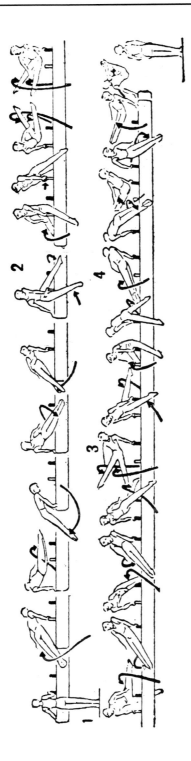

Figure 3.10.

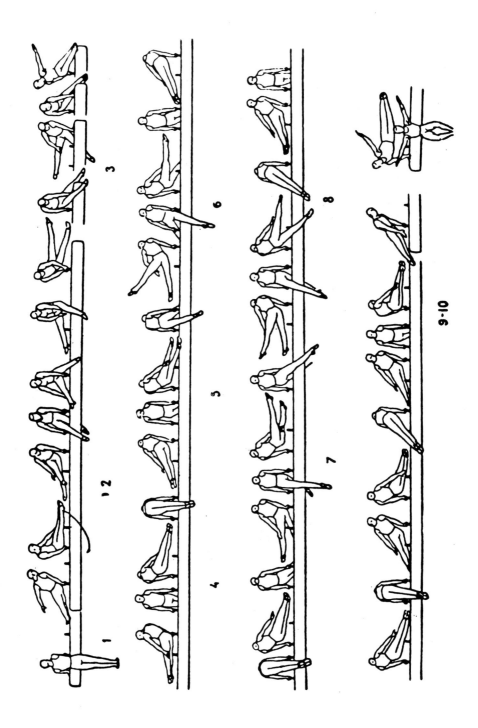

Figure 3.11.

Figure 3.12.

In the course of time, new elements and routines were appearing and gymnastic federations trained their teams to use the horse of new length according to the American model. A 160 cm long horse was used at the 1948 Olympic Games in London. The F.I.G. Technical Committee suggested a 180 cm long horse only in 1955 and latter, in 1960 the horse length became stabilized between 160 and 163 cm. The 1962 World Championships in Prague was the first top competition in which the performances were made on apparatus of constant length. And what a success. The Chinese Yu Lieh-Feng perfomed an original element: the double leg circles in cross support on one pommel.

The Yugoslavian Miroslav Cerar was undefeatable in this event. He won all the top competitions, the World Championships and the Olympic Games in the years 1962 to 1970. His winning routine from the 1970 World Championships in Ljubljana is shown below (Figure 3.13).

Figure 3.13.

Table 3.1. highlights the difficulty of finalists' routines at the 1974 World Championships through to the 1983 World Championships (Jordanov, 1984).

Table 3.1

Rank	Difficulty	Varna (1974)	Strasbourg (1978)	Fort Worth (1979)	Moscow (1981)	Budapest (1983)	Average (Av.)
1	B	3	3	3	2	1	2.4
	C	9	7	8	8	8	8.0
	B + C	12	10	11	10	9	10.4
2	B	3	3	2	3		2.2
	C	5	6	5	8	8	6.4
	B + C	8	9	7	11	8	1.8
3	B	1	2	5	1		1.8
	C	6	5	3	10	10	6.8
	B + C	7	7	8	11	10	8.6
4	B	1	4	4	2		2.2
	C	7	6	5	7	8	6.6
	B + C	8	10	9	9	8	8.8
5	B	4	4	2	1	1	2.4
	C	6	5	5	9	9	6.8
	B + C	10	9	7	10	10	9.2
6	B	2	5	3	4	1	3.0
	C	5	5	5	6	9	6.0
	B + C	7	10	8	10	10	9.0
7	B		5	2	2	2	2.8
	C		5	4	6	8	5.7
	B + C		10	6	8	10	8.5
8	B		3	2	3	2	2.5
	C		5	5	7	8	6.3
	B + C		8	7	10	10	8.8
Av.	B	2.3	3.6	2.9	2.2	0.9	2.4
	C	6.3	5.5	5.0	7.6	8.5	6.6
	B + C	8.6	9.1	7.9	9.8	9.4	9.0

In the 1970s the Hungarian gymnast Zoltán Magyar was unrivalled. Some of the most difficult elements are named after him, such as the Magyar's travels which he did at the 1972 Olympic Games and Magyar spindle which he did at the 1974 World Championships. His winning routine from 1979 World Championships is shown below (Figure 3.14). More difficult elements have required changes of pommels. The officially authorized length changed from 280 to 310 mm as early as 1974. It gave the gymnasts an opportunity to perform their elements in different positions and levels.

Figure 3.14.

The gymnasts always made innovations and new original elements. For example:

Delesalle, Canada, and K. Thomas, USA at the 1976 Olympic Games performed the Thomas Flair. M. Nikolay performed the triple direct Stöckli 'B' at the 1979 World Championships. Tong Fei performed from side support on the end of the horse a Russian Wendeswing without support on the pommels to side support on other end of horse at the 1979 World Championships. Conner and Vidmar (USA) and Korolev and Ditiatin (URS) did handstand in the middle of the pommels at the 1982 World Championships. Sivado did from cross support rearways on end of horse four travel circles backward to cross support frontways on other end of horse (Sivado Travel) at the 1983 European Championships.

The winners on pommel horse at the 1981 World Championships in Moscow were M. Nikolay (GDR) and Li Xiaoping, (CHN) whose routine is shown below (Figure 3.15).

Figure 3.15.

At the 1984 Olympic Games in Los Angeles two trends in pommel horse technique prevailed. The first was based on Magyar travels forward and backward coupled wth single-leg and Thomas Flairs. The second laid emphasis on elements connected with a handstand, preferred by American and Chinese gymnasts. Six of the 8 finalists in Los Angeles perfomed combinations with handstand, most of which included Thomas Flairs and scissors swing. Yamawaki of Japan brought a novelty, a jump travel from the end of the horse over the pommels to other end. The combinations also included new elements, for instance Zellweger's circles with half pirouettes.

The winners here were Li Ning (CHN) with this routine:
From end, Magyar travel to second pommel, travel down, loop, back Moore up, break to front scissor, front scissor to handstand with ½ twist, cut, reverse scissor, pick-up circle in back, circle Flair, Flaired Moore between pommels, Flair on pommels, Flaired hop to end, Flaired loop, Flaired handstand dismount.

and P. Vidmar, (USA)
Back Moore down, spindle, back Moore up, pommel loop, travel to centre, back Moore, back Moore down, Flair-loop around handstand, lower to scissor break to centre, pick-up circles in front back Moore, travel backwards across pommels to end, Flair handstand cartwheel dismount.

At the 1985 World Championships in Montreal the finalists did 16 D difficulty elements , 28 C elements and 9 B elements and connections. The winner was 19 year old V. Moguilni (URS), who won with this routine:
From end, two back loops, back Magyar travel without pommels, Flair spindle on end, Flair back travels to pommel, between pommels, to other pommel, to end, circle, back Moore in, scissor break, pick-up ¾ Bailie to end, Magyar travel to other end, Flaired loop handstand dismount.

At the 1987 World Championships in Rotterdam the exercises of the 177 gymnasts were characterized by the following typical elements (Berczi, 1988):

Mounts:

Direct Stöckli B	47
Direct Stöckli B with double leg circle twice	37
Transverse travel without support on pommel or saddle	26
Magyar travel	16

The most frequent C parts:

Transverse travel without support on pommel or straddle	55
Direct B Stockli with 2 circles	40
Transverse travel	29
Thomas travel with hops	21
Double leg circles in side support, e.g. on one pommel at least twice	18

The most frequent D parts:

Swing into handstand in various forms	89
Tong Fei	23
Magyar travel	23
Double leg circles with travel and ½ spindle	19
Russian Wendeswing on one pommel	13

Dismounts:

Dismount via handstand in various forms	173
Unknown elements were not demonstrated	

The winners at 1987 World Championships were Borkai (HUN) with this routine:

Sivado travel including two loops on each pommel and two loops between pommels, Moore half circle Moore around pommel, circle between pommels, Moore half circle, Moore around other pommel, back Moore in, Flairs, Flaired travel to end Flaired travel with left hand between pommels, then up on pommels, break to leg cuts, 2 front scissors, pick-up, travel to end, loop, straddle handstand dismount.

Bilozerchev (URS) had this routine:

Magyar travel reaching from 1st pommel to 2nd pommel and down to end, loop, circle, back Moore in, half spindle travel to end, finish spindle, half Flaired spindle around 1st pommel, back Flaired Magyar travel to other end, back Moore in, leg cuts, 2 front scissors, pick-up, Flairs, back Stockli to handstand dismount.

In total at the 1991 World Championships in competition IB 338 D-parts were performed, which were distributed as follows (Kato, 1992):

Travel in cross support forward	167
Travel in cross support backward	32
Direct Stockli B	20
Spindle	68
Wendeswing	37
Connection through the handstand	14

In total in competition IB 309 C-parts were performed, which were distributed as follows:

Travel in cross support forward	45
Travel in cross support backward	18
Travel in side support	35
Circle connections	32
Direct Stockli B	7
Spindle	17
Handstand connections	124
Other C-parts	31

At the 1989 World Championships in Stuttgart V. Moguilni (URS) won with this routine:

Two down loops, Sivado travel up to pommel, to pommel loop direct Stockli B, Sivado travel down to end up to one pommel, loop direct Stockli B to Magyar travel down, Schwaben flank, front travel to centre without pommels, back Stockli to end, Kehre out on end, Flair half spindle on end, Flair circle pommels between hands, half spindle between pommels, back travel without pommels, circle pommels between hands, loop side travel up, back scissor, front scissor, side travel, handstand dismount.

At the 1991 World Championships in Indianapolis the winner on pommel horse was Valery Belenky (URS). Belenky said of his routine: "It was easy!" His routine was:

Two loops, Kehre-in between pommels, back Stockli to end, Kehre-out on end, loop, Magyar travel with 3 back Moores on each pommel, Swiss hop on end, loop, back Moore-in, circle, 2 Flairs, handstand, Healy down with left leg in front, scissor break, pick-up Flairs, back Stockli handstand to end, immediate full pirouette to other end.

At the 1992 Olympic Games in Barcelona, the best routines were from Pae Gil Su (PRK) and Vitaly Scherbo (EUN). However in all fairness, Pae's routine had a little more punch. In fact, Pae's set had 83 hand supports to Scherbo's 57. Here are the winners routines:

Pae:

Magyar on leather, back Moore up, Moore in saddle, circle around pommel, saddle loop to Moore around other pommel, circle around pommel, back Moore down, circle, two pommel loops, two back Moores on one pommel, step across of two loops on other pommel, five back Moores on pommel, scissor break, pick-up, Flairs to spindle around pommel to Flaired spindle travel to other end, Flairs on pommels, handstand on end, pirouette to other end.

Scherbo:

On end, Flair handstand pirouette, lower to Flaired spindle travel to other end, two loops, Magyar with extra loop on first pommel, Swiss hop on end, back Moore up, Flair to scissor break, pick-up to Flaired back Stockli handstand, pirouette to other end.

At the 1993 World Championships in Birmingham the winner was again Pae Gil Su (PRK) with the highest socre in this competition 9.750. Second place was Wecker (GER) with a score of 9.450.

Pae's routine was:

Magyar without pommels, Sivado without pommels, walkaround, back Moore up to 3 Moores around pommel, 5 back Moores on 1st pommel, pommel loop, step across to 4 back Moores on 2nd pommel to circle on pommels, scissor break, pick-up, Flairs to spindles around each pommel, Flairs on pommels to handstand pirouette dismount.

Wecker had this routine:

Sivado without pommels, pike up to handstand, scissor break, pick-up, ¾ Bailie to end, Flaired spindle travel to around far pommel and back again, Flaired Sivado without pommels, back Moore up ¾ Bailie, handstand pirouette dismount.

As we can see, Pae's marathon routine was notable for its difficulty, extension, difficulty, variety and difficulty. This tendency will continue in the future.

The Winners on Pommel Horse

1896	Zutter	(SUI)
1904	Heida	(USA)
1911	Palazzi	(ITA)
1913	Zampori, Palazzi &Aubry	(ITA) & (FRA)
1922	Klinger, Jindrich and Stukelj	(TCH) & (JUG)
1924	Wilhelm	(SUI)
1926	Karafiat	(TCH)
1928	Hanggi & Primozic	(SUI) & (YUG)
1932	Pelle	(HUN)
1934	Mack	(SUI)
1936	Frey	(GER)
1938	Reusch & Petracek	(SUI) & (TCH)
1948	Huhtanen, Aaltonen, Savolainen	(FIN)
1950	Stalder	(SUI)
1952	Chukarin	(URS)
1954	Chaguinjan	(URS)
1956	Shaklin	(URS)
1958	Shaklin	(URS)
1960	Ekmann & Shaklin	(FIN) & (URS)
1962	Cerar	(YUG)
1964	Cerar	(YUG)
1966	Cerar	(YUG)
1968	Cerar	(YUG)
1970	Cerar	(YUG)
1972	Klimenko	(URS)
1974	Magyar	(HUN)
1976	Magyar	(HUN)
1978	Magyar	(HUN)
1979	Ditiatin & Guczoghy	(URS) & (HUN)
1980	Magyar	(HUN)
1981	Nikolay & Li Xiaoping	(RDA) & (CHN)
1983	Bilozerchev	(URS)
1984	Vidmar & Li Ning	(USA) & (CHN)
1985	Moguilni	(URS)
1987	Borkai & Bilozerchev	(HUN) & (URS)

1988	Gueraskov, Borkai & Bilozerchev	(BUI), (HUN) & (URS)
1989	Moguilni	(URS)
1991	Belenky	(URS)
1992	Pae Gil Su, Scherbo & Li Jing	(PRK), (EUN) & (CHN)
1993	Pae Gil Su	(PRK)
1994	Urzica	(ROM)
1995	Li Donghua	(SUI)
1996	Pae Gil Su	(PRK)

The Development of Difficulty in Men's Rings Exercise

The first note of rings comes from the ancient Roman artists in varieté who performed their exercises on rings. The original name of this apparatus was Roman rings. The German pedagogues started to use rings relatively lately and even the greatest persons of gymnastics: Guts-Muths, Vieth, Jahn, did not know them: they were first introduced by Adolf Spiess.

At the beginning, the rings were triangular-shaped (Figure 4.1) and only in the middle of the 19th century obtained their shape of metal rings covered with leather or wood (Figure 4.2).

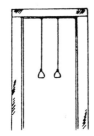

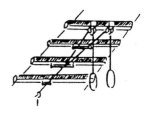

Figure 4.1.   Figure 4.2.

In the 1880s the French gymnasts performed their exercises on wooden rings with steel inserts which allowed them to perform more difficult elements. The Swiss gymnasts created a sensation at the competition held in Paris with their combinations consisting of cross and vertical pull-up with straight arms to support, press to handstand with bent arms and bent body. Rings were undervalued in Bohemia as a result of the fact that the construction of steel rings covered with leather was unsuitable and they could not be fixed up anywhere. The first official competition on rings was held in Bohemia in 1901. The gymnasts performed pulled exercises, such as Felge upward to support and handstand without leg supports.

Rings were included into the programme of the Olympic Games and World Championships as well as into the programme of other international competitions, but their content and forms of evaluation were different. The first prescribed compulsory routine was for the second Olympic Games in Paris 1900. This was the routine:

From front hang, pike hang, backward swing, Felge upward and swing to handstand, lower to free support scale and hold, slowly lower to hanging scale frontway and hold, backswing into inlocate to pike hang, kip uprise to 'L' support, straddle dismount.

The Czech gymnast, Frantisek Erben, saw the Felge upward swing to handstand for the first time at the 1900 Olympic Games in Paris (Figure 4.3). For the 1ˢᵗ World Championships in Antwerp 1903 there were two compulsory exercises (Figure 4.4, 4.5).

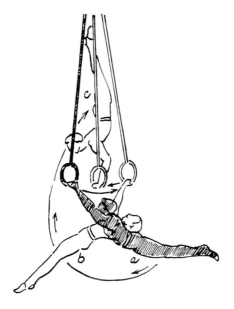

Figure 4.3.

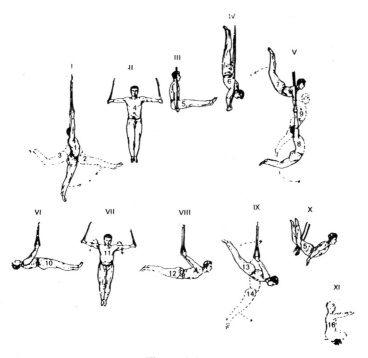

Figure 4.4.

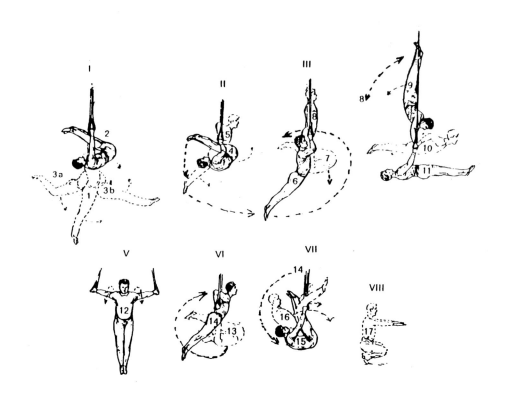

Figure 4.5.

From my analysis of compulsory exercises 1900-1938 (besides competition in 1905) we know that, in the past, gymnasts had to prepare, especially for strength, because 'held' skills predominated. For example, skills such as free support scales, hanging scales frontway and crosses. Dismounts were relatively simple and often repeated. Of fifteen compulsory exercises reviewed, a straddle dismount rearward was used six times, a straddle dismount forward was used five times, and a layout back salto was used four times. The number of elements has changed from the least number, six in 1911 to the highest number, twelve in 1938. The combination of skills changed very little. A new concept of 'combination' was seen for the first time in the Olympic Games in 1936 and the World Championships in 1938 when more swing and dynamic skills were included in the compulsory exercises. The compulsory exercises for the 1932 Olympic Games and for 1938 World Championships are shown in Figures 4.6 and 4.7.

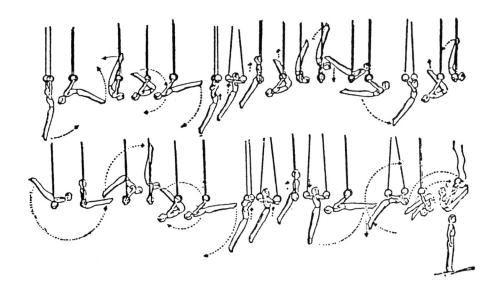

Figure 4.6.

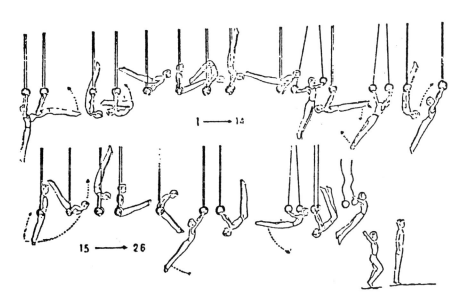

Figure 4.7.

The absolute World Champion Ferdinand Steiner (TCH) became the star of the 1911 World Championships in Torino where he performed an inverted cross. In the 1930s the best gymnast on the rings was Czech Alois Hudec (Figure 4.8). He won at the 1934 World Championships and at the 1936 Olympic Games as well as the 1938 World Championships. A. Hudec died on January 23rd 1997 in Prague.

Figure 4.8.

His routine at 1936 Olympic Games in Berlin was:

Vertical pull-up, arms sidewards and straight, to 'L' support, press to handstand bent body with straight arms, lower to inverted cross, arms horizontal and straight, lower to cross, lower to front lever, inlocate with straight body, Stemme backward to cross, Felge forward with straight body and slowly press to handstand, Felge backward to cross, 'L' cross, lower with straight body to straight inverted hang, inlocate forward with straight body, inlocate to piked inverted hang and dislocate layout flyaway.

Hudec says about his career and experience, "Artistic gymnastics is a wonderful sport. It makes the whole personality strong but it requires toughness and perseverance. One can rely on his own only. I was never satisfied with what I had reached. I began to exercise giant circles on parallel bars and also attempted one-arm giants on high bar. Todays gymnastics is very difficult but, like in our times, gymnasts should not neglect elegance of exercising and inventing new elements."

For the 1948 Olympic Games in London the F.I.G. composed this compulsory exercise (Figure 4.9).

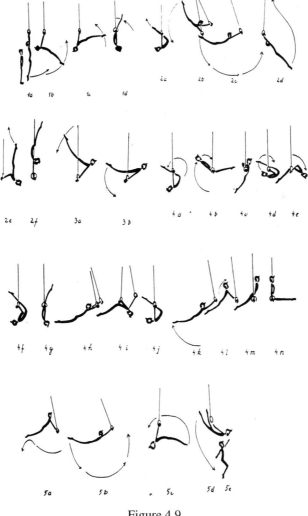

Figure 4.9.

In the 1950s the most expressive person on rings was Albert Azarian (URS) (Figure 4.10). He won at the 1954 World Championships held in Rome. His winning routine from this World Championships is shown in Figure 4.11. He then won at the 1956 Olympic Games in Melbourne, at the 1958 World Championships in Moscow and at the 1960 Olympic Games.

Figure 4.10.

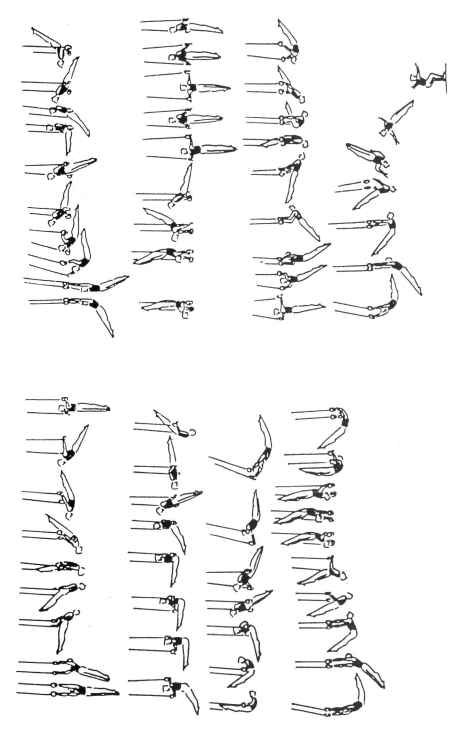

Figure 4.11.

At the 1962 World Championships in Prague the most frequently performed elements were (M. Libra, 1966):

C - parts

Giant swing backward	55
Cross in 'L' position	27
Stemme backward to handstand	23
Giant swing forward	17
Vertical pull-up with straight arms to cross	13
Free support scale	12
Inverted cross	9
Stemme backward to cross	8

Mounts:

From hang - Felge backward with straight body to handstand	36
Dislocate backward - Felge backward to handstand	15
Stemme backward to handstand	12
Vertical pull-up with straight arms to cross	11

Dismounts:

Dislocate backward - salto backward stretched with full twist	24
Dislocate backward - salto backward with pike and stretch	21
Felge backward straddled to stand	16
Dislocate backward - double salto backward tucked	13
Dislocate backward - salto backward straddled	14
Dislocate backward - salto backward stretched	13
Dislocate backward - salto stretched backward with half turn	14

At the 1966 World Championships in Dortmund the winner was M. Voronin with this routine:

Dislocate backward, Felge upward swing with straight arms to handstand, giant swing backward to handstand with straight arms, fall forward and Stemme to cross, lower to pike and Stemme backward to 'L' position, press to handstand with straight body and bent arms. lower through free support scale to hanging scale rearways, dislocate backward, dislocate backward and salto backward stretched with 360° twist.

Here we saw for the first time a new technique for execution of giant backward swing with straight arms. Figure 4.12 shows both the old and new techniques.

OLD   **NEW**

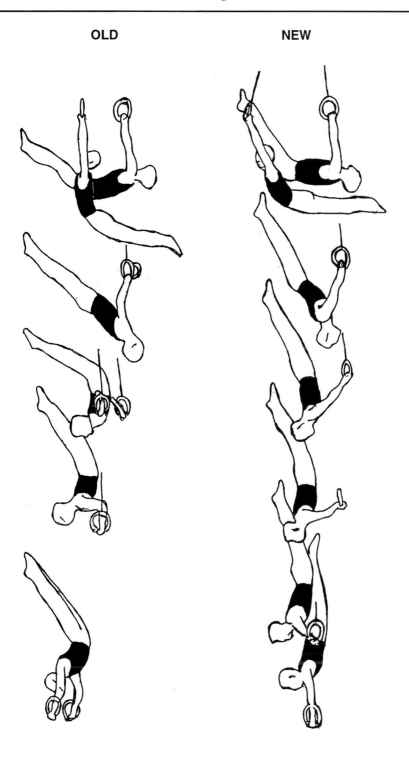

Figure 4.12.

At the 1968 Olympic Games, the 1970 World Championships and the 1972 Olympic Games the best on rings was A. Nakayama (JPN). His winning routine from the 1972 Olympic Games is shown in Figure 4.13 (by Kaneko). At the 1970 World Championships in Ljubljana we saw a new element, from Fumio Honma of Japan, the Honma Stemme to 'L' support (Figure 4.14).

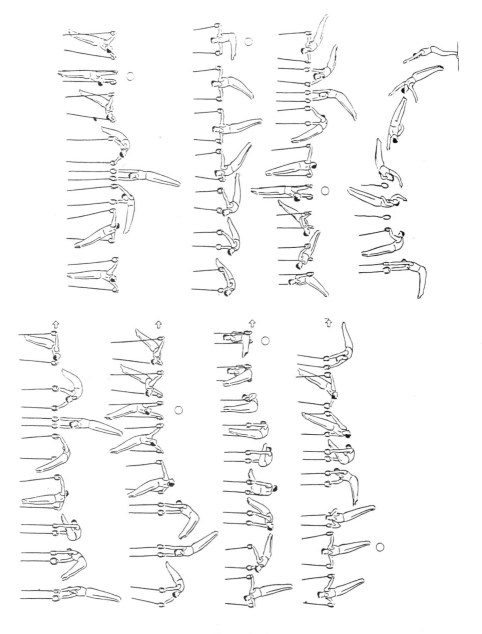

Figure 4.13.

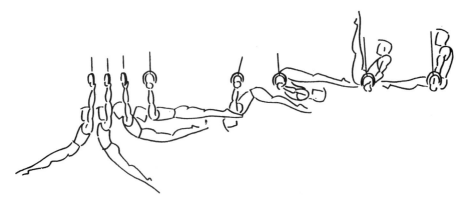

Figure 4.14.

The difficulty of routines has had a rising tendency. Table 4.1 lists the difficulty of the routines performed by the finalist at the 1974 World Championships through to the 1981 World Championships (Jordanov, 1984).

In the 1970s and at the beginning of 1980s N.Andrianov was the best on rings. His winning routine at the Olympic Games 1976 was:

Pull to inverted hang, cast, inlocate to high inlocate to handstand, giant, high dislocate, lower to immediate 'L' cross, drop forward and kip to 'L', slow press to handstand, high dislocate, full-in, back-out.

A. Ditiatin won in 1979, 1980, 1981 and his winning routing at the 1979 World Championships was:

Shoot through planche and lower to cross, inverted hang, kip to support and swing to planche, front uprise to 'L', straight body press to handstand, Honma and swing to handstand, front giant, handstand, bail to immediate piked double.

Table 4.1

Rank	Difficulty	Varna (1974)	Montreal (1976)	Strasbourg (1978)	Fort Worth (1979)	Moscow (1980)	Moscow (1981)	Average (Av.)
1	B	2	3	5	2	3	1	2.7
	C	5	4	4	6	7	9	5.8
	B + C	7	7	9	8	10	10	8.5
2	B	2	4	3	3	4	5	3.5
	C	6	5	6	6	5	6	5.7
	B + C	8	9	9	9	9	11	9.2
3	B	2	5	2	4	5	5	3.8
	C	5	4	6	5	6	6	5.3
	B + C	7	9	8	9	11	11	9.1
4	B	2	6	5	4	3	5	4.2
	C	4	5	3	6	5	6	4.8
	B + C	6	11	8	10	8	11	9.0
5	B	2	2	4	3	4	3	3.0
	C	6	4	5	4	6	7	5.3
	B + C	8	6	9	7	10	10	8.3
6	B	2	4	5	4		4	3.8
	C	5	3	3	4		5	4.0
	B + C	7	7	8	8		9	7.8
7	B			6	4		7	5.7
	C			4	4		7	5.0
	B + C			10	8		14	10.7
8	B			4	5		5	4.7
	C			3.	3		6	4.0
	B + C			7	8		11	8.7
Av.	B	2	4	4.3	3.6	3.8	4.4	3.7
	C	5.2	4.2	4.3	4.8	5.8	6.5	5.1
	B + C	7.2	8.2	8.6	8.4	9.6	10.9	8.8

From 1956 the whole construction of the apparatus as well as the rings themselves was improved achieving maximal constant flexibility and dimensions guaranteeing equal conditions for all. Today the rings with the load up 400 kg do not show any deformation.

Recently gymnasts and their trainers have surprised the experts with many original elements most of all swings composed of combinations. Tucked double Felge backward to forward swing in hang, Guczoghy, performed by the Hungarian Guczoghy (Figure 4.15). "I started to learn this element according to the description of our former top gymnast R. Csanyi who is now a trainer", remembers Guczoghy. "He was preparing this element for many years but a courageous gymnast was not found. After some talks and consultations with my trainer A. Kisteleki I began step-by-step to learn it and after two weeks training I did it. I performed it for the first time in public at the World Cup competition in Zagreb in 1982."

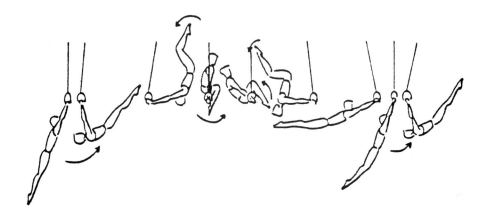

Figure 4.15.

At the 1983 World Championships in Budapest we saw a new element: from support-back toss to hang rearways and Stemme forward to support from Li Ning (CHN), (Figure 4.16).

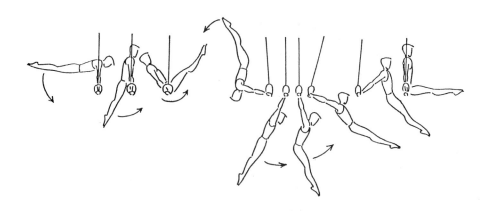

Figure 4.16.

At the 1984 Olympic Games in Los Angeles was another new element, double Felge forward tucked to rearward in hang, from Yamawaki (JPN). At the 1984 Olympic Games on rings two gymnasts were in 1st place, Li Ning (CHN) with this routine:

Dislocate to German uprise 'L', planche, cross, inverted hang, kip to L, straight arm, straight body press, back giant, front giant, giant dislocate, half-in half-out.

and K. Gushiken (JPN) did this routine:

Pull to inverted hang, kip press to inverted cross, drop to inverted hang, kip to planche, bail shoot through inverted cross lower cross, inlocate, cast Japanese inlocate, back uprise handstand, back giant front bail to whippet, forward roll to hollow back press handstand, giant dislocate, double twisting double flyaway.

The routines by the end of the 1980s were more and more difficult. Its very good to see from this example-analysis of D-elements from the 1987 World Championships in Rotterdam compared with the 1989 World Championships in Stuttgart, Competition II. (D. Copeland, 1990).

Element	Stuttgart 1989	Rotterdam 1987
Piked Yamawaki	21	4
Inverted cross	10	15
Full twist double layout	10	1
Kip to 'L' cross	6	1
Giant to inverted cross	6	10
Honma swing handstand	6	2
Back roll cross	6	2
Double twisting double	4	1
Maltese	2	2
Guczoghy	2	2
Back uprise Planche	2	1
Li Ning	1	1
Planche press handstand	1	2

The winner in the 1989 World Championships was Aquilar (GER) with this routine:

Back roll cross, kip to 'L', pike layout straight arm press, inlocate, back uprise handstand front giant, lower through planche to back lever bounce cross, kip 'L', straight body press, dislocate, half-in half-out tucked.

At the 1991 World Championships in Indianapolis the winner was Misutin (URS) with this routine:

Back roll to cross, back kip to 'L', planche, press-out to handstand, piked Yamawaki back uprise hand, back giant, bail layout half-in half-out.

In total 257 D-parts were performed in Competition IB. The most frequent were (I. Berczi, 1992):

Double Felge forward to hang (Jonasson)	73
Double Felge rearward to hang (Gucoghy)	8
Kip to cross 'L' position	57
Lower to inverted cross	34
Press to 'L' support from cross	20

Mounts:

Kip to cross in 'L' position	53
Kip to 'L' support	25
Kip to free support scale	12
Azarian	26
Kip to support, lower to cross	14

Dismounts:

Double salto backward tucked with $^1/_1$ turn (Tsukahara)	86
Double salto backward piked with $^1/_1$ turn	3
Double salto backward tucked with $^2/_1$ turn	8
Double salto backward picked stretched	7
Double salto backward tucked	16
Double salto backward stretched	33
Double salto backward stretched with $^1/_1$ turn	33

Here at the 1991 World Championships there were new elements:

Sin Myong Su (PRK) Back roll to two Olympic crosses, regular cross, pull-out

Miguel Runio (ESP) Yamawaki to barani-in

Vitaly Scherbo (URS) Swing half turn, dislocate half turn, back uprise handstand

Jean-Claude Legros (FRA) Swing half turn, dislocate, half-in half-out (through crossed cables).

At the 1992 Olympic Games in Barcelona the winner was V. Scherbo (EUN) with this routine:

Back roll to cross, inlocate kip to 'L', straight-arm straight-body press, planche, cross, dislocate swing front ½ turn, dislocate immediate ½ turn, back uprise handstand, back giant, giant dislocate, layout half-in half-out.

The gymnasts at the 1992 Olympic Games did these elements (K. Schläger, 1993):

Double Felge forward to hang (Jonasson)	34
Honma Stemme to rearward swing to handstand	24
Kip to cross in 'L' position	19
Felge backward slowly with straight arms to cross (Azarian)	16
Double salto backward tucked with $^2/_1$ turns (double Tsukahara)	4
Triple salto backward	3

At the 1992 World Championships in Paris V. Scherbo won rings again. At the World Championships in Birmingham the winner was Yuri Chechi (ITA). His routine was very difficult and with excellent execution. After the competition, when he finished ahead of A. Wecker (GER) he said: "I think I have done better than Wecker. I am sorry, but I am happy to win". His routine is shown in Figure 4.17 (picture by D. Pellecchia, 1993). This was to be the first of four record World Championships gold medals for the rings by Y. Chechi (ITA).

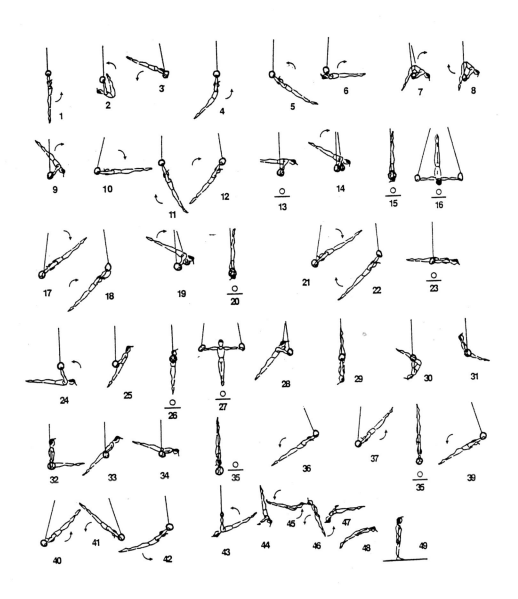

Figure 4.17.

The Winners on Rings

1896	Mitropoulos	(GRE)
1903	Martinez and Lux	(FRA)
1904	Hermann	(USA)
1909	Romano and Torres	(ITA) & (FRA)
1911	Steiner, Follaci & Bianchi	(TCH), (FRA) & (ITA)
1913	Grech, Torres, Zampori and Boni	(FRA), (FRA), (ITA) & (ITA)
1922	Karasek, Maly, Stukelj and Sumi	(TCH), (TCH), (YUG) & (YUG)
1924	Martino	(ITA)
1926	Stukelj	(YUG)
1928	Stukelj	(YUG)
1930	Löffler	(TCH)
1932	Gulack	(USA)
1934	Hudec	(TCH)
1936	Hudec	(TCH)
1938	Hudec	(TCH)
1948	Frei	(SUI)
1950	Lehmann	(SUI)
1952	Chaguinjan	(URS)
1954	Azarian	(URS)
1956	Azarian	(URS)
1958	Azarian	(URS)
1960	Azarian	(URS)
1962	Titov	(URS)
1964	Hayata	(JPN)
1966	Voronin	(URS)
1968	Nakayama	(JPN)
1970	Nakayama	(JPN)
1972	Nakayama	(JPN)
1974	Andrianov & Grecu	(URS) & (ROM)
1976	Andrianov	(URS)
1978	Andrianov	(URS)
1979	Ditiatin	(URS)
1980	Ditiatin	(URS)
1981	Ditiatin	(URS)
1983	Bilozertchev & Gushiken	(URS) & (JPN)
1984	Gushiken & Li Ning	(JPN) & (CHN)

1985	Korolev & Li Ning	(URS) & (CHN)
1987	Korolev	(URS)
1988	Behrendt & Bilozertchec	(GDR) & (URS)
1989	Aquilar	(GER)
1991	Misutin	(URS)
1992	Scherbo (Olympic Games)	(EUN)
1992	Scherbo (World Championships)	(CEI)
1993	Chechi	(ITA)
1994	Chechi	(ITA)
1995	Chechi	(ITA)
1996	Chechi	(ITA)

The Development of Difficulty in Men's Vault

Horse vault belongs to the oldest of physical activities. This discipline recorded its greatest boom in the 18th century. It helped the control of some special horse-riding activities. French court nobility used a wooden horse hanging in space or fixed to the board for learning to ride. At the beginning it was horse-shaped with a saddle but in the course of time it was simplified to the shape of schematic symbol. Jump on and off as well as vaulting were thoughtfully worked-out and a whole range of special motions combined into different variants and combinations was created. Vault was changing from the originally preparatory purpose into an expressive and difficult elegant exercise.

The horse-riding section of Sokol Prague was interested in vaulting as early as 1892 and it was the sole sport club on the Continent with such aims. Highlighted in Figure 5.1 & 5.2 'gymnasts' performed difficult acrobatic elements.

Figure 5.1.

Figure 5.2.

In the course of time, the horse obtained its well-known style of shape in philanthropist schools, Vieth, Basedow, Guts-Muths of the German as well as the Czech movement, Jahn, Eiselen, Tyrs. Development of this apparatus is the same as that of the pommel-horse. The only difference is in the content of exercises. The greatest propagandist of vaults in Bohemia was Dr. M. Tyrs who prepared dynamic group exercises for public performance in 1867 (Figure 5.3, 5.4 & 5.5).

Figure 5.3.

Figure 5.4.

Figure 5.5.

In the 1870s the horse vault was included into regular competition programmes in Bohemia. Vaults were difficult because the length of the horse was 2 m with a width of ½ m and only seldomly without pommels. Frequently used vaults with a springboard were scissors with ½ turn (Figure 5.6) or handsprings.

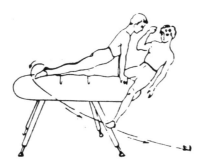

Figure 5.6.

The springboard was discovered by Jahn's follower Eiselen. At the beginning, they were wooden boards, (Figure 5.7, 5.8 & 5.9), later flexible ones, (Figure 5.10) and today the Reuther-Spieth springboard.

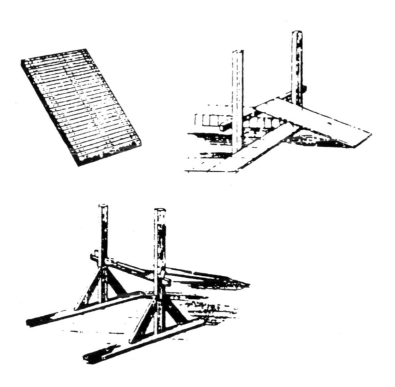

Figure 5.7, 5.8 & 5.9.

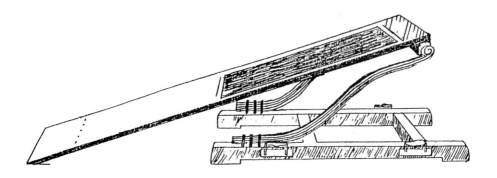

Figure 5.10.

Vault as an event was included into the 1896 Olympic Games programme in Athens. The winner was Karl Schumann (GER) from 15 competitors. At the first World Championship in 1903 in Antwerp the prescribed compulsory vault was jump to handspring and ½ turn dismount (Figure 5.11). The scoring was five points per gymnast and per vault, plus one point for walking up to and one point for leaving the horse.

Figure 5.11.

At the beginning of the 1890s gymnasts did, for example, handspring over two horses from a flexible springboard, (Figure 5.12: in 1902), straddle over two horses and partner (Figure 5.13: in 1904) and handspring from wooden boards (Figure 5.14: in 1905).

Figure 5.12.

Figure 5.13.

Figure 5.14.

Vaults were always the topic of the experts' dispute and for that reason they were excluded from all top competitions between the years 1908 and 1912. It was included again in the programme of the 1913 World Championships in Paris. Then after World War I the vault was in the programme of the 1924 Olympic Games in Paris. Here the gymnasts had a compulsory vault only.

The high jump long horse vault, (Figure 5.15), was an unusual event, in that you had to high jump first over 1.70 m, which is about 5ft. 7 in., and then fly far enough to vault over the long horse.

Compulsory Long Horse Vault.

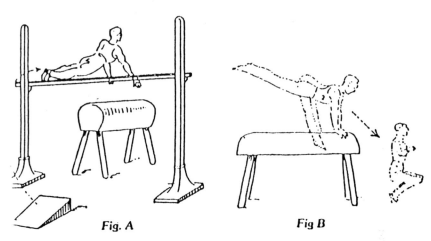

Fig. A   **Fig B**

Figure 5.15.

The winner on this vault was Frank Kriz (USA). Koutny (TCH) was 2nd and 3rd was Morkovsky (TCH). Frank Kriz was 30 years old when he won the high jump long horse at the Olympic Games 1924. Frank Kriz was a product of the Bohemian Gymnastics Association, Sokol, of New York City. He made his third Olympic Team at the age of 34, the 1928 team, a remarkable record. The second compulsory vault was: the side horse vault. With no pommels the vault was a handspring. The winner was Seguin (FRA).

For the 1928 Olympic Games in Amsterdam there were special rules for horse vaulting. The horse was sideways with the pommels-beating board 3 ft. 9 in. away from horse. Height of horse to the top of pommels was 4 ft. 9 in. and the beating board was 4 in. high.

Run, place hands on pommels vault to handstand with straight body, place the right hand on the neck of the pommel, make ¼ left turn releasing the left hand to cross-stand arms sidewards. Screw vault forward.

Horse lengthways without pommels. Height of the horse from the floor was 5 ft. 10 ½ in. with the springboard 15 ¾ in. high. The length of board was 6 ft. 6 in. and 24 in. wide. Voluntary vault with support of one or both hands over the length of the horse.

Here in the 1928 Olympic Games the winner was Eugene Mack (SUI) who won again at the 1934 World Championships in Budapest and at the 1938 World Championships in Prague (Figure 5.16).

Figure 5.16.

By the end of the 1920s and in the 1930s among the best gymnasts of the world were the Czech gymnasts E. Löffler, J. Gajdos and L. Vácha. For a nice example of the difficulty and technique from this 'old' time see Figure 5.18. L. Vácha is doing a Hecht vault. The coach, Dr. M. Klinger, honorary member of the F.I.G., died in 1979 in Prague. This figure is from the preparation of our gymnasts for the 1928 Olympic Games. J. Walter (SUI) finished in 4th place at the 1934 World Championships (Figure 5.19).

Jan Gajdoš

Figure 5.17.

Figure 5.18.

Figure 5.19.

At the 1932 Olympic Games in Los Angeles there were two prescribed compulsory vaults, the cartwheel and the Hecht vault.

The winner was only 20 years old, Savino Guglielmetti (ITA), (Figure 5.20).

Figure 5.20.

At the 1934 World Championships in Budapest, the compulsory vault was stoop with support on the neck of the horse. The horse was 1.30 m high and the length was 1.80 m. The winner was E. Mack (SUI). At the 1936 Olympic Games in Berlin the compulsory vault was stoop with support on the croup of the horse. The winner was

K. Schwarzmann (GER). At the 1938 World Championships in Prague, the compulsory vault was stoop with support on the neck of the horse. This same compulsory vault was in the 1948 Olympic Games in London. The winner was P. Aaltonen (FIN). At the 1950 World Championships in Basle the compulsory vault was scissors with ½ turn with support on the neck of the horse, but from a flexible springboard.

The Soviet gymnasts participated for the first time at the 1952 Olympic Games in Helsinki. The compulsory vault here was stoop with support on the neck of horse. The winner on vault as all-around winner was V. Chukarin. At the 1954 World Championships in Rome the compulsory vault was squat with immediate stretching of knees after the squat through with support on the croup of the horse. The winner was L. Sotornik (TCH) (Figure 5.21). At the 1956 Olympic Games in Melbourne the compulsory vault was jump to handstand and ¼ turn to turnover sideways, a simple Hollander. At the 1958 World Championships in Moscow the compulsory vault was stoop with support on the neck of the horse. The winner was Yuri Titov: President of the F.I.G. from 1976-1996. Figure 5.22 shows his Hecht vault.

Figure 5.21.

Figure 5.22.

This event did not see any visible development until the beginning of the 1960s. In 1956 the disputes were still going on, but this time they were of a technical nature: whether the length of the horse should be 180 cm or 160 cm and whether its height should be 130 cm or 135 cm. No decision was made and the horse remained as it was.

At the 1960 Olympic Games in Rome the compulsory vault was scissors with ½ turn with support on the neck of the horse. The final competition was a very interesting fight between 3 Soviet gymnasts and 3 Japanese gymnasts. From the Soviet Union were B. Shaklin who performed a handspring with support on the neck: Titov did a Hecht vault with support on the croup of the horse and Portnoi did Hecht vault with support on the neck of the horse. From Japan were T. Ono, who did handspring with support on the neck and he took the gold medal with B. Shaklin: Tsurumi and Endo did Hecht vault with support on the neck. So, we see that at this Olympic Games there was not any new structure of vaults.

After the 1960 Olympic Games in Rome, where the Japanese defeated the Soviets for the first time, the war for leadership began. National teams of both countries underwent a strenuous preparation for the following 1962 World Championships in Prague. A year before, October 8th 1961, the Soviet team went to Tokyo to compete with its greatest rival. The competition was extraordinarily balanced. Young Haruhito Yamashita performed an original never seen vault in his optional programme for the first time in an official competition: the Yamashita with support on the croup of the horse (Figure 5.23). This revolutionary vault delivered thanks to the exact physical computations of the Japanese experts who were in search of new content of exercises. This adventurous and physically fit experimenter was found to perform the vault. It was officially certified by the F.I.G. at the 1962 World Championships in Prague.

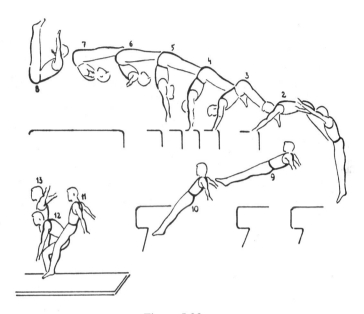

Figure 5.23.

Haruhito Yamashita-Macuda, born 15th of November 1938 was a member of the winning Japanese team at the 1962 World Championships, the 1964 Olympic Games in Tokyo and the 1966 World Championships in Dortmund. Even though he did not succeed in other events of competition, he always belonged to the first ten best gymnasts and he attracted the experts by his vault performance. Yamashita perfected his vault all the time and he won convincingly at the 1964 Olympic Games where he performed the Yamashita with $1/_1$ turn. He also won vault at the 1966 World Championships in Dortmund under the name Macuda, after his wife.

During the 1962 World Championships in Prague the gymnasts performed various vaults:

Handspring with support on the neck	79
Stoop with support on the croup	51
Hecht vault with support on the croup	50
Jump with ¼ turn to turnover sideways, Hollander	27

Stoop with support on the neck   11

Squat with immediate stretching of knees after the squat through

     with support on the croup   6

Scissors with ½ turn with support on the neck   2

The World Champion was Premysl Krbec (TCH) with an excellent vault, Hecht with support on the croup, (Figure 5.24).

Figure 5.24.

In the 1968 Olympic Games in Mexico City the winner was M. Voronin, (USR). But here all were captivated by Sergei Diamidov (URS) with a new vault Hecht vault with $^1/_1$ turn although at the end he took only 3rd place and the bronze medal.

In spite of all this news, opponent voices became stronger and stronger. The Swiss J. Gunthard expressed his attitudes at the meeting of gymnastic experts in Magglingen in 1969 this way.

"Vault is not a complex of elements as other gymnastic events are and gymnasts obtain a non-adequate number of points for their performance. The limited area of hand support on the horse back limits more difficult vaults because gymnasts must concentrate themselves to hand-support: incorrect area of hand support means a big point reduction. The surface of the horse is inelastic which may cause numerous injuries.".

In spite of this argument, the technical committee of F.I.G. correctly decided not to exclude vaults from gymnastic competitions.

The next years brought the confirmation of vault as a popular and developing event. Tsukahara surprised experts with his new vault at the 1970 World Championships in Ljulbjana, which was a round-off backward somersault vault tucked. Tsukahara improved and in finals perfected the round-off backward somersault vault piked (piked Tsukahara) (Figure 5.25).

Figure 5.25.

Experts didn't believe it! Tsukahara, for many years the trainer of the national women's gymnastic team said about it:

"My vaults were never excellent. My run-up was too slow and my kick was poor as well. I wanted to improve it by means of special advanced training but without any successes. Then I began to think of a new vault consisting of turns which would not require any dynamical run-up or strong kick. Because of this extremity I made up a new original vault called the Tsukahara vault."

In the 1970 World Championships we saw a new vault, the handspring-salto forward tucked, performed by Szajna (POL).

In the year 1968, the Technical Committee of the F.I.G. prepared new rules of evaluation in artistic gymnastics, that refers also to the evaluation of the vaults. The evaluation of the long horse vault was divided into four individual factors:

1. Difficulty of the optional jump, or interpretation of the compulsory jump.
2. The support of the hand or hands.
3. The pre-flight and flight of the body from a technical standpoint.
4. The form in execution of the jump.

Especially important was the rule of the support of hand or hands and grip zones. The horse was divided into five different grip zones according to the following figure (Figure 5.26).

In the 1972 Olympic Games in Munich Klaus Köste (GDR) won vault in front of V. Klimenko. Here we could have seen new original vaults such as the handspring and salto forward piked performed by Szajna (POL) and the handspring with $^1/_1$ twist with support on the neck performed by Stan Wild (GBR), (Figure 5.27).

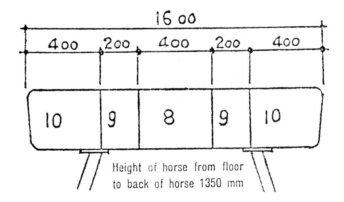

Figure 5.26.

The "Wild" vault performed by Stan Wild, first seen at the Munich Olympics.

Figure 5.27.

In the 1974 World Championships in Varna the World Champion was Shigeru Kasamatsu (JPN), who as his second vault in the final competition presented his original vault, Kasamatsu piked, (Figure 5.28). Second place in these World Championships was N. Adrianov (URS), whose first vault was handspring and salto-forward tucked. His second one was handspring forward with support on the croup and with ½ turn.

Figure 5.28.

In the year 1976 the Technical Committee of the F.I.G. prepared new rules of evaluation of vaults. According to these rules the body of the horse was divided into two parts. (Figure 5.29).

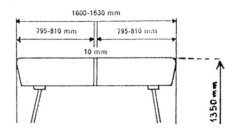

– Figure 5.29.

Another peculiarity was that the individual vaults were divided into special groups: A, B, C, D, E, F where the basic score expressed the difficulties and risks of vaults. The scores for each group was following: A = 7.0 points, B = 8.0 points, C = 9.0 points, D = 9.4 points, E = 9.8 points, F = 9.4 points. For vaults in groups from A to E it was possible to give bonus of 0.2 points for virtuosity. The new vaults which belonged to the group F = 9.4 points with a possible bonus to the full extent for the risk, difficulty and originality of 0.2 points for each factor.

Example

A = 7.0 points	Straddle
B = 8.0 points	Squat with ½ turn
C = 9.0 points	Stoop, handspring, Hecht.
D = 9.4 points	Tsukahara tucked, handspring with ½ turn
E = 9.8 points	Tsukahara piked, handspring with $^1/_1$ turn

At the 1976 Olympic Games in Montreal there shaped up an interesting duel between Andrianov and Tsukahara. Not even the Tsukahara stretched has helped M. Tsukahara to win this wonderful fight. Tsukahara stretched was a new vault.

The winning vaults of Nikolai Andrianov were handspring with 1½ salto and barani out from the near end, and the second one was Tsukahara with full twist, but the direction of the twist appeared opposite to the ¼ turn on.

In these Olympic Games 1976 was a new vault from the gymnast from Cuba, Cuervo, who performed handspring forward with ½ turn and salto backward tucked.

In the 1978 World Championships in Strasbourg the winner was from Japan, Junichi Shimizu, who did as his first vault handspring 1½ front barani out off the far end. As his second vault he did layout Tsukahara. In the second place finished N. Andrianov with the first vault of handspring 1½ front barani out from near end and the second vault was layout Tsukahara. Ralph Barthel, (GDR) finished in third place with his first vault Tsukahara with full twist and second one handspring 1½ front barani out from near end.

In the year 1979 the Technical Committee of F.I.G. prepared further changes in the evaluation of gymnastic routines and vaults. Especially big changes concerned the evaluation of vaults. The changes were as follows: All vaults must be executed with support of one or both hands, over the horse without support zones. The length of running approach is optional, however, it must not be longer than 25 m, counted from the vertical line of the near horse-end.

Bonus points in all three competitions:

The vaults numbered from A-C were divided according to their difficulty into 3 groups with the following base score:

A = 9.0 points   stoop, Hecht vault, handspring sideways, Hollander.

B = 9.4 points   stoop with ½ turn, Hecht vault with ½ turn, handspring sideways with ¾ turn, Tsukahara tucked.

C = 9.8 points   Tsukahara piked, Tsukahara stretched, Kasamatsu tucked, Kasamatsu piked.

Bonus points for virtuosity must be within the frame of 0.2 points, and can be given in the categories A to C. New vaults may be awarded with bonus points in all three categories, risk, originality and virtuosity, each with 0.2 points.

In this year, 1979, were the World Championships in Fort Worth where after 19 years the gymnasts of the Soviet Union won the men's team competition. After all these years they finally beat the team of Japan. Also on the vault, the World Champion was Alexander Ditiatin (URS) who performed as his first vault handspring 1½ front barani out from near end. His second vault was layout Tsukahara. Second was N. Andrianov with the same pairs of vaults as Ditiatin and in the third place finished B. Conner (USA), who performed layout Tsukahara and full twisting Tsukahara. In the year 1979 in the sporting festival 'Spartakiade' of the nations of the Soviet Union we saw the gymnast from Cuba, Roche performing a very difficult original vault, handspring and double salto forward tucked. Roche, (Figure 5.30).

Figure 5.30.

Later on in the 1980 Olympic Games in Moscow we saw a new and original vault performed by Markelov (URS): the Tsukahara stretched with $^1/_1$ turn.

In the 1981 World Championships in Moscow from 170 gymnasts in competition IB we saw 54 vaulted handspring full twist. The second most popular vault was the tucked Kasamatsu which was performed by 21 gymnasts. The third most often seen vault was a layout Tsukahara, performed by 19 gymnasts. There was a total of 13 different vault combinations performed. In these World Championships we saw a new and original vault Tsukahara stretched with a double twist, 720° (Figure 5.31). Ralf-Peter Hemmann (GDR) GDR became World Champion. He performed: Handspring piked somersault with ½ turn, Tsukahara with 360° twist.

Figure 5.31.

In the European Championships in 1982 we saw a new and original vault performed by Boda (HUN): handspring with support of only one hand, salto forward tucked. Also we saw a new vault handspring forward with ½ turn salto backward with $^1/_1$ turn, performed by Brylok (GDR) and Fischer (GDR).

In the 1983 World Championships in Budapest the winner was Akopian (URS) performed: Tsukahara stretched with 720° twist, Handspring forward salto forward with ½ turn. Second finished Li Ning (CHN) with these vaults: Tsukahara stretched, Tsukahara stretched with $^1/_1$ turn.

In these World Championships from 173 gymnasts, 34 did handspring salto forward tucked. In the 1984 Olympic Games in Los Angeles, the attraction was partly due to the

AMF springboard that helped the gymnasts present longer and higher vaults than earlier. In these Olympic Games we saw also a new original vault performed by Lou Yun (CHN) Cuervo stretched with 1½ turn or call it handspring front with 1½ twists (Figure 5.32). Lou Yun became Olympic Champion.

Figure 5.32.

In the 1985 World Championships in Montreal Y. Korolev (URS) won. He performed: 1-arm handspring piked front, 1-arm layout Tsukahara (Figure 5.33). Equal second was Lou Yun (CHN) with: handspring half turn layout back, handspring front layout with 1½ twists. In second place was also Barbieri (FRA) with: 1-arm piked Kasamatsu, 1-arm tucked Kasamatsu.

In 1985 the Technical Committee of the F.I.G. again prepared new rules according to which the vaults are categorized A, B, C and D-value groups with the following base score:

A = 9.0 points stoop, Hecht vault, handspring.

B = 9.2 points handspring with ½ turn, handspring and salto forward tucked.

C = 9.4 points handspring with $^1/_1$ turn, handspring and salto forward piked.

D = 9.6 points handspring and salto forward stretched, Cuervo piked.

Additional bonus points up to 0.2 may be awarded for virtuosity for vaults in A, B, C and D categories. Bonus points for courage are already included in the base score. For new vaults shown in the C and D categories, bonus points may be awarded up to 0.2 for originality.

Figure 5.33.

In 1987 during the World Championships in Rotterdam vaults of the following groups were demonstrated:

	A	B	C	D
Competition IB	1	9	60	105
Competition II	0	0	5	36

The most frequent vaults were:

Stretched Kasamatsu	34
Stretched Tsukahara	30
Stooped Cuervo	15
Tucked Cuervo	11

There were two winners at these World Championships. Lou Yun (CHN) with 1½ twisting front layout and layout Cuervo. Also Kroll (GDR) with layout front-half, and 1½ twisting front tuck.

In the year 1989 the Technical Committee of the F.I.G. again prepared new rules according to which the vaults are categorised into the following 4 value categories of: 8.7 points, 9.0 points, 9.3 points, 9.6 points.

and six structure groups:

Stoop

Hecht

Handsprings forward

      Yamashita

      front handspring

Handsprings sideways with turns

      Hollander

      Tsukahara

      Kasamatsu

Vaults with turn in the first flight phase

Vaults from a preparatory element

Vaults executed with support on 1 arm now have the same value as if executed with support on both arms and will not be recognized as different vaults in Competition III. According to these rules it is possible to give bonus points for originality and / or virtuosity. For illustration we show the values of some of the vaults:

Stoop	8.70 points
Stoop with ½ turn	9.00 points
Hecht with $^1/_1$ turn	9.30 points
Hecht with $^2/_1$ turns	9.60 points

In the 1989 World Championships in Stuttgart Behrend (GDR) won with these vaults: handspring 1½ front layout ½ turn, handspring 1½ front tuck $^1/_1$ twist.

In the 1991 World Championships in Indianapolis the following vaults from different value levels in competition IB were performed: A - 2, B - 10, C - 62, D - 138.

From groups 3 and 4, the most frequently performed were:

Tsukahara stretched	31
Handspring, salto forward piked	12
Kasamatsu tucked	10

| Handspring, salto forward tucked with $^1/_1$ turn | 10 |
| Round-off, salto backward stretched with $^1/_1$ turn | 10 |

At these World Championships in 1991 the winner was You Ok Youl (KOR) with these vaults: layout Cuervo, handspring piked front 1½ twists.

Second was V. Scherbo (URS) with his vaults: layout Yurchenko-full, layout Yurchenko-double full.

Third was Aihara (JPN) with: layout Kasamatsu-full, handspring piked front with 1½ twists.

In the 1992 Olympic Games in Barcelona in competition IB 93 gymnasts participated. They used vaults from 3 different structure groups. Structure group 3 had 28 vaults while structure group 4 had 59 vaults.

These vaults were from following value categories: A - 0, B - 1, C - 5, D - 87.

In these Olympic Games we saw two new vaults, round-off 1½ somersaults into handspring forward performed by May (GBR) and round-off $^1/_1$ twist salto backward. stretched with $^1/_1$ twist performed by Scherbo (EUN).

The Olympic Champion was V. Scherbo with these vaults: double-twisting layout Yurchenko, round-off onto the board, full twist onto horse, Yurchenko-full.

Second was Misutin with: handspring tucked double front, layout Cuervo.

The bronze medal went to You (KOR) with: layout Cuervo, handspring layout front with 1½ twists.

In the year 1993 has the Technical Committee of the F.I.G. prepared new rules, where the vaults are categorized into the following 5 value categories: A = 8.60, B = 8.90, C = 9.20, D = 9.50, E = 9.80.

For example, 8.6 point value vaults were: Yamashita, Yamashita with ½ turn, handspring forward, handspring forward with ½ turn, round-off handspring backward and salto backward tucked. Vaults of 8.9 point value included: Yamashita with $^1/_1$ turn, handspring forward with $^1/_1$ turn. 9.2 point value vaults included: handspring forward with 1½ turn, Cuervo piked or handspring salto forward, ½ turn piked, Tsukahara stretched. 9.5 point value: Hecht with $^2/_1$ turns, handspring with $^2/_1$ turns, handspring with ¼ turn and salto forward stretched, Yurchenko straight with $^1/_1$ twist. For a 9.8 point value vaults were: Yurchenko straight with $^2/_1$ twist, Tsukahara stretched with 1½ or $^2/_1$ turns.

In the 1993 World Championships in Birmingham V. Scherbo (BLR) won with a first vault: layout Yurchenko-double twist, round-off onto board, ¾ turn onto horse, layout Tsukahara-full.

A big surprise for all experts was the second place of Feng Chih-Chang (TPE) with these vaults: layout Kasamatsu-full, handspring piked front 1½ twists.

Four of the eight finalists showed two types of Kasamatsus.

In the 1994 World Championships in Brisbane all around 86 gymnasts participated. The winner in the final was V. Scherbo. The big surprise was a new vault executed by Yeo Hong-Chul (KOR) with double tucked Tsukahara. He received for his original vault only 9.425 and he took third place.

The Winners on Men's Vault

1896	Schumann	(GER)
1903	Dejaeghere, Lux & Thysen	(FRA), (FRA) & (HOL)
1904	Heida and Eyser	(USA)
1905	Dejaeghere	(FRA)
1907	Erben	(TCH)
1913	Stary, Sadoun, Palazzi & Vidmar	(TCH), (FRA), (ITA), & (YUG)
1924	Kriz	(USA)
1928	Mack	(SUI)
1932	Guglielmetti	(ITA)
1934	Mack	(SUI)
1936	Schwarzmann	(GER)
1938	Mack	(SUI)
1948	Aaltonen	(FIN)
1950	Gebendinger	(SUI)
1952	Chukarin	(URS)
1954	Sotornik	(TCH)
1956	Bantz & Mouratov	(GER) & (URS)
1958	Titov	(URS)
1960	Shaklin & Ono	(URS) & (JPN)
1962	Krbec	(TCH)
1964	Yamashita	(JPN)
1966	Matsuda & Yamashita	(JPN)
1968	Voronin	(URS)
1970	Tsukahara	(JPN)
1972	Koste	(GDR)
1974	Kasamatsu	(JPN)
1976	Andrianov	(URS)
1978	Shimizu	(JPN)
1979	Ditiatin	(URS)
1980	Andrianov	(URS)
1981	Hemman	(GDR)
1983	Akopian	(URS)
1984	Lou Yun	(CHN)
1985	Korolev	(URS)
1987	Lou Yun & Kroll	(CHN) & (GDR)
1988	Lou Yun	(CHN)

1989	Behrend	(GDR)
1991	You Ok Youl	(KOR)
1992	You Ok Youl (World Championships)	(KOR)
1992	Scherbo (Olympic Games)	(EUN)
1993	Scherbo	(BLR)
1994	Scherbo	(BLR)
1995	Nemov	(RUS)
1996	Nemov	(RUS)

The Development of Difficulty in Men's Parallel Bars Exercise

This apparatus was constructed in 1810 by Ludwig Jahn. Its name was derived from the word 'barrier'. Jahn used his bars for perfecting the art of vaultage as well as other elements performed on the horse.

Originally the apparatus consisted of two wooden horizontal bars firmly connected with wooden posts fixed on the floor without any opportunity of raising, lowering, or widening them (Figure 6.1) and (Figure 6.2).

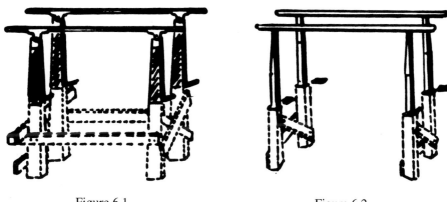

Figure 6.1.   Figure 6.2.

Triple bars were mentioned in German terminology. Bars of different length from ½ m up to 4 m were used and the bars were supported by 6 posts: the common length was 2.75 m. The increased interest for bars exercises after their transfer into gyms caused the fixation of their posts on the wooden frame (Figure 6.3). The widening of exercise content required some changes in construction to the adjustable bars. Their first makers were the Swiss expert Phokion Heinrich Clins (1819), Amoros Y Odeans (1830) from Spain and the German Hermann Otto Kluge (1857).

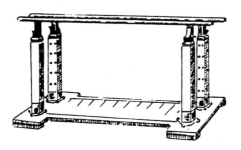

Figure 6.3.

The difficulty of exercises raised in the 1850s and controversy broke out between ·the defenders of Swedish and German gymnastics. The results of the Swedish Lings system investigation made by Major Hugo Rothstein, the head of Royal Central Institute in Berlin concluded that bars were harmful for youth. Scientists from the Berlin University, Rudolf Virchov and Dubois Reymond, a well-known neuro-physician sharply protested against this conclusion and they upheld the benefit of bars exercises and introduced them into the training process again in 1863.

Bars exercises were performed in Czechoslovakia as early as the 1840s when the German apparatus routine was introduced into private gymnasiums. Here gymnasts performed only simple elements consisting of two-three combinations. The main aim was the training of the Tyrs system. Elements were performed at first in mixed hangs and supports, climbing, simple leg swings and handstands. (Figure 6.4).

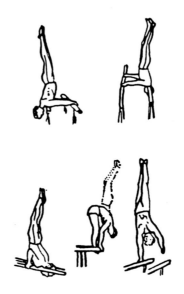

Figure 6.4.

Secret contests were held to show the greater versatility of athletes and the 3rd Sokol Rally in 1895 introduced optional routines prepared beforehand and directed by the main judge at the beginning of the competition.

Parallel bars as a piece of apparatus was included in the programme of Olympic Games and· World Championships as well as into the programme of some other international competitions. The first compulsory routine was at the 1900 Olympic Games in Paris. This was the routine:

Cross stand at end of bars facing inward, jump, straddle cut mount to 'L' support, hold, double leg circle clockwise over right bar to front support, backswing, through bent arm support, jump to straight arm 'L' support, hold, press bent arms and straight body to handstand, hold, lower to shoulder stand, hold, lower to pike underarm, support, kip uprise to support, backswing, straddle cut to 'L' support, hold, backswing to underarm support, back shoulder roll to support, drop to pike hang, kip uprise to support, backswing, double rear dismount.

For the 1st World Championships in Antwerp in 1903 two compulsory exercise routines were used (Figure 6.5 & 6.6). A very difficult competition was the 1907 World Championships in Prague where there were 18 disciplines. The compulsory routine here was:

From underarm support in centre, slowly pull to pike, kip uprise to support, backswing, handstand, hold, drop to underarm support, back shoulder roll to free support scale, hold, 'L' support, hold, Czechkehre straddle, frontswing, front scissors to seat, off-swing to rear to underarm support; frontswing, back shoulder roll to shoulder stand, hold, press to support, frontswing, backswing, handstand, front dismount over both bars.

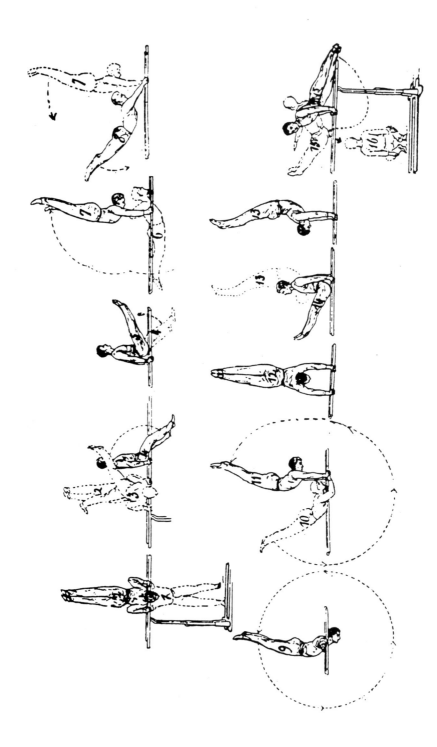

Figure 6.5.

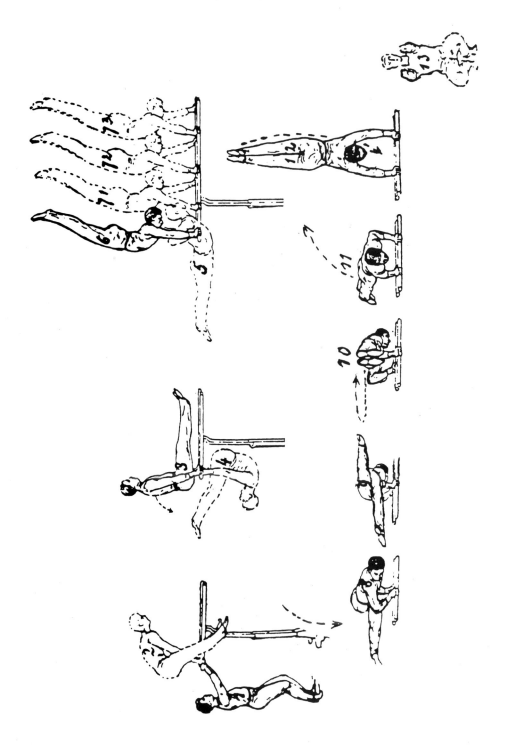

Figure 6.6.

Here in 1907 the Czech gymnasts did very difficult elements such as from forward swing in support basket to upper arm hang (F. Erben). Also from cross stand basket to 'L' support (F. Erben and J. Cada). J. Cada (Figure 6.7) did Czechwende to forward swing in support. A very big surprise was an element from the Czech K. Sála, backward salto in upper arm hang. Dismounts were mostly these elements: Front dismount over both bars, half pirouette forward to handstand on one bar-squat dismount, double rear dismount.

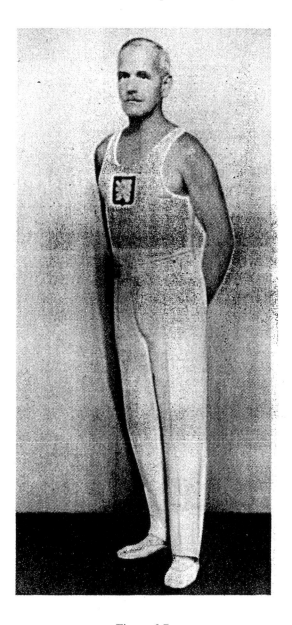

Figure 6.7.

At the 1909 World Championships in Luxembourg, the Czechs gymnasts did mostly strength elements. These included press to handstand with straight body and bent arms. K. Stary did press to handstand with straight body and straight arms. Also the Czech gymnasts did new elements and connections: J. Cada did slide kip and double leg circles 3 times.

K. Stary did a very nice connection from handstand roll backward to handstand backward salto to upper arm hang! A. Braglia from Italy did backward salto to handstand.

After the First World War the gymnasts did their combinations of elements under the bars, such as Stukelj, Indruch, Vanecka, Vácha and Pechácek. Pechácek in 1922 did salto backward to support and basket in upper arm hang. Before the 1924 Olympic Games the Czech Peninger did Stützkehre forward to shoulder stand.

There was a very difficult compulsory routine for the 1928 Olympic Games in Amsterdam:

From cross stand at end of bars facing outward, grasp in outer grip, jump, basket to handstand, through bent arm support, frontswing, Stützkehre to support, drop to pike hang, kip uprise to support, backswing, handstand, hold, lower to shoulder stand, forward shoulder roll to Stemme backward with straddle cut forward to support, offswing to underarm support, Stemme forward to support, rear vault with 90° turn to 'L' hand on one bar, pull uprise support, back shoulder roll to shoulder stand, salto rearward to regrasp left to undergrip and press with straight arms and bent body to handstand, half pirouette forward to handstand on both bars, cartwheel dismount.

At this Olympic Games 1928 the winner was a Czech, L.Vácha (Figure 6.8). He had this routine:

Kip to momentary handstand, press to handstand with straight body and bent arms, free support scale in cross support, Stemme forward to support and Czechwende to 'L' support.

Figure 6.8.

An original dismount was performed by the very good gymnast Mack (SUI): handstand with ¼ turn from backswing, handstand on one arm and straddle dismount. Also a very nice and difficult connection from Neri (ITA), salto backward to support and salto backward to upper arm hang.

At the international competition of 'Slovan Sokols' in Belgrade 1930 J. Primozie (YUG) did a new connection. From cross stand basket to support and immediately basket to handstand.

At the 1st individual World Championships in 1931 in Paris, it was a celebration of the 50th anniversary of the foundation of the F.I.G. and the winner on all around and on the parallel bars was the Czech A. Hudec. He was equal first on bars with I. Pelle (HUN) A. Hudec in the middle of the routine did a new nice connection, basket to support cast to upper arm hang Stemme backward to handstand. Pelle did one arm handstand. But a very difficult element was done by Romeo Neri (ITA) a salto backward to handstand (Figure 6.9) and as dismount salto backward to outer cross stand.

Figure 6.9.

At the 1934 World Championships in Budapest there were excellent routines performed by gymnasts from Germany. They participated for the first time in the World Championships. An element performed by Lorenz was from handstand lower to straddled 'L' position. Volz performed Salto forward to outer cross stand. From Czech gymnasts came the new element, Kolinnger, a Czechwende stretched.

At the 1936 Olympic Games in Berlin the gymnasts did very difficult routines and connections. Armelloni (ITA) did basket to handstand salto backward to handstand, salto backward to outer cross stand. With salto backward out to dismount also from Neri and Bonoli. The winner on parallel bars in 1936 was Konrad Frey, Germany, with this routine:

From stand and jump on the end of bars, slide kip to support double leg circles, two and half circles to 'L' position, press to handstand with bent body and straight arms, jump, hop, to bent support forward rearward swing to shoulder stand, Stemme backward to support with $^1/_1$ turn, rearward swing, handstand, turn in handstand, lower to upper arm hang, Stemme forward to support, front dismount to right on left arm.

At the 1938 World Championships in Prague the gymnasts did not perform new elements. The winner was M. Reusch (SUI) with this routine:

From cross stand, basket, shoot up, to handstand, turn in handstand, lower backward and Felge, salto, under bars to hang, slide kip to 'L' position, press to handstand with straight body and bent arms, salto bow, to support, cast to rearward swing in upper arm hang, Stemme backward and straddle cut to bent support and swing to handstand, lower to upper arm pike position, kip to support, backward swing to handstand, ¼ turn, one arm handstand, on left, straddle dismount.

With this routine M. Reusch won also on the bars at the 1948 Olympic Games in London.

A new element was performed at the Championships of Germany in 1939 (Frisch): Cast with ½ turn to forward swing in upper arm hang. In 1940 in competition in Germany there was a new element, cast to rearward swing in support, Teräsvista from Finland.

After World War II a new generation started in gymnastics. At the 1948 Olympic Games in London the winner was Reusch (SUI). Here the gymnast from France, Sirota, did a new element, cast rearward swing in upper arm position, pike and immediately roll backward to handstand. R. Dot did from jump to support, salto forward to support and immediately to handstand.

In Berlin 1951 at an international competition, Festival of Youth, V. Chukarin (URS) did salto backward with ½ turn dismount. This element was devised by Professor Alekperov from St. Petersburg, for many years the head of gymnastics department on Lesgaft Physical Education Institute.

At the 1952 Olympic Games in Helsinki the winner was Hans Eugster (SUI). He started his routine with basket to handstand and ended with straddle dismount from one arm handstand. Here at these Olympic Games for the first time was the Soviet Union. V. Mouratov did as a dismount salto forward with ½ turn. Czech, F. Danis did at the beginning from outer side stand frontways, slide kip straddle.

In the 1950s the best performers on bars were V. Chukarin and B. Shaklin from the Soviet Union. The winner's routine, B. Shaklin from 1958 World Championships and 1960 Olympic Games is shown below (Figure 6.10).

H. Bantz did front out ½ turn in competition in Berlin in 1940. Then V. Chukarin (URS) did salto with $^1/_1$ turn to outer cross stand at the 1954 World Championships. Also very interesting research by J. Göhler 1993 in an article 'Turns on Bars' in the magazine Olympische Turnen Aktuel N5/1993 where he wrote that, "Salto backward with ½ turn to upper arm hang was performed first by Phillips (USA) at the 1936 Olympic Games in Berlin."

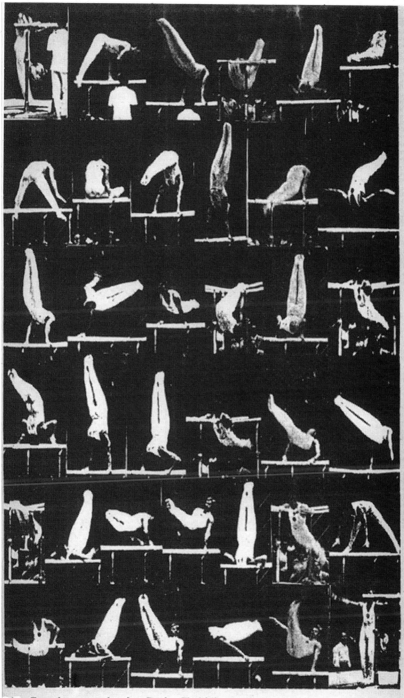

Complete exercise by Boris Chakhline (U.S.S.R.) World Champion 1958 Olympic Champion 1960

Figure 6.10.

At the 1962 World Championships in Prague the winner was M.Cerar (YUG) after a long discussion between the judges. Here M. Cerar did a very interesting new connection in the middle of routine, Stutz forward with ¼ turn to forward swing in hang on one rail, stoop through and shoot up rearways forward to 'L' support, press to handstand with straight arms and bent body. Second place went to B. Shaklin (URS) with the same routine from 1960 Olympic Games. At the 1962 World Championships the most frequent 'C' elements were (Libra, 1969):

Salto backward to forward swing in support-Stützkehre to support	43
Salto forward with ½ turn to outer cross stand	32
Cast to rearward swing in support/to 'L' support/and connection	21
Stützkehre forward to handstand	14
Press to handstand with straight body and straight arms	13
Handstand on one arm	10
From support-basket to handstand	9
Salto backward to handstand	8
Free support scale	6
Salto backward to support twice	4
Roll backward to handstand-salto backward to support	3
Basket to upper arm hang-roll backward to handstand	3
Salto forward to support	2

As dismounts:

Salto backward to outer cross stand	43
Salto forward to outer cross stand with ½ turn	34
Salto forward to outer cross stand	12
Straddle dismount from handstand	10
Straddle dismount from one arm handstand	9
Salto backward with ½ turn to outer cross stand	3

Opinion about the bars construction and specifications began to be unified in 1951. The apparatus was broken 4 times at the 1952 Olympic competition in Helsinki. Two years later the German expert Reuther introduced a new construction. The length of the bars was 3 to 3.5 m and the diameter of the bars 40 to 50 mm with an adjustable maximum height of 175 cm. In 1963 Reuther perfected the apparatus with laminate inserts. Two thin laminate rods were inserted into the lower part of a bar. The adjusment of bars was the same in years 1965-1979 from 42 to 52 cm and the distance between the uprights was 48 cm.

At the 1964 Olympic Games in Tokyo Jukio Endo won on bars (Figure 6.11). But here at this Olympic Games was a new element. From support, forward swing with $^1/_1$ turn with support of one arm to handstand, Diamidov, by S. Diamidov (URS). At the 1966 World Championships in Dortmund S. Diamidov won on bars. In 1964 Peter Healy (USA) performed a new element, the Healy to support. This element is now often in routines of the best gymnasts.

Figure 6.11.

A. Nakayama (JPN) won the parallel bars competition in the 1968 Olympic Games and the 1970 World Championships. His routine is shown (Figure 6.12). The Japanese dominated the 1970s. At the 1972 Olympic Games S. Kato did forward swing on bent arms to ½ jump turn to rearward swing in support. In 1978 in Strasbourg for the World Championships E. Kenmotsu did back giant. At these Games also Willy Moy (FRA) introduced the Moy swing, underbar swing to forward uprise into support. New elements were many at this time: Richards (CUBA) Stemme forwards with full turn to handstand, Y. Korolev (URS) back giant with straddle cut (Figure 6.13), K. Gushiken (JPN) back giant to half upper arms, a Gienger inside the bars.

Figure 6.12.

Figure 6.13.

The difficulty of routines of the finalists at the World Championships and at the Olympic Games has had an increasing tendency. Table 6.1 shows the increase in difficulty of routines of finalists from the 1974 World Championships to the 1981 World Championships.

Table 6.1

Rank	Difficulty	Varna (1974)	Montreal (1976)	Strasbourg (1978)	Fort Worth (1979)	Moscow (1980)	Moscow (1981)	Average (Av.)
	B	2	7	4	2	4	3	3.7
1	C	5	3	4	6	5	7	5.0
	B + C	7	10	8	8	9	10	8.7
	B	2	4	3	2	2	3	2.7
2	C	5	4	4	7	6	8	5.7
	B + C	7	8	7	9	8	11	8.4
	B	8	9	10	10	8	10	9.2
3	C	5	3	6	8	5	9	6.9
	B + C	8	9	10	10	8	10	9.2
	B	1	5	2	3	4		2.5
4	C	7	3	7	5	4	8	5.7
	B + C	8	8	9	8	8	8	8.4
	B	4	5	2	5	1	3	3.3
5	C	4	5	6	5	6	7	5.5
	B + C	8	10	8	10	7	10	8.8
	B	5	5	3	2	2	4	3.5
6	C	4	4	5	6	7	5	5.2
	B + C	9	9	8	8	9	9	8.7
	B			3	1		4	2.7
7	C			6	6		6	6.0
	B + C			9	7		10	8.7
	B			4	4		4	4.0
8	C			5	5		5	5.0
	B + C			9	9		9	9.0
	B	5.7	5.3	3.1	2.6	2.7	2.8	3.7
Av.	C	5.0	3.7	5.4	6.0	5.5	6.9	5.4
	B + C	10.7	9.0	8.5	8.6	8.2	9.7	9.1

As we know, the F.I.G. composed compulsory exercises for each World Championships and Olympic Games. From my analysis of compulsory exercises from 1900, 1989 and 1992 where I evaluated difficulty of routines according to the rules of the F.I.G. which applied from the year 1985, I have these results. At the 1900 Olympic Games the compulsory exercises had: 3 N elements (meaning no difficulty according to present day rules), 6 A elements and 2 B elements. In the 1989-92 Olympic Cycle compulsory exercises had 4 A and 6 B elements.

Generally we can say that the content of compulsory exercises for World Championships was more difficult than for the Olympic Games.

Compulsory exercises in the period 1928-1976 were composed from 73 different elements and the most frequent elements were: Stemme forward, Stemme forward with ½ turn, Stemme backward with ½ turn, Stemme backward and straddle cut to 'L' support, handstand pirouette forward, from handstand, cartwheel dismount.

An example of the content and of the difficulty of compulsory exercises from many years ago can be seen in Figures 6.14, 6.15, 6.16, 6.17, 6.18, 6.19. They are the compulsory exercises for the 1932 Olympic Games, the 1936 Olympic Games, the 1938 World Championships, the 1948 Olympic Games, the 1950 World Championships and 1958 World Championships.

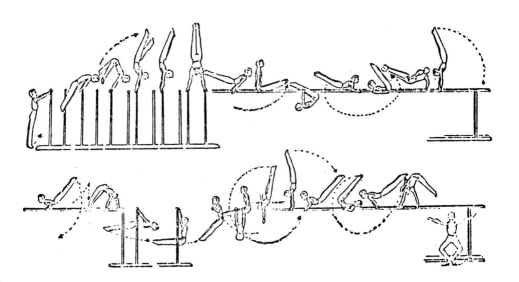

Figure 6.14.

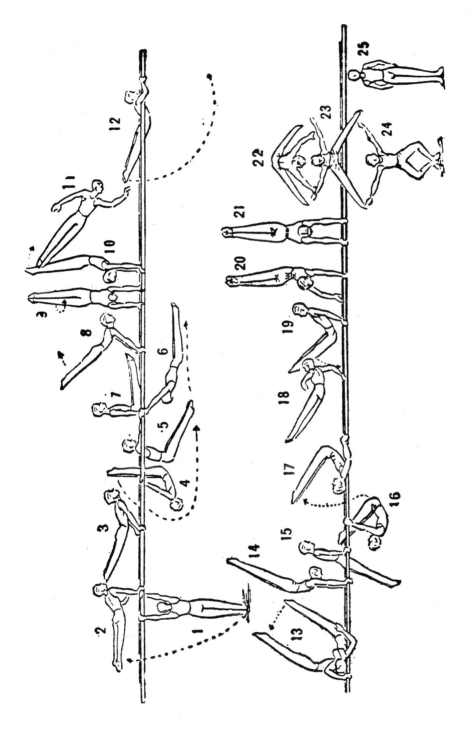

Figure 6.15.

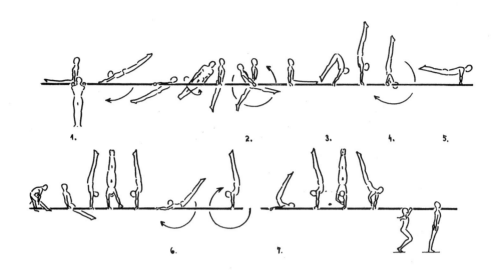

Figure 6.16.

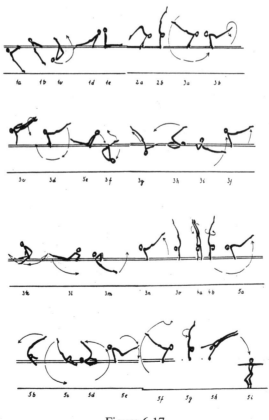

Figure 6.17.

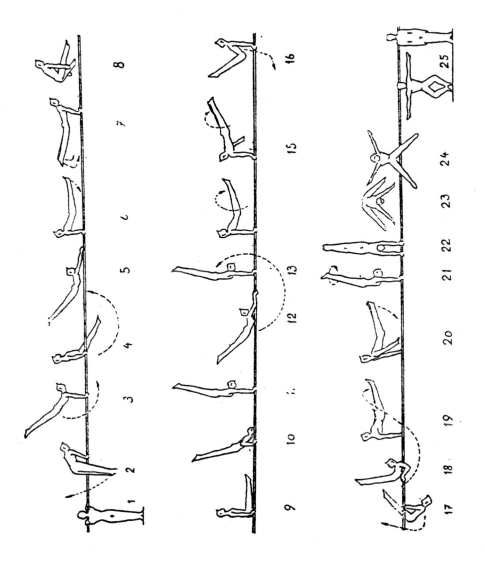

Figure 6.18.

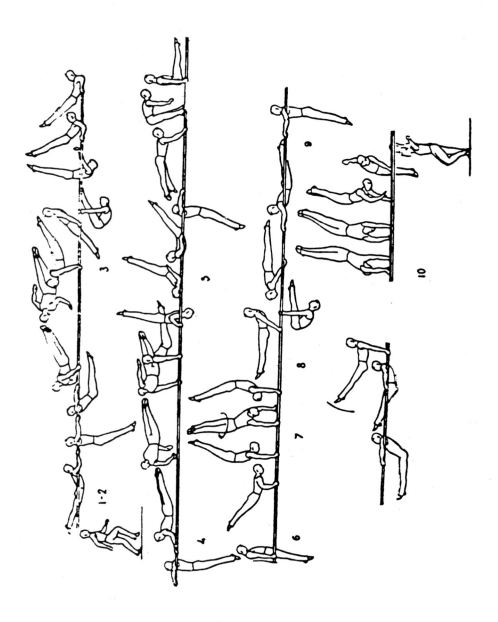

Figure 6.19.

At the competition "Eastern-Bloc friendship" - in Trnava 1984 for the first time a young 16 year old, Sim Myeng Su from North Korea did a new element, double salto backward tucked from giant backward swing (Figure 6.20). Also from Morisue, Japan, at the 1984 Olympic Games, but from handstand.

Figure 6.20.

At the 1984 Olympic Games in Los Angeles 5 years after winning the world title in Fort Worth the winner was again Bart Conner (USA) with this routine:

From side, free hip handstand on far bar, ¼ pirouette to both bars, back toss, back toss, Stutz, to straddle handstand, full pirouette straddled lower to 'L' on one bar, full pirouette in straddle 'L' on one bar, English press to handstand, step-over both bars, Stutz, double back tuck.

At the "Friendship" competition in Olomouc 1984 Balabanov did a new element, a giant backward with $^1/_1$ turn.

At the 1985 World Championships in Montreal parallel bars saw an increase in giant-work with pirouettes at the top (Diamidov) being the most impressive giant skill. Chartrand (CAN) did a tucked Gienger off the end of bars to glide kip. Healys were also common. The gold medal was shared by two gymnasts, S. Kroll (GDR) with this routine:

From side, shoot to handstand on far bar, pirouette in, back toss, glide kip, swing reverse pirouette, Diamidov, Diamidov 1¼ to glide and upstart up on one bar, pirouette in, Stutz, tucked double back.

and V. Mogilny (URS) with this routine:

On the end, glide reverse cut to handstand, Diamidov, giant down to front uprise to centre of bars, Healy twirl, back Stutz, swing pirouette giant, Stutz, back toss, back toss, tucked double back.

At the 1987 World Championships in Rotterdam the gymnasts did 31 D elements; 5 elements as dismount and 2 elements as mounts of the routine. 24 elements were performed in the middle of routines. In 31 routines out of 175 there was no D element (Eckhart, 1988). Several new combinations could be seen on parallel bars. Kwon Soo-Seong (PRK) swung a Gienger from one bar to the other sideways and dismounted with a double flyaway from one bar under the other. Hibert did a back toss with a half turn to upper arms. Chechi (ITA) and Tippelt (GDR) showed the Moy to reverse straddle cut. Belle and Tippelt concluded their routines with double front off the end of the bars. The winner in 1987 was V. Artemov (URS) with this routine:

Peach to handstand, peach half pirouette, giant, Stutz, cast upper arms, back uprise hop pirouette, dip swing reverse straddle cut, high 'V' press, 2 back tosses, double tuck.

The 1988 Olympic Games was won again by V. Artemov (URS) and then at the 1989 World Championships in Stuttgart he won jointly parallel bars with Li Jing (CHN). Li Jing did this routine:

In centre, glide kip reverse straddle cut to handstand, giant full twist, giant, Stützkehre handstand, Moy to support, reverse Stützkehre swing handstand Healy, Healy double front to upper arm, lay away glide kip swing handstand, hold, pirouette, hold, Stützkehre handstand, hold, double pike.

V. Artemov had this routine:

Felge to handstand, Felge to handstand with ½ twist, giant, Stütkehre handstand, cast to upper arm, back uprise top turn to handstand, bent arm reverse straddle cut, 'V' sit, hold, pike press, hold, back salto handstand, back salto handstand, double pike.

At the 1991 World Championships in Indianapolis in total in competition IB, 204 D-parts were performed, of which the following were most frequently performed:

Healy, Healy	34
Double salto forward to upper arm hang	28
Giant swing backward with ½ turn	27
Giant swing backward with $^1/_1$ turn	10
Diamidov with ¼ turn	26
Felge with straddling forward into support	24
Double salto backward tucked to upper arm support	15

In total in competition IB, 657 C-parts were performed. The most frequently performed of these were:

Stützkehre forward to handstand	195
Salto backward stretched to handstand	135
Healy to support	79
Giant swing backward to handstand	58
Diamidov	49
From a handstand, Moy to support	39
From a side hang, kip into straddled	33
'L' support, press to handstand	
Stemme forward and straddle cut backward to support	24

Mounts:

Slide Kip and straddle backward to support	59
Slide kip to support	28
Basket/shoot up/to handstand	32
Cast to rearward swing in support	29
Basket with straddle to rearward swing to support	25

Dismounts:

Double salto backward tucked	141
Double salto backward piked	52
Double salto forward tucked	5

The winner in 1991 was Li Jing, China, with this routine:

Glide reverse cut handstand, giant-Diamidov, giant, Stutz, Moy, reverse Stutz, swing handstand, Healy, Healy, from 1¾ to upper arms, back uprise straddle cut, dip swing handstand, pirouette, Stutz, double pike. (Stoica, 1992).

At the 1992 Olympic Games in Barcelona the best result was received by V. Scherbo, 6 gold medals. He won on the parallel bars with this routine:

On end, jump to straddle cut 'L', piked press, giant-Diamidov, giant 1½ turn, pirouette, Moy, Healy, Healy, hop pirouette, Stutz, back toss, back toss, double pike.

The most frequently performed D-parts in competition IB (Graham, 1993):

Giant backward with ½ or $^1/_1$ turn	30
Double salto forward to upper arm hang	26
Healy-Healy	23
Diamidov with ¼ turn	16

At the 1993 World Championships in Birmingham V. Scherbo (BLR) took gold medal again on parallel bars with a pair of giant Diamidovs on the end and a double front to upper arms in the middle. Very nice and interesting elements and connections performed by Supola (HUN) Diamidov 1¼ to one rail to tucked double flyaway under other rail. Kharkov (RUS) piked and tucked double fronts to upper arms. Jovtechev (BUL): piked double front to upper arms and tucked double back to upper arms. Keswick (USA): tucked double front to upper arms to back uprise planche.

The Winners on Parallel Bars

1896	Flatov	(GER)
1903	Martinez & Hentges	(FRA) & (LUX)
1904	Eyser	(USA)
1905	Martinez & Lalue	(FRA)
1907	Lux	(FRA)
1909	Martinez	(FRA)
1911	Zampori	(ITA)
1913	Zampori & Boni	(ITA)
1922	Stukelj, Derganz & Simoncic, Jindrich & Klinger	(YUG) & (TCH)
1924	Guttinger	(SUI)
1926	Vacha	(TCH)
1928	Vacha	(TCH)
1930	Primozic	(YUG)
1932	Neri	(ITA)
1934	Mack	(SUI)
1936	Frey	(GER)
1938	Reusch	(SUI)
1948	Reusch	(SUI)
1950	Eugster	(SUI)
1952	Eugster	(SUI)
1954	Chukarin	(URS)
1956	Chukarin	(URS)
1958	Shaklin	(URS)
1960	Shaklin	(URS)
1962	Cerar	(YUG)
1964	Endo	(JPN)
1966	Diamidov	(URS)
1968	Nakayama	(JPN)
1970	Nakayama	(JPN)
1972	Kato	(JPN)
1974	Kenmotsu	(JPN)
1976	Kato	(JPN)
1978	Kenmotsu	(JPN)
1979	Connor	(USA)
1980	Tkatchev	(URS)
1981	Ditiatin & Gushiken	(URS) & (JPN)

1983	Artemov	(URS)
1984	Connor	(USA)
1985	Kroll & Moguilni	(GDR) & (URS)
1987	Artemov	(URS)
1988	Artemov	(URS)
1989	Li Jing & Artemov	(CHN) & (URS)
1991	Li Jing	(CHN)
1992	Li Jing & Voropaev (World Championships)	(CHN) & (CEI)
1992	Scherbo (Olympic Games)	(EUN)
1993	Scherbo	(BLR)
1994	Huang Liping	(CHN)
1995	Scherbo	(BLR)
1996	Charipov	(UKR)

The Development of Difficulty in Men's High Bar Exercise

George Kunzle described the beginnings of high bar exercises by means of a citation from Rabelais' Gargantua, written in 1535, as follows:

"They set up a pole fixed between two trees and there he would swing by his hands, his feet touching nothing."

The roots of the horizontal bar event can be traced to the early competitions of the Turners. In Charles Spencer's fourth edition of Modern Gymnast, predating its modern namesake by nearly three quarters of a century, the author recalls the 'invention' of the first flyaway dismount, or 'backaway' to use Spencer's term:

"The first time this graceful evolution was performed was by accident. A young friend of mine was trying a longswing, a sort of giant swing, and the bar being too thick, they were commonly made of wood, he could not retain his grasp when the great strain of the swing took place. His hands slipped.... and the effect was that he turned completely round in the air and came to his feet safely."

Heinrich L. Jahn called the apparatus with a word which has its roots in south German dialect: it means the bar for hanging cloth or cross-bar on which chickens sit. The circus artists of the late Helen era performed their exercises on cross-bars or suspended ropes. There are no documents from the Middle Ages, but a well known picture of Breughels shows children playing on bars. The Japanese performed their exercises on bamboo bars in the 18th and 19th centuries as pictured by Hoikussai (1770-1849). In 1810, L. Jahn taught his pupils to do exercises on limbs. They performed their exercises with such an inspiration that he had to use six limbs (Figure 7.1). In those times they performed half-circles from standing as well as from hanging and backward hip circle. Some pupils even managed sixty backward single knee circles.

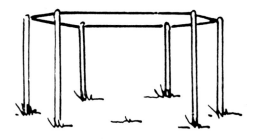

Figure 7.1.

In Czechoslovakia high bar exercises were performed in private in the Institute of Gymnastic Art in Prague, founded by Rudolf Stephany in 1843. The first public exhibition was in June 1862. In those times, elements were drawn out from a hat at the beginning of the competition and gymnasts had to perform them in exact order. The elements were evaluated by 3 judges with 1 to 5 points.

The bar was made of wood, 6 cm in diameter, and competitors performed most of all strength elements. As early as 1875, team competitions were in both compulsory and optional exercises. At this time the most difficult routine was:

Frontswing in reverse grip, back uprise to handstand, half turn in handstand to regular grip, giant swing, squat dismount.

High bar was included in the programme of the Olympic Games and World Championships as well as other international competitions. At the first Olympic Games held at Athens in 1896, the winner on high bar, only optional exercises, was Hermann Weingärtner (GER) with this routine:

From hang in reverse grip kip to momentary handstand, two giant swings forward, ½ turn through handstand. Two giant swings backward, giant swing backward in cross grip, forward swing in regular grip with ½ turn. Half giant backwards to support, free hip circle to straddle dismount.

The first prescribed compulsory routine was at the second Olympic Games 1900 in Paris. The routine was as follows:

From hang frontway with overgrip, Stemme backward to support, flank cut to rear support, drop to rear and underswing forward. Stemme backward to free support scale with bent arms, hold. Back hip circle, lower to hanging scale frontway, hold, hang. Pull uprise to support, press with bent arms and straight body to handstand and squat dismount.

At this second Olympics Games there were no team competitions. There were sixteen events with a maximum score of twenty points per event, giving a cumulative maximum of 320 points for the competition. The gymnast also had an optional exercise on the high bar. Here on the high bar we know that a German from Berlin, Hugo Peitch, performed a double salto at the end of his routine. It was brave, courageous and stupefying! Not only that, but a judge gave him a perfect score of 20.

At the first World Championships 1903 in Antwerp the F.E.G. prescribed two compulsory exercises, one exercise had mostly strength or hold elements (Figure 7.2) and the second exercise had a content of swing elements (Figure 7.3).

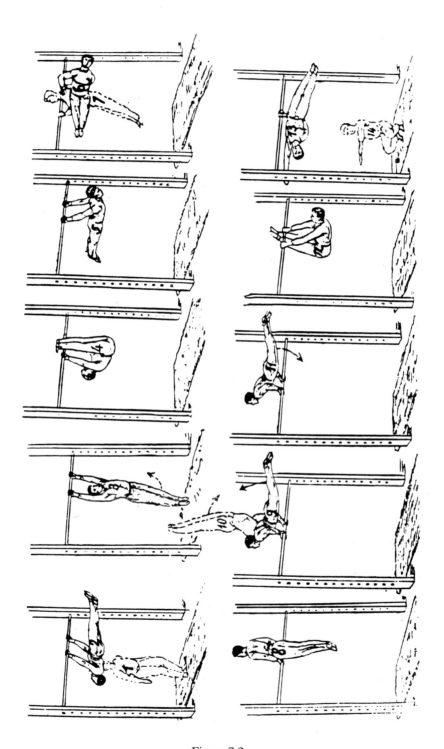

Figure 7.2.

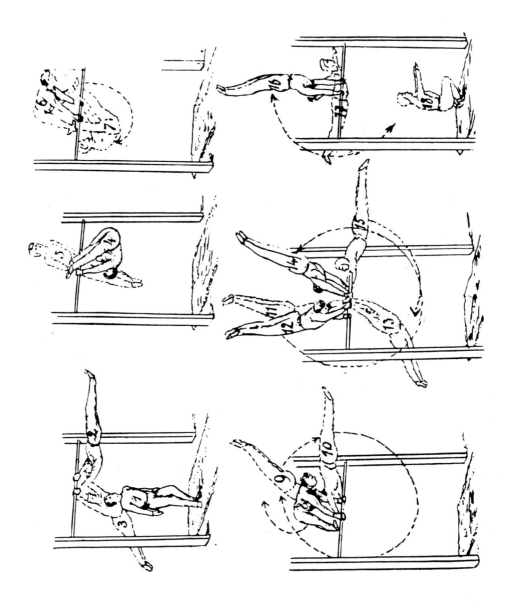

Figure 7.3.

The first time a Czech team participated at the World Championships was in 1907 at Prague. Here they won the team competition, the all around individual competition, J. Cada and on the high bar F. Erben was equal first with N. Charmoille (FRA). Here is

F. Erben's routine which he did at the World Championships in 1907:

From hang, vertical pull-up to support, lower slowly forward to hanging scale frontways, hold, hang 'L' support, hang, kip to support, free hip circle backwards, cross arm giant ½ turn, cross change, giant forward and joined flank, cut catch to hang. In backward swing turn around the left hand to regular grip, kip to support, free hip circle to hang, turn in handstand, back uprise to support. Free hip circle to hang and salto backward stretched to dismount.

As we see F. Erben did a routine with 15 elements, from this 12 elements were swing, 2 hold elements and 1 strength element at the start.

J. Cada, the all round winner at the World Championships had the same structure of routine as F. Erben. But in his routine was a very difficult, interesting connection:

Back uprise to support with immediately joined flank cut catch to hanging scale rearwards (Figure 7.4), and ended with salto backward stretched (Figure 7.5). As I know from Dr. J. Göhler, the German gymnast from Hannover, Fritz Ewert performed as dismount underswing and salto forward and Hermann Wolf did from giant backward salto backward stretched with half turn.

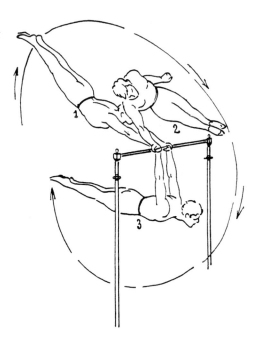

Figure 7.4.

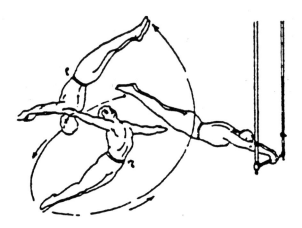

Figure 7.5.

At the 1908 Olympic Games in London and at the Olympic Games in Stockholm the all around competition was won by Alberto Braglia (ITA). At the 1908 Olympic Games he performed for the first time the Steinemann Stemme, which Eduard Steinemann (SUI) did in competition in Stüttgart in 1933. Here is the routine of Braglia from the Olympic Games 1912:

From hang in mixed grip, under cast with ½ turn to hang in regular grip, shoot backward to back hang and schechenStemme to rear support. Lower to piked inverted hang, kip to support, free hip circle to hang. Back kip, free hip circle rearways backwards, Steinemann Stemme (I think it is better that we should call it "Braglia"). Lower to piked inverted hang, kip to support, straddle cut catch to reverse grip, lower back to hanging scale rearways, hold. Raise body to rear support and change grip to regular grip, lower to piked inverted hang, kip to rearward swing to momentary handstand. Back giant swing, whip turn, back turn, blind change, giant forward to support and forward stoop, hang on heels, half circle on heels and forward dismount.

At the beginning of our century the wooden bar was replaced by a steel one covered with a thin layer of ash and fixed on stands. The gymnasts were using resin for their hands which they held in their pockets. At the Olympic Games in 1912 in Stockholm the high bar had a height of 240 cm, a length of 220 cm, a thickness 32 mm and was made of polished steel. It is interesting to compare the principles for judging. At the 1912 Olympic Games they used this principle:

"There shall be three judges at each apparatus. Each judge shall award the points independently and shall not consult with his colleagues regarding the points. Immediately after a squad has gone through its programme at an apparatus the judges' protocols, duly signed, shall be sent in to the Sub-Committee for gymnastics. During the competition the judges may not divulge the points awarded by them. Points will be awarded at each apparatus in the following manner:

For the manner of approaching the the apparatus: maximum of 1 point

For the manner of leaving the apparatus: maximum of 1 point

For execution: 0 - 10 points comprising:

    0 points for no execution

    2 points for bad execution

    4 points for moderate execution

    6 points for satisfactory execution

    8 points for good execution

    10 points for excellent execution

Intermediate points allowed are: 0.75, 0.50, 0.25.

Maximum points to be awarded by judge:

For manner to and from the apparatus:

    2 points x 4 apparatus: 8points

For execution

    10 points x 4 apparatus:40 points

Total maximum 48 points

Teams have the right to bring their own apparatus."

After World War I the F.E.G. prepared for the World Championships of 1922 in Ljubljana. Here this compulsory routine was used:

From front hang with over grip, swing, Stemme backward, free hip circle to handstand. Back giant to handstand, lower to support, drop to rear, underswing forwards. Backswing to frontswing with 180° turn to mixed grip, kip uprise with regrasp to overgrip, lower forward to 'L' hang, hold. Through pike hang pull uprise to rear support, regrasp to under grip, front seat circle, lift to pike support with heels on bar, drop to rear and underswing dismount forward.

At this World Championship in 1922 there was a big fight for first place. After the competition five gymnasts were on first place: Stukelj, Derganc, Simoncic, (YUG) and Czechs Klinger and Jindrich. What they performed on high bar:

From hang in over grip, back uprise joined flank, cut with ¼ turn to front support, lower to piked inverted hang, kip to support. Free hip circle backwards to front support, giant backwards, giant backwards and lower to hanging scale front ways. Pull to support, press to handstand with straight body and bent arms, lower to free support scale. Cast squat to 'L' support, free hip circle rearways backward, lower back, underswing with ½ turn in backswing to reverse grip, kip and swing to handstand, Giant swing forward and straddle dismount.

M. Klinger had as a beginning:

From hang in under grip, cast to handstand and two giant swings forward. As a dismount, kip to handstand and straddle dismount.

In the twenties the requirements of high bar content was not still fully clear. The gymnasts performed routines with swinging elements as well as strength and hold elements. The most frequent elements in routines were (Figures 7.6 - 7.11).

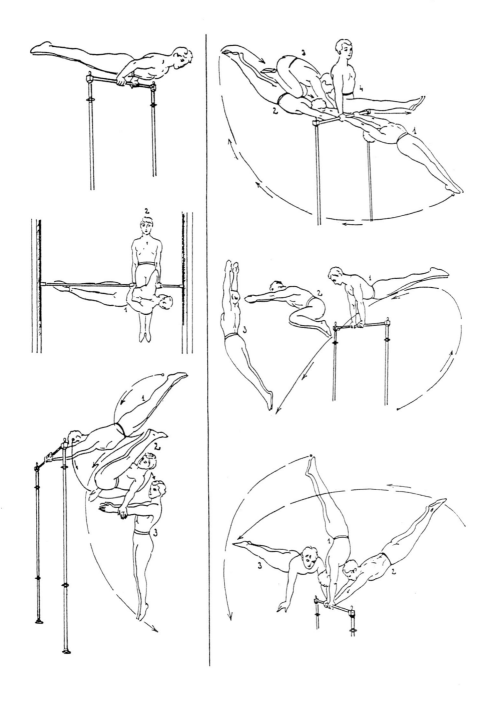

Figures 7.6. - 7.11.

But during this time many gymnasts tried new elements. For example Willi Platzek (GER) in 1924 performed from standing on the bar a stretched salto backward to hang which Olga Korbut used in the 1972 Olympic Games.

At the Olympic Games of 1922 in Amsterdam there began a new composition of compulsory exercise where the content of a routine was only from swing elements. The best gymnasts on high bar were the gymnasts from Switzerland. The winner G. Miez did for the first time a back uprise in mixed grip followed by a straddled double rear vault (Swiss circle). Fourth placed was H. Hänggi (Figure 7.12).

Figure 7.12.

From the Czech team came very difficult parts. From J. Löffler, Steinemann Stemme, giant swing rearways forwards (a Russian giant swing) and as a dismount from handstand a one arm straddle.

At the World Championships in 1930 in Luxembourg the gymnasts performed for the last time routines of strength and hold parts. Stukelj (YUG) was third on high bar and as a beginning did back uprise to free support scale and immediately press to handstand with straight body and bent arms. However in the compulsory exercise there was still hanging scale rearways and hanging scale frontways. New from Primozic (YUG), was elgrip giant swing forward and hop change to giant swing forward.

At the World Championships of 1934 the best gymnasts on high bar were the Germans, Swiss and Czechs. The Czech gymnasts performed some very difficult parts. A. Hudec as a start did backward swing in hang and pirouette to forward swing in hang and kip. E. Löffler performed Stemme backward with straddle vault over the bar with ½ twist to hang, kip. The German gymnast, Sandrock, did as dismount giant swing forward and salto stretched with ½ twist.

The winner, Winter, ended with double salto backward!

For the Olympic Games 1936 the F.I.G. composed a very difficult compulsory exercise (Figure 7.13). The gymnasts did especially difficult dismounts. For example from giant swing forward a Hecht straddle. Schwarzmann (GER) the winner on high bar and Saarvala (FIN) both performed the double back salto backward, while Taräsvirta (FIN) did an underswing and salto forward tucked.

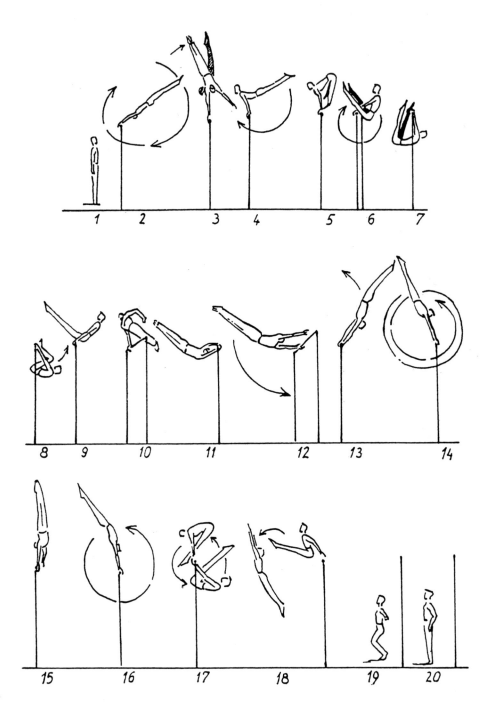

Figure 7.13.

The last big international competition before World War II was the 1938 World Championships in Prague but there was not any progress in content or combinations.

After World War II a new gymnastics generation started. At the 1948 Olympic Games in London this was the compulsory routine (Figure 7.14). The gymnasts had not prepared any new elements. Only a Swiss, Josef Stalder (Figure 7.15), performed a new element: the free straddle circle backwards.

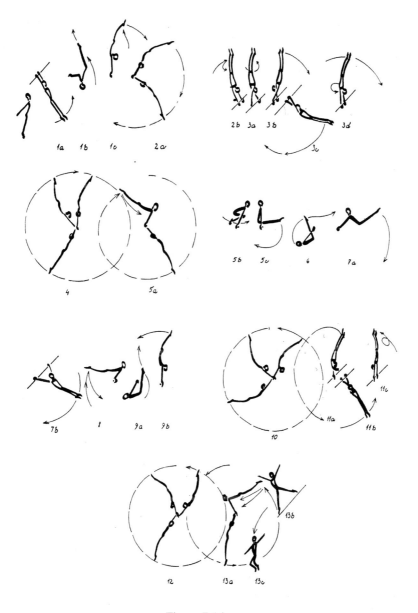

Figure 7.14.

Figure 7.15.

It is true that the most startling turning point was the entrance of Soviet Gymnasts into the 1952 Olympic Games competition in Helsinki. The winner on high bar was Jack Günthard (SUI) with this routine (Figure 7.16).

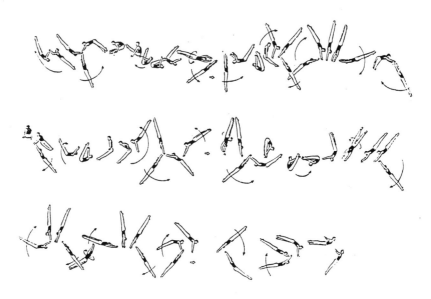

Figure 7.16.

In 2ⁿᵈ place, shared with J. Stalder, was A. Schwarzmann (GER) in his 40ᵗʰ year. Here at these Olympic Games V. Chukarin (URS) did giant swing rearways, forwards, a Russian Giant Swing. However the first time this element was performed was by the Czech E. Löffler at the 1928 Olympic Games. But as Dr J. Göhler knew the very first time this element was invented was by the German, Zink, in 1908. H. Savolainen (FIN) was 4ᵗʰ on high bar in the Olympic Games of 1952 at the age of 45 years (Figure 7.17).

Figure 7.17.

The compulsory exercise of the 1954 World Championships in Rome was not so exacting and the gymnasts aimed themselves at the enrichment of their optional programmes. That was the year in which the F.I.G. established an exact code for optional routines with separate elements divided into groups A, B, and C according to their difficulty. According to this code the exercise had to consist of four elements from group B and at least one of the C group, the most difficult.

At the Olympic Games of 1956 in Melbourne the most difficult routine with very nice technique was T. Ono, with this routine (Figure 7.18). He was for many years the best on high bar. His routine from the Olympic Games of 1956 had 3 Cs, 7 Bs and 6 As. By the 1960 Olympic Games competition in Rome he had 6 Cs, 5 Bs and 5 As.

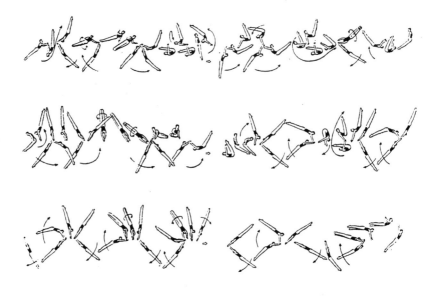

Figure 7.18.

At the World Championships of 1962 in Prague the finalists on high bar had 18 to 21 elements in each routine and the time of their routine was between 35.0 - 46.0 seconds. The most elements in a routine was from Stolbov (URS) with 21 in total and lasting for 46 seconds. The most difficult and frequent elements parts at the 1962 World Championships were (M. Libra, 1969):

Elgrip giant swing forward and hop change to the another grip   73
Steinemann Stemme (separate)   57
Free straddle circle (Stalder)   19
Shoot with full turn to rearward swing in hang and rear vault over
   the bar with ½ turn to forward swing in hang   14
Giant swing rearwards forward (Russian giant) twice   13
Steinemann Stemme twice   10
Giant swing rearways forward (separate once)   6

As beginnings of routines at the 1962 World Championships were:
From hang, stoop through and free hip circle rearways forward   29
Back uprise in mixed grip and rear vault over bar with ½ turn to
   forward swing hang   23

Slight forward swing underswing to handstand	18
Backward swing in hang and pirouette to forward swing in hang	8
As dismounts:	
Salto backward stretched	40
Double salto backward tucked	19
Hecht straddle	13
Hecht	10
Straddle dismount	7
Salto stretch with full turn	7

At the Olympic Games and at the World Championships 1964-1968 the best performers were Soviets and Japanese. Especially A. Nakayama who won in 1966 and 1968. His winning routine from the 1968 Olympic Games is shown below (Figure 7.19). This time only gymnasts who had new elements or connections in their routine could be winners. This fact forced the coaches and their gymnasts to perform more intensive work to create original elements.

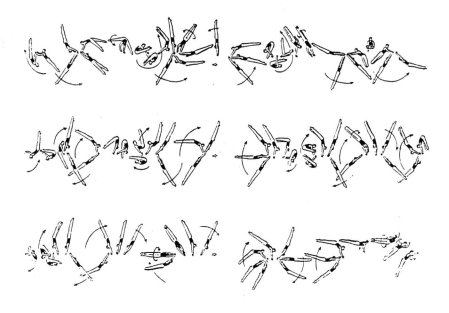

Figure 7.19.

Such a new element was V. Skoumal's giant swing (Figure 7.20 & 7.21).

Figure 7.20.

Figure 7.21.

Václav Skoumal, the best Czech gymnast of the years 1966-1974, performed it for the first time in 1966 at a competition in Hungary:

"It was in April 1966 when I relaxed after a warm up on wall bars. My shoulders were very mobile and I could turn, or rotate, them in any direction to the envy of my colleagues. Performing such a turn I felt a position I had never been in before. After a while I came to the conclusion that such a position could be done on high bar too. It was a kind of body dislocation in ordinary grasp with head on chest. I worked this position for a little longer and my coach J. Kejr was with me for this training. I suggested to try it on high bar. He had no objections but he did not believe I could do it. My first attempts were not very successful. I could not swing over the bar. Only the sixth attempt was right. I did it before the opening of the World Championships 1966 in Dortmund and I performed it at the Olympic Games 1968, World Championships 1970 in Ljubljana as well as at the Olympic Games 1972." (Vaclav Skoumal).

New elements were appearing in top competitions every year. For example at the 1966 World Championships M. Voronin (URS) did back uprise in reverse grip and stoop vault over the bar with ½ turn to forward swing in hang (Voronin) (Figure 7.22).

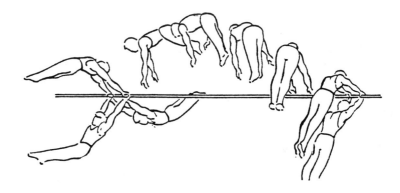

Figure 7.22.

At this 1970 World Championships we also saw a new dismount from the Swiss gymnast W. Straumann which was a double salto forward over the bar to dismount (Straumann forward). At the Olympic Games in 1972 as a dismount M. Tsukahara did double salto backwards tucked with full twist (Figure 7.23). At the 1974 World Championships in Varna B. Jaeger did salto forward piked with straddled legs to forward swing (Jaeger). At the European Championships of 1977 in Vilnius the Bulgarian S. Deltchev performed forward swing in hang and salto backward straddled with ½ turn to forward swing. Also here A. Tkatchev (URS) performed swing backward down through a hang and backward straddle over the bar and regrasp to forward swing in hang. (Figure 7.24).

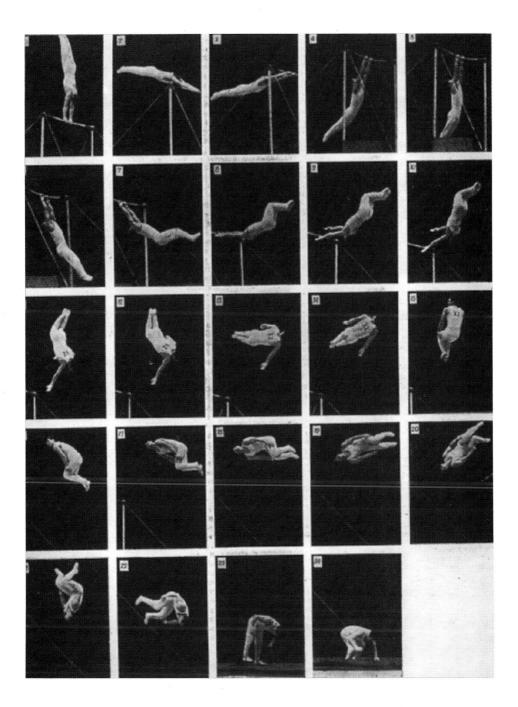

Figure 7.23.

Figure 7.24.

"After the European Championships of 1977 I found out that my routine on high bar was somehow not in," remembers E. Gienger (GER). "I urgently started to train Tkatchev's release as well as other flying elements. I had a feeling I could could never manage them. I started to train Deltchev's salto. Firstly I did not catch the bar and landed five metres far from it. Later on this distance lowered and some time I caught the bar at least with one hand. I wanted to to do it with straight legs in the piked position. I tried it at least thirty times. My forearms were swollen from constantly hitting them on the bar but without any result. My friend proclaimed sceptically that I would never manage it. He provoked the bet for fifty bottles of wine. Finally I caught the bar with the tips of my fingers at the 41st attempt and on the 46th attempt I caught it with both hands. The next day I succeeded twice. I came to the 1977 Universiade final in Sofia with a low score. I decided to do my element, I had nothing to lose. I did my routine successfully and I got a medal."

From that time on Gienger won on the high bar at the World Cup in 1977 and 1978 and he finished his active career with a silver medal from the World Championships of 1981 in Moscow, when he was 30 years of age.

In the 1970s there were new dismounts. For example double salto stretched by N. Andrianov at the 1977 World Cup and triple salto backward tucked at the World Championships of 1974 also by N. Andrianov.

But in 1979 at the World Championships we saw at first time a new element which was a 'revolution', a new possibility of movements on the high bar. Here Tong Fei (CHN) did a one arm giant swing backwards. However the question is who did this element first? E. Gienger said that he saw this element for the first time in Moscow by Saifulin (URS) 1979, and J. Titov said that Maxim Zygankov (URS) did it first time in 1979. This element is shown below (Figure 7.25).

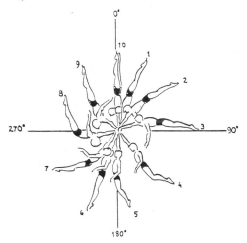

Figure 7.25.

The difficulty of routines has a rising tendency. Table 7.1 highlights the difficulty of finalists at the World Championships from 1974 till 1983 (Jordanov, 1984).

Table 7.1

Rank	Difficulty	Varna (1974)	Montreal (1976)	Strasbourg (1978)	Fort Worth (1979)	Moscow (1980)	Moscow (1981)	Budapest (1983)	Average (Av.)
1	B	3	4	4	4	1	2	3	2.7
	C	6	5	7	6	9	13	11	8.1
	B + C	9	9	10	9	10	15	14	10.8
2	B	1	5	3	3	2	2	1	2.4
	C	8	3	6	6	7	10	9	7.0
	B + C	9	8	9	9	9	12	10	9.4
3	B	2	3	4	3	4	2	2	2.8
	C	7	7	5	6	6	11	10	7.4
	B + C	9	10	9	9	10	13	12	10.2
4	B	2	4	4	2	2	2	2	2.5
	C	5	7	7	6	8	8	13	7.7
	B + C	7	11	11	8	10	10	15	10.2
5	B	4	3	3	4	2	2	2	2.8
	C	5	4	5	6	6	7	9	6.0
	B + C	9	7	8	10	8	9	11	8.8
6	B	4	4	2	3	5	1	1	2.8
	C	8	5	8	5	5	7	10	6.8
	B + C	12	9	10	8	10	8	11	9.7
7	B			5	3		2	2	3.0
	C			3	5		8	10	6.5
	B + C			8	8		10	12	9.5
8	B			5	4		1	2	3.0
	C			5	4		7	10	6.5
	B + C			10	8		8	12	9.5
Av.	B	2.7	3.8	3.6	3.1	2.7	1.7	1.8	2.7
	C	6.5	5.2	5.7	5.5	6.8	8.9	10.2	6.9
	B + C	9.2	9.0	9.3	8.6	9.5	10.6	12.1	9.7

By the end of the seventies you can see the level from the winning routine at the World Championships 1979 in Fort Worth (K. Thomas (USA)):

Overgrip, back uprise, immediate Stalder. Half turn, Deltchev straddled, kip change, pirouette. Giant, stoop in, back German, half turn, Stalder out, pirouette. Forward giant swings, full-in double.

The gymnasts also came with some new elements to the World Championships and Olympic Games. So for example at the World Championships of 1981 in Moscow a new element was seen: Goto (JPN) and Tong Fei (CHN) one arm giant swing forward, M. Gaylord (USA) 1½ salto forward tucked over the bar to forward swing in hang (Figure 7.26). J. Def (FRA) forward swing in hang and salto backward with 1½ turns to forward swing in hang (Def) (Figure 7.27).

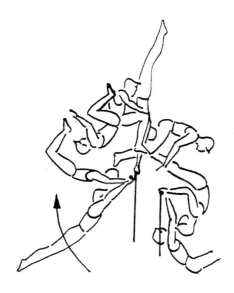

Figure 7.26.

Figure 7.27.

Pogorelov (URS) and Winkler (GER) performed salto forward stretched with full turn to hang. Hemmann (GER. East) double salto backward tucked with full over the bar (Tsukahara).

At the Olympic Games in Los Angeles the 71 participants in the competition IB showed the following dismounts:

Different double saltos	61
Triple saltos	9
Straumann forward with ½ turn	1

Frequency of flying elements:

Exercises with a single flying element	38
Exercises with two flying elements	21
Exercises with three flying elements	4

A new element at the 1984 Olympic Games was performed by M. Gaylord (USA), Deltchev over the bar to forward swing in hang (Gaylord II). The winner was Shinji Morisue (JPN) with this routine:

Straight arm shoot to handstand, pirouette on one arm, two one arm giants. Reverse Hecht twice, hop change, Markelov kip. Czech giant swing, double layout back somersault dismount. The mark was 10 points.

At the international competition in 1984 in Olomouc (TCH), the alternative Olympiade, we saw for the first time these new elements: Jaeger salto stretched by Balabanov (URS) and from one arm giant swing backward Gienger salto to one arm hang by Borkai (HUN).

At the 1985 World Championships in Montreal one-arm Tkatchevs were quite common, while the most spectacular high bar release was the 'Pineda'. T. Pineda (MEX) did a full-twisting flyaway over the bar to catch in over grip giants (Gaylord II with ½ twist). S. Kroll (GDR) and Y. Balabanov (URS) performed nice double fronts with 1½ twists off high bar and B. Preti (ITA), G. Guczoghy (HUN) and Balabanov (URS) did Jaeger fronts in the layout position. Full-twisting Giengers are scarce but A. Tumilovich (URS), J. Hasse, and R. Mendez (CUB) performed them. Mendez's was performed from one arm. Tong Fei did a new dismount, the side somersault-in with ¾ twisting layout-out. His winning routine was:

Free hip circle, back giant, one arm giant, one arm Tkatchev with legs together. Two back giants, one arm Tkatchev, hop kip cast, front giant, jam dislocate, invert, hop pirouette. Two back giants, straddled side somersault-in ¾ twisting layout-out.

At the World Championships of 1987 in Rotterdam we were waiting for a come back from D. Bilozerchev after enduring an auto accident that had shattered his left leg into forty pieces. After this competition we could say that it was his big fight. He won the all-around competition as well as the pommel horse and horizontal bar. His routine on horizontal bar was:

Back uprise free hip circle, two backward giants, one arm backward giant, turn to 1 arm elgrip giant, immediate ½ turn to one arm back giant. Blind to two front giants, one arm forward giant, pirouette to one arm back giant, one arm Gienger, kip cast pirouette. Back giant, Tkatchev-Gienger, kip cast pirouette, two back giants, double layout dismount.

At the World Championships of 1987 during competition IB, 265 flight elements were demonstrated, in competition II 72 were demonstrated and in competition III there were 15 (75 of them with one arm only). Two consecutive flight elements were performed 50 times and three were performed twice. 89 flight elements were accepted as D parts. The most frequent elements demonstrated in competition IB were:

Tkatchev	58
Gienger	41
Gienger front one arm giant circle	32
Jaeger-salto	22
Cuervo	10
Markelov	8

Dismounts:

Stretched backward double somersault	49
Tucked backward double somersault with full turn	23
Tucked backward double somersault with double turn	20
Tucked backward triple somersault	17
Backward double salto, stooped-stretched	12
Stooped backward double salto with full turn	11
Tucked backward double salto	9
Tucked forward double salto with ½ turn	6
Stretched backward double salto with full turn	5
Stooped backward double salto	3

Other examples of frequently performed elements:

Stalder circle	82
From backward giant circle to handstand with ½ turn	49
Endo circle with ½ turn	33
Endo circle	29
Underswing with ½ turn to momentary handstand	17

We can compare the difficulty of high bar routines to those of 30 years ago. The most frequent elements of 'C' grade difficulty at the 1962 World Championships in Prague were:

Elgrip giant swing	73
Steinemann-Stemme	57
Stalder circle	19
Russian giant swing (twice)	13
Steinemann-Stemme (twice)	10

Dismounts:

Stretched salto backwards	40
Tucked double salto backwards	19
Hecht straddle	13
Stretched salto backwards with full turn	7

At the World Championships 1989 in Stüttgart the finalists performed on average 2.50 D, 3.00 C, and 1.9 B elements. The winner was Li Chunyang (CHN) with this routine:

Back uprise Stalder, blind change, back giant ½ turn to reverse grip, Gaylord I piked. Giant, endo, stoop in dislocate to handstand, Russian giant swing, eagle, Jaeger, full twisting double layout dismount.

At the 1991 World Championships in Indianapolis during competition IB the most frequently performed D parts were:

One arm giant swing backwards, Gienger salto	44
One arm giant swing backwards, Tkatchev	11
Counter stoop	3
Hecht backwards (counter Hecht)	17
1½ salto forward tucked over the bar to hang (Gaylord)	17

Mounts:

Back uprise, free straddle circle backwards	77
Underswing giant swing backwards	38
Underswing reverse grip with ½ turn	16
Underswing mixed grip with ½ turn	16
Underswing reverse grip	15
Underswing reverse grip, free straddle circle forward	6

Dismounts:

Tsukahara piked	54
Tsukahara tucked	38
Double Tsukahara	23
Double salto backward stretched	35
Triple salto backward	30
Double salto backward stretch - piked	8
Double salto tucked	8

The most difficult and unusual highlights were: Reverse grip back giant to piked double flyaway (M. Monteiro (BRA)) and Xiao Ruizhi to one-arm regrasp (unintentionally) followed by ½ turn to kip all without an immediate swing. Also Kovacs to Gienger, one-arm Gienger to one-arm regrasp (C. Fajkusz (HUN)) and Stoop Stalder immediate Higgins roll to inverts (Y. Hatakeda (JPN)).

First place was taken by Li Chunyang (CHN) with this routine:

Back uprise Stalder, blind, two front giants, piked Gaylord, endo. Front giant, jam dislocate, invert, piked Jaeger, kip cast pirouette. Two backward giants layout half in half out.

and R. Buechner (GER):

Free hip circle, back giant, Kovacs, two back giants, Tkatchev. Back giant, Stalder immediate blind, front giant, jam dislocate, two inverts, hop to front giant, pirouette. Two back giants, layout half in half out.

At the Olympic Games of 1992 in Barcelona the winner on high bar was Trent Dimas (USA), which was a big surprise for everyone. His routine was:

Cast immediate overgrip inside endo, overgrip endo, reach under pirouette immediate overgrip endo, pirouette. Two back giants, Kovacs, two back giants, Tkatchev to Gienger. Swing ½ turn to mixed grip, swing forward and hop right hand to undergrip, immediate jam dislocate, eagle, hop pirouette. Two back giants, triple flyaway.

After the final T. Dimas said "I am totally numb. I can't believe I've won. It all came together at the time I needed it to...... My coach Burch who trained me since I was 6 years old peaked me at the right time, at the Olympic Games."

At the 1992 Olympic Games in Competition I, 91 exercises were performed: The most frequently performed elements:

Dismounts were:

Triple salto backward tucked	25
Double salto backward stretched with full turn	18
Double Tsukahara	15
Double salto backward stretched with double turns	8
Double salto backward stretched	7

Flight element connections:

Tkatchev - Gienger	15
Tkatchev - Tkatchev	8
Tkatchev with closed legs - Gienger	1
Tkatchev - Tkatchev piked	1
Tkatchev piked - Gienger	1
Kovacs - Gienger	1
Giant swing hop full turn - Gienger	1
Tkatchev piked - Tkatchev piked - Tkatchev	1
Voronin - Gienger	1

At the 1993 World Championships in Birmingham the winner was Sergei Kharkov (RUS) with this routine:

Mixed grip layout, immediate pirouette, back giant, Kovacs to Tkatchev, piked Tkatchev piked Tkatchev to Gienger. Kip cast hop to front giant, jam dislocate, invert, hop pirouette, two back giants, triple flyaway. 9.450 points.

Kharkov's Kovacs to Tkatchev and A. Pegan's (SLO) tucked Gaylord I were sensational.

The Winners on High Bar

1896	Weingärtner	(GER)
1900	Team and All around only	
1903	Martinez & Pissie	(FRA)
1904	Heida & Hennig	(USA)
1905	Lalue	(FRA)
1907	Charmoille & Erben	(FRA) & (TCH)
1909	Martinez, Cada & Erben	(FRA) & (TCH)
1911	Cada	(TCH)
1913	Cada, Torres, Aubry, Demol & Palazzi	(TCH), (FRA), (BEL) & (ITA)
1922	Klinger, Stukelj & Sumi	(TCH) & (YUG)
1924	Stukelj	(YUG)
1926	Stukelj	(YUG)
1928	Miesz	(SUI)
1930	Pelle	(HUN)
1932	Bixler	(USA)
1934	Winter	(GER)
1936	Saarvala	(FIN)
1938	Reusch	(SUI)
1948	Stalder	(SUI)
1950	Aaltonen	(SUI)
1952	Günthard	(SUI)
1954	Mouratov	(URS)
1956	Ono	(JAP)
1958	Shaklin	(URS)
1960	Ono	(JAP)
1962	Ono	(JAP)
1964	Shaklin	(URS)
1966	Nakayama	(JAP)
1968	Voronin & Nakayama	(URS) & (JAP)
1970	Kenmotsu	(JAP)
1972	Tsukahara	(JAP)
1974	Gienger	(GER)
1976	Tsukahara	(JAP)
1978	Kasamatsu	(JAP)
1979	Thomas	(USA)
1980	Deltchev	(BUL)

1981	Tkatchev & Gienger	(URS) & (GER)
1983	Bilozerchev	(URS)
1984	Morisue	(JAP)
1985	Tong Fei	(CHN)
1987	Bilozerchev	(URS)
1988	Artemov & Liukin	(URS)
1989	Li Chunyang	(CHN)
1991	Li Chunyang & Buechner	(CHN) & (GER)
1992	Misutin	(CIS)
1992	Dimas	(USA)
1993	Kharkov	(URS)
1994	Scherbo	(BLR)
1995	Wecker	(GER)
1996	Carballo	(ESP)

The Development of Difficulty in Women's Vault

Women's vault was under the influence of the men's conception of apparatus selection and exercise content right from the beginning. Vaults in competition were firstly mentioned at the end of the 19th century, where women gymnasts tried simply to jump up kneeling and down from the horse. Women jumped over the long horse as well as side horse with or without pommels in their competitions in the years 1920 to 1938.

They took part in the Olympic Games competition for the first time in 1928 in Amsterdam where they performed flank and straddle vaults. Optional vault was included into the programme of the World Championships for the first time in 1934 in Budapest. A compulsory vault was not prescribed. Every gymnast had to jump over the side horse with pommels using the normal wooden springboard or flexible beating board. Every gymnast had to perform one vault different from the vaults performed by her team mates. Also the judging at this time was interesting compared to today's. Judges were divided into 4 groups, each consisting of three judges, however only two of them were judging. The third judge was relaxing. If a team competing was from the same country as the judge, she had to stop judging. At these 1934 World Championships the winner in the team competition was Czechoslovakia and all around winner was Vlasta Dekanova. V. Dekanova is shown in handstand position in Figure 8.1.

Figure 8.1.

The first compulsory vault was prescribed for the 1936 Olympic Games in Berlin (Figure 8.2). One of the participants, a member of the German Olympic team, was Anita Barwirth. Her vault is shown below (Figure 8.3).

Figure 8.2.

Figure 8.3.

At the 1938 World Championships in Prague only the optional vault was used. The best were M. Palfyeva, (TCH), and N. Majovska (POL).

At the 1948 Olympic Games in London women performed their exercises on the 150 cm high horse with pommels, jumping off the beating board, for the last time. The compulsory vault consisted of handstand with ¼ turn with cross grasp and cartwheel. The optional vaults were mostly front vaults.

The first World Championships after World War II were the ones in 1950 held in Basle. The prescribed compulsory vault was the stoop vault (Figure 8.4).

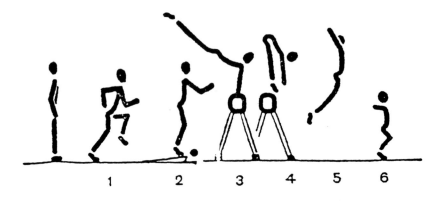

Figure 8.4.

The Technical Committee of F.I.G. prepared 21 optional vaults, which each gymnast was free to choose from. These 21 vaults are shown in Figure 8.5. The best gymnast here on vault was Rakoczy of Poland who was also the all around winner.

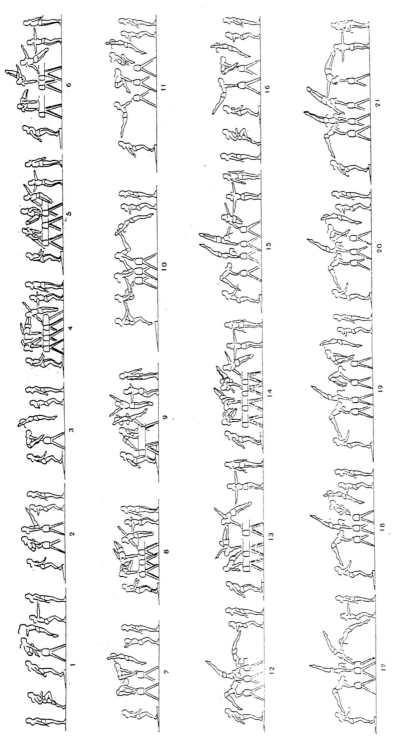

Figure 8.5.

The Soviet Union competed for the first time at the 1952 Olympic Games in Helsinki. The gymnasts mostly performed straddle and stoop vaults but for the first time gymnasts performed front handspring vaults. In the final competition the best was a Soviet, E. Kalintshuk, ahead of the all around winner M. Gorokhovskaya. The compulsory vault used at this competition is shown below (Figure 8.6).

Figure 8.6.

At the 1954 World Championships in Rome the largest number of gymnasts performed. In all 15 teams and 126 gymnasts from 18 countries competed. For the first time gymnasts from Japan participated and they achieved good results. On vault the F.I.G. prescribed the straddle vault as the compulsory vault. The winner was T. Manina (URS) equal with A. Petersson (SWE).

For the 1956 Olympic Games in Melbourne the compulsory vault was handspring forward. The gymnasts mostly performed the stoop jump to handstand with front dismount, the cartwheel, the handstand with cartwheel and the handspring. The best again was a Soviet gymnast, Latynina. Also at the 1958 World Championships in Moscow the best gymnasts were again from the Soviet Union. First place was Latynina, then Mouratova, Kalinina and Manina.

The vault at the 1960 Olympic Games in Rome was the apparatus which registered the least development compared with the others. Mostly the gymnasts performed cartwheel and handspring vaults. But at these Olympic Games we saw a new vault performed by M. Nicolaeva (USSR): the Hecht. Again the best gymnasts were from the Soviet Union. The winner was Nicolaeva ahead of Mouratova and Latynina.

From the 1962 World Championships until the 1968 Olympic Games in Mexico City Vera Cáslavská (TCH) ruled (Figure 8.7). She was the first woman gymnast to perform a new vault, the Yamashita, at the 1964 Olympic Games in Tokyo. Her excellent successes not only in vault were the result of very hard training, which she remembered with these words, "During one month I have performed 120 vaults, out of which three quarters of vaults were perfect." At the present time she is a member of the International Olympic Committee.

Figure 8.7.

At the beginning of the 1970s, the Technical Committee of F.I.G. decided to allow only four identical vaults in a team competition which forced the development of more complicated vaults. The 1972 Olympic Games winner, K. Janz (GDR), performed Yamashita with $^1/_1$ turn. Also Khitrova from Bulgaria performed handspring and salto forward tucked for the first time. According to the men's example, women too were training the Tsukahara tucked vault. This vault was performed for the first time by L. Tourischeva at the 1973 European Championships in London, by Bogdanova (USSR) at the Universiade in Moscow and by Romanian Goreac at the Balkan Championships, all in the same year.

At the 1974 World Championships in Varna Olga Korbut (USSR) enriched the vault's register when she performed handspring forward with $^1/_1$ turn in the first as well as in the second flight phase (Figure 8.8). The new era began.

Figure 8.8.

At the 1976 Olympic Games in Montreal the winner N. Kim performed a new and very difficult vault, ½ twist on with 1½ saltos with full twist to land facing the horse

(Figure 8.9). She received 9.95. For her second vault she performed 1½ twisting handspring. L. Tourischeva took silver with a first vault of Tsukahara tucked and a second vault of handspring with $^1/_1$ turn. The bronze medal went to C. Dombeck (GDR) with a first vault of handspring with 1½ salto tucked and a second vault of handspring with 1½ salto piked for the first time.

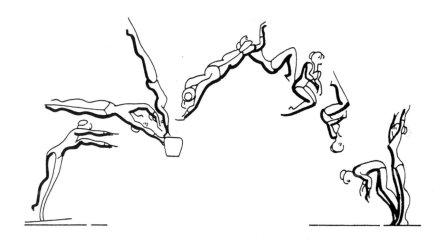

Figure 8.9.

In 1976 the Technical Committee of the F.I.G. raised the height of the horse according to the results of a scientific investigation to 120 cm from 110 cm. The advantage of vaulting over the higher horse is that the gymnast arrives higher in the transition over the horse from which she lengthens the second phase of the flight to allow saltos in this phase. It was also logical that the height of the springboard was increased from 12 cm to 15 cm.

At the 1977 World Cup gymnasts performed more difficult structures of Tsukahara vaults in the stretched position. This vault was performed by Egervary (HUN), as well as by Filatova and Shaposhnikova (USSR).

N. Kim was again the winner at the 1978 World Championships in Strasbourg. She performed as a new vault, the Tsukahara stretched with $^1/_1$ turn and scored 9.80. This new vault was also performed by N. Shaposhnikova (USSR). Silver was won by N. Comaneci with a first vault of handspring 1½ saltos and a second vault of Tsukahara piked.

For the 1978 World Championships and the 1980 Olympic Games the F.I.G. Technical Committee prescribed the compulsory vault as handspring forward with ½ turn in first and second flight phase (Figure 8.10).

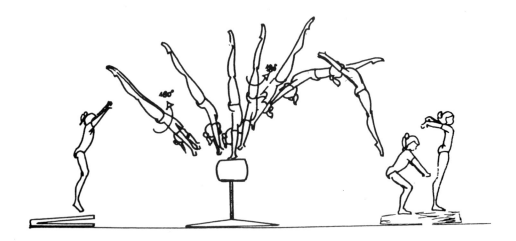

Figure 8.10.

At the 1979 World Championships in Fort Worth the winner was D. Turner (ROM) with a first vault of handspring 1½ salto and a second vault of handspring 1½ barani out. She scored 9.90 and 9.95 for the vaults respectively. Silver was taken by S. Zacharova (USSR) with a new vault as her second vault, handspring Rudi Fliffis piked (Cuervo). C. Canary (USA) also performed a new vault, handspring 1½ salto barani to back out. She took 6th place in the final.

At the beginning of the 1980s the horse-vaulting was classified in groups, which were formed according to the following criteria:

1. Yamashita with or without a turn around the longitudinal axis
2. Handspring with a 540° turn around the parallel axis, in the second flight phase forward somersaults
3. Handspring with a 540° degree turn around the parallel axis and subsequently around the longitudinal axis in the second flight phase
4. Tsukahara tucked and then stretched body
5. Tsukahara with a turn around the longitudinal axis
6. Tiger vault with turn around the longitudinal axis
7. Vaults with more than 540° turns around either the longitudinal parallel axis in the first or in the first and second flight phase

Only groups 1 to 6 contain vaults which are worth less than 9.00 points. These are the handspring, 8.80: ½ turn in the first flying phase and ½ turn in the second phase, 9.00: Yamashita with ½ turn in the second flying phase 9.00: lateral turning 8.80: lateral turning with a 10% turn in the second phase 8.80: lateral turning with ½ turn in the second flying phase 9.00: tiger jump 9.00. These vaults are A-elements. Those vaults that are classified as B-elements can be judged with points between 9.10 and 9.50. C-category vaults can be judged between 9.60 - 10.00 points. The following vaults are worth 10.00 points:

Group 1:
Handspring with a 720° rotation in the second flight phase.
Handspring with a 360° rotation in both flight phases.
Yamashita with 720° turn in the second flight phase.
Yamashita with a 360° turn in both flight phases.

Group 2:
There is no jump worth 10.00 points.

Group 3:
Turning somersault with 360° turn.
Turning ½ turn in the second flight phase and backward somersault.
Yamashita with tucked or bent body or with a turn in the backward somersault.

Group 4:
There is no vault worth 10.00 points.

Group 5:
Tsukahara stretched and 180° turn in the second flight phase.
Tsukahara tucked or stretched with 360° or more turns in the second flight phase.

Group 6 and 7:
Tiger vault backward somersault, tucked, bent or stretched in the second flight phase.
During the somersault a 180° turn or more around the longitudinal axis of the body.

Group 8:
All the vaults grouped here with handspring and turning together with a 1½ somersault in the second flight phase.

At the 1980 Olympic Games in Moscow the gold medal was won by N. Shaposhnikova (USSR) with Tsukahara layout and Tsukahara layout with $^1/_1$ turn. Silver medal, S. Kraker (GDR) with the same vaults as Shaposhnikova. New vaults performed here included half twist on, half twist off front salto by M. Ruhn (ROM) and full on and 1½ front salto by E. Davydova (USSR) (Figure 8.11).

Figure 8.11.

At the 1981 World Championships in Moscow the winner was M. Gnauck (GDR) with Tsukahara layout with $^1/_1$ turn and with Tsukahara layout. One of the best vaulters in the field was O. Bitcherova (URS) but she did not make it into the finals because of a mistake committed during the team competitions. But she became the all around winner, the youngest women's World Champion at that time. Her weight was only 29 kg and height 137 cm. She married V. Mogylny and now works in Paris. She is shown in Figure 8.12.

Figure 8.12.

A surprise at the 1982 World Cup in Zabreb was Natalia Yurchenko (URS) with a new and unusual vault, round-off, flic-flac on followed by a stretched 1½ salto backward with full turn (Figure 8.13).

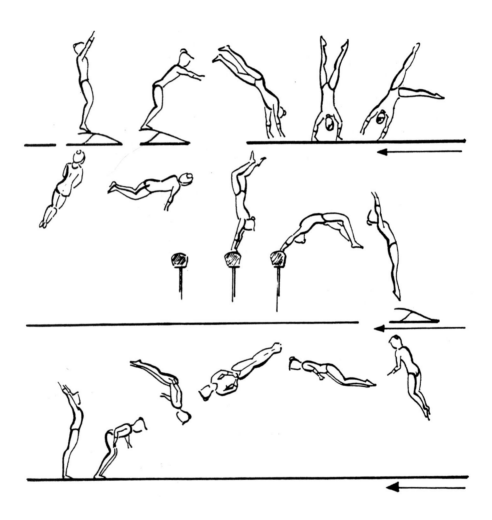

Figure 8.13.

Who is N. Yurchenko? Born on January 26th 1965 in Norilsk in the Northern Soviet Union. In 1982 her weight was 45 kg and her height was 156 cm. Her coach was very famous, Vladislav Rastovski from Rostov-on-Don. From the same club, Dynamo Rostov where she practised was N. Shaposhnikova and L. Touricheva. Her great year was 1982 when she took the Soviet all-around title and came also first in vault, bars and floor. In the same year she became all-around World Cup winner in a tie with O. Bitcherova. However her big success was in Budapest at the 1983 World Championships where she became all-around winner. But in the final competition on vault she had a bad injury and could not continue in the competition. The last time she competed was at the 1985 World Championships in Montreal where she was a member of the gold medal team, USSR.

Figure 8.14.

At the 1983 World Championships in Budapest the winner was B. Stoyanova (BUL) in front of two Romanians, Agache and Szabo.

At the 1984 Olympic Games in Los Angeles the big star was E. Szabo (ROM) who took 3 gold medals in the finals. On floor she had beaten Retton on Retton's best event. She performed Cuervo tucked and then Cuervo piked with average score of 9.925. Retton took silver medal with handspring front pike half and with Tsukahara layout with $^1/_1$ turn. L. Agache took bronze with Tsukahara tucked with 1½ turn and Tsukahara tuck with a ½ turn.

At the international competition in Olomouc in 1984 Shushunova (USSR) performed a difficult vault, the Yurchenko with 1½ turns.

At the 1985 World Championships in Montreal the winner on vault was E. Shushunova (USSR) a 16 years old gymnast from Leningrad, now at St. Petersburg (Figure 8.14).

She performed as her first vault Yurchenko layout with $^1/_1$ turn and as a second vault Yurchenko layout with 1½ turn. D. Silivas took silver with Yurchenko tucked with $^1/_1$ turn and Yurchenko piked with $^1/_1$ turn as her second vault. The bronze medal was won by Kersten (GDR) with a first vault of Cuervo piked and a Tsukahara tucked with $^1/_1$ turn as her second vault.

At this World Championships we saw a new vault from Luconi of Italy, round-off onto board flic-flac with $^1/_1$ turn on salto backward stretched.

Since January 1st 1986 a new vaulting horse has been used in F.I.G. competitions. The construction was designed by the Spieth company, with the proposal of several prominent gymnastic experts in Europe and the U.S.A. Gymnasts were given the chance to test the new horse in the 1983 World Championships in Budapest. The trunk of the horse consists of two parts. Due to its flexible material the joints of gymnasts are exposed to less strain. The apparatus is covered by synthetic leather, and its height is variable between 110 cm and 150 cm.

E. Shushunova again won at the World Championships 1987 in Rotterdam with a Yurchenko layout with $^1/_1$ turn as a first vault and a Yurchenko layout with 1½ turns as a second vault. Golea (ROM) took silver medal with a Yurchenko layout with $^1/_1$ turn followed by a Yurchenko layout with $^2/_1$ turns. These vaults were also performed by S. Baitova (USSR), but she took 'only' 4th place. At this World Championships Omeliantchik (USSR) performed round-off to the board, ½ turn to the horse, piked front off.

At the 1988 Olympic Games in Seoul the majority of the vaults, 88 out of 149 performed during the team optional competitions were from the round-off entry family. That proves the rapid increase of vaulting difficulty compared to the Olympic Games 1984, when there were only 12 round-off entry vaults performed by gymnasts from four countries: it was unbelievable. In the 1984 final all of the gymnasts were performing Yurchenko vaults, except B. Johnson who made her front handspring pike with half turn. E. Shushunova made a commendable effort. She tried to perform a layout Yurchenko with 1½ turns but fell forward on landing. Her second vault, Yurchenko layout, was better but on average she scored only 9.712 and took last place. The best here was S. Boginskaya (USSR) in front of two Romanians, Potorac and Silivas.

At the 1989 World Championships in Stuttgart seven gymnasts performed Yurchenko layout with $^1/_1$ turn as a first vault. Only the winner O. Dudnik (USSR) performed Yurchenko layout with $^2/_1$ turns. As a second vault she used front handspring salto forward tucked with ½ turn and her score was 9.987. In second place and silver medal were two gymnasts, B. Johnson (USA) and C. Bontas (ROM). B. Johnson (USA) performed a Yurchenko layout with $^1/_1$ turn and front handspring pike salto forward with ½ turn giving a score of 9.950. Johnson's World Championship silver medal on vault was the highest placed finish ever received by a U.S.A. gymnast for that event.

At the 1991 World Championships in Indianapolis the winner was L. Milosovici (ROM) with Yurchenko layout with $^1/_1$ turn, scoring 9.962. This was followed by handspring tucked front with ½ turn and 9.937, winning with an average score of 9.949. The silver medal was shared. Chusovitina (USSR) performed handspring 1½ piked front, and Tsukahara layout with $^1/_1$ turn as did H. Onodi (HUN).

The new and unusual vaults performed here were by Dungelova (TCH), double twisting tucked Yurchenko, Mroz (POL) round-off onto the board, half onto horse, Cuervo (in podium training), Mermet (FRA) handspring layout front (in podium training).

At the 1992 World Championships in Paris the winner was H. Onodi (HUN) in front of Boginskaya and Chusovitina, both now are C.I.S..

H. Onodi took gold again at the 1992 Olympic Games in Barcelona equal with L. Milosovici. Both of them performed Yurchenko layout with $^1/_1$ turn. For a second vault Milosovici performed handspring tucked front 1½ and for her first vault H. Onodi did handspring piked front 1½. In 3rd place was Lisenko (USSR) with Yurchenko layout with $^2/_1$ turns and handspring tucked front 1½.

The Women's Technical Committee of the F.I.G. published in January 1993 a new edition of the Code of Points for Women's Artistic Gymnastics. According to these new rules were the following:

General:
1. All vaults are to be performed with the support of both hands on the horse.
2. The length of the run can be individually arranged. The arrival on the board is possible from a run or from an element.
3. The vault may not have more than one preparatory element before the arrival

on the board.

4. The compulsory vault may not be performed as an optional vault in a competition with a compulsory programme.

The vaults will be classified into the following groups:

Group 1:
Handsprings, Yamashitas, cartwheels without and with longitudinal axis turn.

Group 2:
Saltos forward. With and without longitudinal axis turn and Cuervos without and with additional longitudinal axis turns.

Group 3:
Saltos backward with and without longitudinal axis turns, Tsukaharas

Group 4:
Vaults from a round-off, Yurchenkos.

All vaults are illustrated with a number tucked, piked and stretched. The gymnast is responsible for the flashing of the correct vault number.

Starting Values were as follows:
A vaults	to 9.00
B vaults	from 9.10 to 9.50
C vaults	from 9.60 to 9.70
D vaults	from 9.80 to 9.90
E vaults	10.00

All judges evaluate the vaults from the Starting Value (SV) according to the Vault Table. The Starting Value of the performed vault and not the flashed vault is decisive.

In Competition IA the gymnast is allowed only one vault. In Competition IB two vaults are permitted. The two vaults may be the same or different and the better vault score is counted. In Competition II the gymnast must show two vaults, which may be the same or different. In Competition III two vaults from different Vault Groups must be shown. The vault number is to be flashed manually or electronically before the optional vault.

So, according to these rules, the lowest value vaults include the handspring forward, 8.50: the Yamashita, 8.60: and the cartwheel on ¼ turn, 8.60. The highest value E vaults include handspring on tucked 2½ saltos forward off, 10.00: Tsukahara stretched with 1½ turns, 10.00 points and Yurchenko stretched 1½ salto backward with 1½ turn off, 10.00.

The new Code of Points worked very well for women's vaulting. The best gymnast at the 1993 World Championships in Birmingham was E. Piskun (BLR) who took the gold medal with a Yurchenko stretched with $^2/_1$ turn, getting 9.857 and handspring piked front half scoring 9.687. Her average score was 9.762. Second was L. Milosovici (ROM) with Yurchenko layout with $^1/_1$. Chusovitina Oksana (UZB) took the bronze medal with handspring piked front ½ turn and Tsukahara layout with $^1/_1$ turn.

In the final only four of the 16 vaults started from a 10.00. They were: Yurchenko stretched with $^2/_1$ turn by Piskun (BLR): Yurchenko stretched with 1½ turn by Strug (USA): round-off half on, handspring-tucked front by Kudilko and round-off Yurkenko straight half turn to layout front by Jova (CUB).

In Competition II, four gymnasts performed vaults with a start value of 10.00. Lisenko (UKR), Dawes (USA), Fabrichnova (RUS) and Piskun (BLR).

At the 1994 World Championships in Brisbane gold went to a 16 years old gymnast from Romania, Gina Gogean with Yurchenko stretched with 1½ turn and Cuervo piked, giving an average of 9.812. Second was Svetlana Chorkina (RUS) with Yurchenko with half turn on and Cuervo off and the second Cuervo from a conventional forward take off, an average of 9.80. Milosovici was third. Other finalists made big errors especially in landing such as Lisenko, Podkopayeva, Miller, Kochetkova and Piskun.

The Winners on Women's Vault

1950	Ratoczy	(POL)
1952	Kalintshuk	(URS)
1954	Manina & Petersson	(URS) & (SWE)
1956	Latynina	(URS)
1958	Latynina	(URS)
1960	Nicolaeva	(URS)
1962	Cáslavská	(TCH)
1964	Cáslavská	(TCH)
1966	Cáslavská	(TCH)
1968	Cáslavská	(TCH)
1970	Zuchold	(GDR)
1972	Janz	(GDR)
1974	Korbut	(URS)
1976	Kim	(URS)
1978	Kim	(URS)
1979	Turner	(ROM)
1980	Shaposhnikova	(URS)
1981	Gnauck	(GDR)
1983	Stoyanova	(BUL)
1984	Szabo	(ROM)
1985	Shushunova	(URS)
1987	Shushunova	(URS)
1988	Boginskaya	(URS)
1989	Dudnik	(URS)
1991	Milosovici	(ROM)
1992	Onodi (World Championships)	(HUN)
1992	Onodi & Milosovici (Olympic Games)	(HUN) & (ROM)
1993	Piskun	(BLR)
1994	Gogean	(ROM)
1995	Amanar	(ROM)
1996	Amanar	(ROM)

The Development of Difficulty in Women's Asymmetric Bars Exercise

As early as 1830, the Spanish Don Francisco et Ondeano, 1770-1848, mentioned uneven bars in his text book Manuel d'Education et Morale. This was an unknown source for many years. Its original name, 'Women's Physical Education on Apparatus' was influenced by men's exercises. According to opinions and research, the impossibility of mechanical transfer of men's exercises for women in respect of a woman's body mechanics was confirmed. Women's trainer Hanusova used uneven bars in her physical education lessons as early as 1875 because they offered more possibilities of exercise for women of all age groups. The different height of bars made it possible to perform exercises in hang as well as in support. The first women's gymnastic competition was held at the end of the 19th century. Its character was identical with that of men's only its content was less difficult. The athletes drew the content of their routines before the start of the competition. Routines were, of course, short and consisted only of few elements, simple as well as complicated swings in mixed hang, forward and side sittings, positions and balanced elements (Figure 9.1, 9.2 & 9.3).

Figure 9.1.

Figure 9.2.

Figure 9.3.

Only in 1928 in Amsterdam did the programme of the Olympic Games also include a women's competition on uneven bars. Exercises were most of all of static character and strength elements were preferred. Little publicity of this gymnastic event is shown by the fact that compulsory exercises prescribed at the 1936 Olympic Games competition in Berlin and the optional programme could be performed also on parallel bars. All of the gymnasts with the exception of the Czechoslovakians, chose the parallel bars.

The first compulsory exercise was prescribed at the 1936 Olympic Games in Berlin (Figure 9.4).

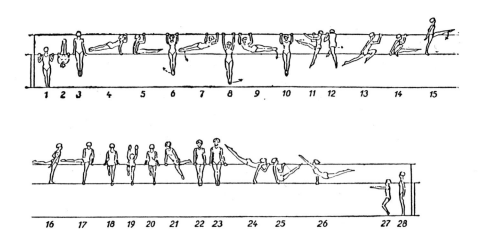

Figure 9.4.

The best Czechoslovakian gymnast at this time was V. Dekanova (Figure 9.5). She became the all around Champion at the 1934 and 1938 World Championships.

Figure 9.5.

In the 1938 World Championships there was also a compulsory exercise, the most difficult parts were swing down from outward front support on the high bar to Felge on the low bar with grip change and later, from front transverse hang, with both hands grasping the high bar and the legs on the low bar, two-leg circle round and along the low bar. The dismount was a cast from the high bar across the low bar.

Uneven bars were slowly accepted after the World War II. This event was not included in the programme of the 1948 Olympic Games in London. Even at the 1950 World Championships in Basle, the gymnasts could choose parallel bars or rings in place of uneven bars. The compulsory exercise for the 1950 World Championships is shown in Figure 9.6. This event became a fixed part of the eight events competition of women only at the 1952 Olympic Games in Helsinki.

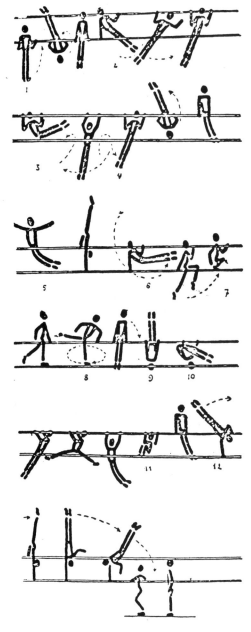

Figure 9.6.

At the competitions before the 1952 Olympic Games in Helsinki the gymnasts performed their routines with mainly static elements, such as bridges, splits, arched hangs, 'L' support and handstands. These elements were linked together with swing elements, but only sometimes. For example links included back hip circle, front hip circle, astride uprise and overhang uprise.

Later, the content of the optional exercises become more and more difficult and the static elements exchanged for swing and dynamic elements. Such a huge difference was seen in the 1952 Olympic Games in Helsinki, where for the first time the Soviet Union gymnasts competed. The routines on the uneven bars took around 20-25 seconds and the gymnasts performed their routines without stopping. One of the most difficult and original elements and connections on the Olympic Games 1952 were:

Glide kip, forward hip circle, cast straddle forward, rear support, lower back, glide stoop mount to rear support. From standing on the low bar handstand and straddle dismount. From front support on the high bar handstand on the low bar with ½ turn and backward hip circle.

In the 1952 Olympic Games and the 1954 World Championships the winners were from Hungary, M. Korondi in 1952 and in A. Keleti 1954. A. Keleti also won in the 1956 Olympic Games.

At the 1956 Olympic Games in Melbourne the all around winner was L. Latynina (USSR) who won second place on the uneven bars with this routine:

From a running start, jump to grasp the low bar with a regular grip, squat over the low bar grasping the high bar, swing forward under the high bar, extend the legs forward with a ½ turn left about the left arm and regrasp the high bar with a regular grip to an underswing. Swing forward, swing backward and on the next forward swing, single leg swing up to a side stride support right on the high bar, immediate ½ turn left about the left arm, regrasping the high bar under the right hand, to a side balance straddle leg support. Swing backward with the hips bent and legs straddled, disengage the legs in front of the bar and extend with a ½ turn left regrasping the high bar with a regular grip to a long hang. Swing forward and backward and on the next forward swing, bend knees and place the feet on the low bar, Stemme rise to an outer side support, turn over the high bar and grasp the low bar with the right hand to a cross handstand. Swing the body downward between the bars and double rear about the right arm, regrasping the left hand to an under grip on the low bar. Seat circle forward grasping the high bar with an under grip to a long hang, swing the legs upward to an inverted bent hip hang backward. Place both feet on the low bar with knees bent, release the left arm and make a ¾ turn right about the right arm to a cross straight stand on the low bar. Swing the right leg forward and right sideward over the high bar with a ¼ turn right to an inner side stand facing the high bar and grasp the high bar with a regular grip. With straight arms jump off the low bar to a side handstand on the high bar and stoop vault dismount.

L. Latynina, one of the best and most successful gymnasts in history won on the uneven bars at the 1958 World Championships in Moscow (Figure 9.7).

Figure 9.7.

The change of content in routines demanded the change of apparatus construction. The first bars where the high bar was connected with wires were produced in 1953 in Hamburg. This construction really allowed the gymnasts to use dynamic swinging elements to a greater extent.

In the 1960 Olympic Games in Rome the winner was Polina Astachovova (USSR), winning with this routine (Figure 9.8).

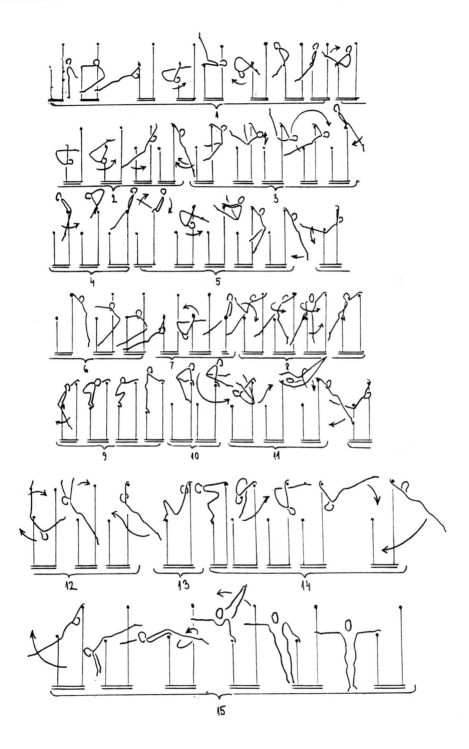

Figure 9.8.

The most surprising in 1960 were the Japanese gymnasts with the most difficult routines.

At the 1962 World Championships in Prague the winner on the uneven bars was I. Pervuschina (USSR), but a very interesting routine was performed by V. Cáslavská (TCH) who is a world famous gymnast. Her routine from the World Championships, 1962, is shown in Figure 9.9 by Frederick (1962). She was also one of the innovators of bars exercises, when she surprised the experts at the 1964 Olympic Games in Tokyo with a new connection, after the straddle backward leg swing to hang, full turn to hang through backswing grasping the lower bar (Figure 9.10).

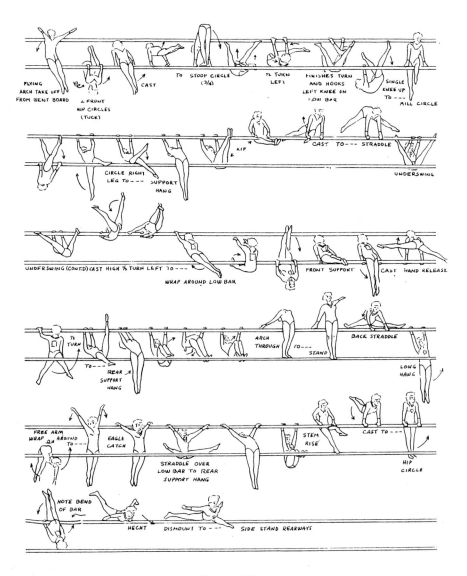

Figure 9.9.

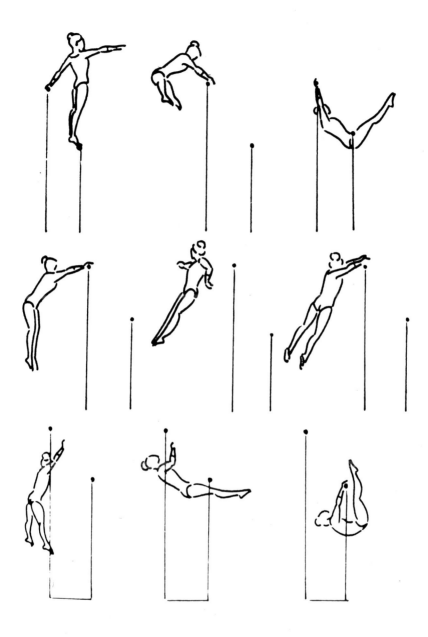

Figure 9.10.

At the Gymnaestrade in 1965 at Vienna, Reuther presented a perfect double horizontal bar of excellent stability and easily arranged, which weighted only 75 kg. The original weight of the bar was 750 kg.

The American Doris Fuchs-Brause indicated new concepts possible with her routine performed two years later at the 1966 World Championships in Dortmund. She, (Figure 9.11), was awarded only 9.766 for her perfect routine. Spectators protested against this evaluation with a deafening whistle and attempts to appease them were useless. The floor exercise of U. Stark was interrupted after the first acrobatic pass. The protest lasted for 65 minutes and stopped only after the F.I.G. threatened to finish the Championship prematurely.

Figure 9.11.

At the 1968 Olympic Games in Mexico City the average value of the six final routines was 15.2 elements, consisting of 3.2 C elements, 5.3 B elements and 6.7 A elements. The required difficulty at this time was 3 Cs and 4 Bs. The most difficult routine was performed by Z. Voronina (USSR) which contained 5 Cs, 5 Bs and 6 As.

At the 1970 World Championships there was a very interesting new mount, jump with ½ turn and immediately kip to free hip circle backward to momentary handstand. Noack (GDR) also did a new element 'Wip-salto' straight with $^1/_1$-turn dismount.

In the 1972 Olympic Games final in Munich three of the gymnasts were from GDR, 2 were from the USSR and 1 from Hungary. The winner, K.Janz, performed the most difficult routine with 3 As, 3 Bs and 8 Cs. She performed new elements such as the straddle salto forward between bars to hang on the high bar, 'Janz's salto' and full twisting Hecht off low bar. This same element was done by L.Touricheva and T. Lazakovitz from the USSR. But O. Korbut (USSR) performed a very interesting routine here. As a new element she performed stretched backward salto to hang from the high bar (Figure 9.12 & 9.13).

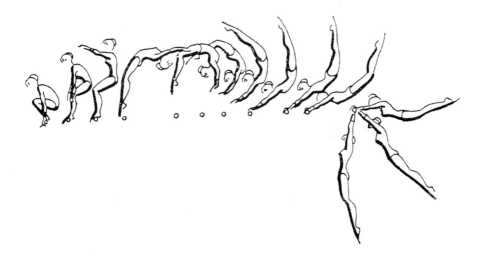

Figure 9.12.

Figure 9.13.

The average value of the six final routines was 14.5 elements, consisting of 5.8 C elements, 3.8 B elements and 4.8 A elements. The longest routine was performed by Tourischeva, 17 elements and the shortest routine was by Bekesi and Hellman consisting of

13 elements.

In the 1974 World Championships there was a very interesting fight between A. Zinke (GDR) and O. Korbut. The gold medal went to A. Zinke. At these World Championships we saw the following new elements. As a mount, salto forward over low bar to the seat on the low bar by Egervary and Medveczky from Hungary. As a dismount Egervary did underswing salto forward tucked and underswing salto forward tucked with ½ turn. Schorn and Woehrle from Germany also used as dismounts underswing and salto forward tucked. Ungureanu (ROM) performed underswing and salto forward tucked with ½ turn.

At the 1976 Olympic Games in Montreal for the first time in many years, the Russians came away without a medal on the uneven bars. Romanians Comaneci and Ungureanu and Hungarian Egervari took the victory stand following this event. The average value of the six final routines was 14 elements, consisting of 6.5 C elements, 3.7 B elements and 3.8 A elements. The longest routine came from Ungureanu with 18 elements. The shortest was by N. Kim, with only 11 elements. The most difficult and with perfect technique was performed by the winner, N. Comaneci (Figure 9.14). Her routine consisted of 5 As, 3 Bs, 9 Cs and 1 D. Her score was 10.00. Here is her winning routine:

Jump to low bar with ½ turn, kip and grab the high bar, kip, straddled front somersault to regrasp the high bar, full twisting pirouette on high bar to low bar, kip, front hip circle, straddled somersault to grab high bar, ½ turn, pirouette, stomach whip on low bar, to free hip circle, toe-on, undershoot ½ in back somersault. In her routine we must point out new elements. Salto forward on high bar to the hang and as dismount underswing with ½ turn and salto backward tucked.

Figure 9.14.

Also at these Olympic Games we saw a new dismount, performed by Chatarowa (BUL): double salto backward tucked.

At the 1978 World Championships in Strasbourg the most difficult routine was performed by M. Frederick (USA). She had 3A, 4B, 12C and 2D elements. All together 19 elements! The average value of the eight final routines was 14.5 elements, consisting of 7.6 C elements, 3.7 B elements and 3.1 A elements. The value of the original elements in the final was 1.4 D elements.

The winning routine of M. Frederick was:

Flip under the low bar and kip to the high bar, forward hip circle, Stalder to handstand, pirouette, body whip, long hang, kip, towards handstand, Stalder, toe on circle and shoot, body whip, double twist, full twist, drop to low bar and straddle glide, kip, to high bar, over the low bar, kip to high bar, forward hip circle, toe on pike front salto over low bar.

New and original elements on the 1978 World Championships included a dismount, underswing with ½ turn and salto backward with $^1/_1$ turn by Arshannik (USSR) and Kraker (GDR). A very difficult element performed by J. Mukhina (USSR), from standing on the high bar salto backward stretched with $^1/_1$ turn, (Figure 9.15).

Figure 9.15.

Again as a dismount Sube (GDR) did underswing and salto forward piked.

M. Frederick did the most difficult element: Stalder backward with $^1/_1$ turn in the handstand. Shaposhnikova (USSR) did Deltchev salto and Pyfer (USA) did Endo forward to the handstand. Turnbov (USA) performed Endo forward to the handstand with ½ turn. M. Filatova (USSR) showed a very difficult element in the middle of her routine, giant swing backward, which had been performed for the first time by Shaposhnikova (USSR) at the 1977 World Championships.

At the 1979 World Championships in Fort Worth the winner was Y. Ma (CHN) with this routine:

From high bar side, reach under the low bar with ½ turn kip to handstand, drop, glide, seat circle up to grab high bar, kip, free hip circle to handstand, full pirouette, beat on the low bar, wrap around, grab high bar, drop, glide, kip to high bar, kip to handstand, beat to low bar, free hip circle to handstand, Stalder, beat low bar, over low bar to glide kip, dismount with Hecht action to full twist tucked salto. Her new dismount is shown in Figure 9.16. As a new dismount at these World Championships we saw Hecht with ½ turn and salto forward tucked by Z. Zheng (CHN) and Hecht and salto backward tucked with a $^1/_1$ turn.

Figure 9.16.

In the 1980 Olympic Games in Moscow the winner on uneven bars was G. Gnauck (GDR). Her routine consisted of 4 C elements, 4 B elements and 2 A elements. She did 1 risk element and 1 original element. M. Gnauck was the most successful participant at the 1981 World Championships in Moscow. She was born on October 10th 1964 in Berlin. She burst onto the scene at the GDR's world famous Spartakiade for Children and Youth in 1977 and a year later at the Chunichi Cup in Japan she gave evidence of her talent by taking 4th place among the seniors. She was 143 cm tall in 1979, 146 cm a year later, and reached 152 cm in 1981. At the 1981 World Championships she won again on uneven bars.

In the 1980 Olympic Games J. Davydova (URS) performed a Tkatchev for first time (Figure 9.17).

Figure 9.17.

Amongst the most difficult elements on the 1981 World Championships was from swing forwards 1½ turn to hang and immediately change the grip on low bar by Davydova

(USSR) (Figure 9.18). As a mount round-off with $^1/_1$ turn and jump straddle over low bar to the hang on high bar by Kano (JPN) (Figure 9.19), and round-off with ½ turn and salto forward piked on the low bar to hang on high bar, Brannekamper (GER) and Goodwin (USA) (Figure 9.20).

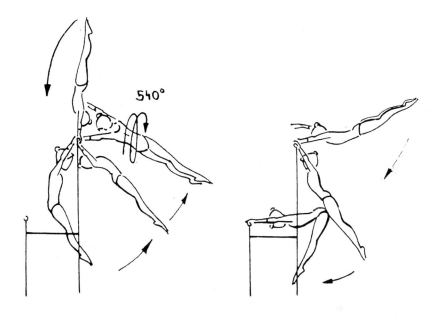

Figure 9.18.

Figure 9.19.

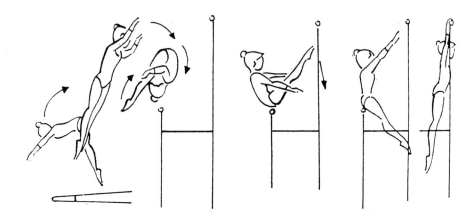

Figure 9.20.

As a dismount from handstand salto backward with $^2/_1$ turn by Johnson (USA).

How visible the increasing difficulty of the routines on uneven bars was, we can see on the following statistics made by the Technical Committee of the F.I.G. under the leadership of Ellen Berger. The increasing number of risky and original elements has resulted in a shift towards R-elements:

1981 World Championships: 50% R-element, 50% R-connection
1983 World Championships: 58% R-element, 42% R-connection

This advance is mainly due to an increase in the following elements:

	World Championships 1981	World Championships 1983
Release Elements		
Jaeger-salto	3	27
Regular Delchev	4	18
Delchev with ½ turn	2	9
Counter-straddle	2	16
Comaneci salto	1	2

Dismounts		
Double back $^1/_1$ turn	7	35
Hecht with salto backward $^1/_1$ turn	7	4
Comaneci dismount, $^1/_1$ turn	4	2
Mounts as a C element	25	42

At the 1984 Olympic Games in Los Angeles the gold medal was shared by two gymnasts, M. Yonhong (CHN) with:

In front with board. Straddle vault over the low bar to high bar, kip cast handstand, Tkatchev, kip cast free hip circle handstand, reverse wrap, Hecht ½ catch high bar, drop glide kip catch high bar, straddle over low bar, kip cast handstand, pirouette, beat low bar, straddle over low bar, kip cast handstand, back hip circle Hecht back with full twist.

Also J. McNamara (USA) with her routine:

Behind with board. Jump to high bar with mixed grip, high start to handstand, pirouette, giant, Tkatchev, drop ½ turn to glide on low bar, kip catch to high bar, straddle Peach to Stalder on low bar, pirouette to glide on low bar, double leg squat on low bar catch high bar, kip cast handstand, Stalder, underswing front with ½ turn.

At the international competition in Olomouc in 1984 was a new original mount from Senff (GDR), round-off and salto backward tucked over the low bar to the hang on the low bar.

In the 1985 World Championships in Montreal the winner was G. Faehnrich (GDR) with this routine:

In front of bars. Round-off onto the board, straddle over low bar to Stalder on low bar, glide kip catch high bar, kip cast hop to undergrip, Jaeger immediate underswing half turn over low bar, glide jam, kip cast hand on high bar, 2 giants, toe-on front-half.

At this World Championships we saw a new mount from G. Faehrich, salto forward over the low bar to the elgrip hang on low bar.

We also saw giant swing backwards with $^1/_1$ turn in the handstand by Garrison (USA) and Kasakova (BUL), Luconi (ITA) and Stojanova (BUL).

At the 1987 World Championships in Rotterdam again two gold medals, Silivas (ROM) with this routine:

Straddle vault over low, kip cast hand, Stalder full pirouette, giant, Deltchev, drop glide kip, cast hand, Stalder pirouette to glide squat, hop to high, kip cast hand, Tkatchev, kip cast hand, giant, underswing tucked front-half.

And Thuemmler (GDR) with her routine:

From behind bars, jump to handstand on low, pirouette to glide squat, hop to high bar, kip cast hand, Tkatchev, kip cast handstand, Deltchev, underswing-half over low, glide straddle, hop to high bar, kip cast handstand, free hip handstand, giant, toe-on with one foot first to tucked front-half.

At these World Championships we saw several new mounts:

Jentsch (GDR), round-off back tuck over low to a glide on low bar, Gurova (USSR) round-off to the board, full twisting back dive to a glide on low bar.

In the middle of routines we saw these new elements:

W. Kiaoyan (CHN) tucked Tkatchev, Jaegar to cross grip, drop full twist to glide on low bar by Boucher (FRA) and full-twisting Tkatchev by Shushunova (USSR).

At the 1990 World Championships in Brussels, Belgium, the Chinese gymnast L. Li used original elements double salto forward tucked with ½ twist and from rear support on high bar circle swing backward in clear pike support, Steineman-uprise, with stoop out backward to hang.

At the 1991 World Championships in Indianapolis the winner was only 135 cm tall and 27 kg in weight, Kim Gwang Suk, North Korea, with this routine:

From front stand facing the low bar run to straddle jump with hand support over low bar to hang on high bar, cast backward to handstand-legs together, Tkatchev, release high bar with ½ turn to drop into glide kip up on low bar, cast backward to handstand, legs together with ½ turn in handstand on low bar, glide, stoop through kip up, glide squat, through rear support on low bar, long hang kip on high bar, cast backward to handstand on high bar, giant circle backward with $^1/_1$ turn through handstand, double salto backward tucked dismount.

At this World Championships gymnasts performed may new elements and connections such as:

Kreiskehre to Stalder by Y. Li (CHN). German giant to reverse Hecht by L. Li (CHN). Jaeger to layout flyaway to low bar by Pak Gyong Sil (PRK). Shaposhnikova immediate full turn by Lisenko (USSR). Tkatchev to giant by Galieva (USSR).

At the 1992 Olympic Games in Barcelona the winner was L. Li (CHN) with a perfect 10.00 and a very difficult routine:

Jump to kip on high bar, cast hop to undergrips, front giant, full pirouette to inverted giant, Jaegar, overshoot ½ to Stalder on low bar, free hip, underswing release, straddled to catch high, kip cast handstand, Tkatchev, kip cast handstand, Tkatchev, kip cast handstand, giant, double layout.

The silver medal went to Gutsu (UKR) and she performed Gienger, Tkatchev releases and double layout as dismount. The bronze medal was won by S. Miller (USA) who finished giant full, full-in back-out.

In the 1993 World Championships in Birmingham S. Miller (USA) won the gold medal with this routine:

On low bar, glide kip cast handstand, free hip Hecht-half to high bar, kip cast handstand pirouette, giant, giant hop full, Gienger, overshoot-half to glide on low bar, straddle over, kip cast handstand on high bar, giant-full, Tkatchev, kip cast handstand, giant double layout.

The silver medal was won by D. Dawes (USA) with a start of straddle over the low bar, kip cast handstand on high bar and as a dismount did giant, tucked half-in half-out. S. Miller did 7 Bs, 1 C, 2 Ds and 2 Es. The average value of final routines was 3.1 Bs, 2.4 Cs, 1 Ds and 0.6 Es.

At the 1994 World Championships in Brisbane the gold medal went to L. Li (CHN) with very difficult elements including inverted giants and double layout as a dismount. She had the longest routine of 40 seconds. The shortest routine was by Kochetkova's (RUS) at only 28.7 seconds. The average of all final 8 routines was 33.2 seconds. But here the most exciting new element performed by a gymnast from China, Huilan Mo and this element was eagle grip circle swing over high bar with 1½ salto forward tucked to a hang in reverse grip. Huilan Mo wasn't in the final but for the illustration we inform you about her unique very difficult routine:

Glide kip-up on low bar, cast backward to handstand on low bar, clear underswing with release and counter straddle movement forward in flight to hang on high bar, long hang kip-up on high bar, giant circle backward to handstand with ½ turn in handstand phase into eagle grip, giant swing forward to handstand in eagle grip on high bar, a Mo salto, release to drop into glide kip-up on low bar, cast backward to handstand with ½ turn in handstand, glide kip-up on low bar, cast backward, clear hip circle backward on low bar with Hecht to hang on high bar, long hang kip-up on high bar, cast backward to handstand on high bar, giant circle backward with ½ turn in handstand phase to eagle grip, giant swing forward in eagle grip on high bar, giant swing forward in eagle grip on high bar with ½ turn after handstand, Tkatchev, long hang kip-up on high bar, cast backward on high bar, giant circle backward on high bar, double backward stretched dismount.

The Winners on Asymmetric Bars

1938	Dekanova	(TCH)
1950	Kolar & Petersen	(AUT) & (SWE)
1952	Korondi	(HUN)
1954	Keleti	(HUN)
1956	Keleti	(HUN)
1958	Latynina	(URS)
1960	Astakhova	(URS)
1962	Pervuschina	(URS)
1964	Astakhova	(URS)
1966	Kuchinskaya	(URS)
1968	Cáslavská	(TCH)
1970	Janz	(GDR)
1972	Janz	(GDR)
1974	Zinke	(GDR)
1976	Comaneci	(ROM)
1978	Frederick	(USA)
1979	Ma Yan Hong & Gnauck	(CHN) & (GDR)
1980	Gnauck	(GDR)
1981	Gnauck	(GDR)
1983	Gnauck	(GDR)
1984	Ma Yan Hong & McNamara	(CHN) & (USA)
1985	Faehnrich	(GDR0
1987	Silivas & Thuemmler	(ROM) & (GDR)
1988	Silivas	(ROM)
1989	Fan Di & Silivas	(CHN) & (ROM)
1991	Kim Gwang Suk	(PRK)
1992	Milosovici (World Championships)	(ROM)
1992	Milosovici (Olympic Games)	(ROM)
1993	Miller	(USA)
1994	Miller	(USA)
1994	Luo Li	(CHN)
1995	Chorkina	(URS)
1996	Chorkina	(URS)

The Development of Difficulty in Women's Beam Exercise

J.C.F. Guts-Muths, 1759 - 1839, dedicated a whole chapter of his book 'Gymnastics for Youth' to balance exercises. Beam, on which the youths performed balance exercises, was made of horizontal rounded spruce. The height of the beam was adjustable. Vieth, the Guts-Muths contemporary, described beam in the second part of his book 'Encyclopaedia of Exercises' as follows, "Its length is 20 or more feet, its big end is placed on a post, another a little lower, lies in the middle which makes it nearly horizontal. Its thinner part is not supported, it lies free and can be moved in any direction.". Jahn's beam is thin, its wood is branchless and it stands between two pairs of big stems placed on iron stands which can be moved up and down (Figure 10.1).

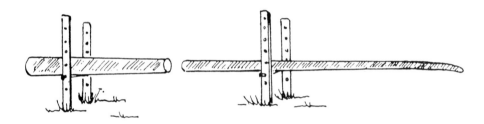

Figure 10.1.

According to the Swedish gymnastics of Peter Henrik Ling, 1777-1839, the beam, balanscribba, belongs to apparatus and balanced exercises combined with Swedish bench exercises and are the basis of the daily training routine. Low beam was later introduced into the German school system. The gymnastic pioneers Spiess and Klops considered it suitable mainly for schoolgirls. The Swedish low beam penetrated into European schools as well, and along with the Swedish vaulting box it belongs to the standard equipment of school gyms but it was never accepted as a competitive apparatus. In the Czech Republic Hanusova taught her gymnasts to perform exercises on a low beam in her Sport Club of Prague for Ladies and Girls. The height of the beam was 25 cm, width 14 cm and length 5 m (Figure 10.2).

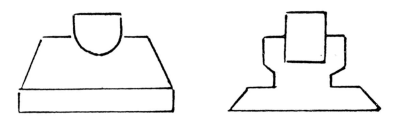

Figure 10.2.

In 1920, women were competing on the beam according to their level of performance at the 6th Sokol Rally. Routines were evaluated by 0 to 10 points. A fall caused a 2 points deduction. If an element was somehow replaced, added or avoided, routines were evaluated to 0. Accurate reports of exercises are not preserved but we know that they were restrained by the moral rules of those times. Squats, straddle stands, bent standing positions with step, scales, front, side, as well as ordinary straddling forward were forbidden. Therefore, elements in exercises were performed only in standing positions or walking with different step variations, hopping and turning.

Beam exercises were not used abroad. When Czech gymnasts came to Paris in 1921, they had to perform their routines on a board supported by props. The Germans performed front horizontal scales of 4 counts endurance for the first time in 1928 at the sport festival in Cologne. There is no report of beam competitions in gymnastic competitions until 1929, when only mass platform routines on the beam were performed (Figure 10.3). The Norwegians showed some progress when they performed backward pull-over on the beam at the sport festival in Finland in 1929. The gymnasts performed dynamic routines at the 130 cm high beam in Poznan in the same year.

Figure 10.3.

In the 1930s the French and Yugoslavian gymnasts enriched their routines by dance steps and variations. Beam changed in 1930, when the beam became oblong in cross-section, the props allowing a height from 50 cm to 120 cm. But the stability of the beam was insufficient, which made it more difficult to 'start and finish the routines (Figure 10.4).

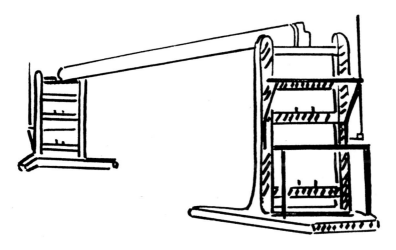

Figure 10.4.

Exercises of the first World Championships in 1934 in Budapest were performed on the 120 cm high, 8 cm wide and 5 m long beam. The optional exercise was time limited to a maximum of 55 seconds and evaluated by 0 to 10 points. The most incredible element was the splits, performed by G. Meszarosz (HUN). From that time on, beam became standard apparatus at international competitions. The 14 years old Italian, Elda Lividin, showed some new opportunities of artistic gymnastics in her compulsory routine (Figure 10.5). The best Czech gymnast in this event was Foltova (Figure 10.6). Exercises were more and more directed to acrobatics and therefore a beam of better stability was needed. To secure more safety for complicated saltos and handsprings the beam is widened to 10 cm. Its sides were rounded and the diameter of the beam became 13 cm. Absolute stability of apparatus was formulated in the book of specifications, "It cannot have any vibration during performance, is adjustable from 800 mm up to 1200 mm, each step of 50 mm. Its height on international competitions should be 120 cm and its length 5 m. Security the of beam requires certain elasticity. In 1200 mm height and 135 kg load its maximum deflection should be 8 mm."

Figure 10.5.

Figure 10.6.

The first improvements of the apparatus brought changes of exercise content. From Czechoslovakia, Honcova attracted experts with her dismount, salto backward tucked, at the 1948 Olympic Games in London. Also Srncova (TCH) performed a new original connection, handstand-forward roll. The winning Czechoslovakian team at these Olympic Games is shown below with Srncova third from left and Honsova seventh (Figure 10.7).

Figure 10.7.

At the 1950 World Championships in Basle the optional routines were evaluated by 10 points for execution and 5 points for difficulty. The gymnasts mostly performed, handstand, headstand, shoulder stand, splits, straddle 'L' and as dismounts, handspring, handstand squat and salto backward tucked. For the judges these elements were shocking and they didn't see any future in them. It meant a reduction of points because they said the elements deflected from the principles of 'women's elements'. The difficultly of the compulsory exercise at these World Championships is shown in Figure 10.8.

Figure 10.8.

At the 1952 Olympic Games in Helsinki the gymnasts for the first time competed on all apparatus in compulsory and optional exercises. There were eight gymnasts in a team, the best six results were counted into the competition. For the first time here gymnasts from the USSR competed and they were the best on the beam. The winner was M. Botsharova and second was M. Gorokhovskaya who also won the all around competition (Figure 10.9).

Figure 10.9.

At the 1956 Olympic Games in Melbourne most elements and connections were static, with only the gymnasts from Japan doing dynamic elements but not with good stability. The winner A. Keleti (HUN) did as a mount, jump squat to the 'V' position on the of beam. Then she did from scale, forward roll to shoulderstand, handstand. As a dismount she performed a salto backward tucked. The new elements at these Olympic Games were cartwheel on 1 arm, two connected cartwheels on 1 arm and as dismount handspring at the side of the beam and lift to handstand with bent body and straight arms, handspring with ½ turn at the side of the beam.

At the 1958 World Championships in Moscow in the final on the beam were three Soviets. The winner was L. Latynina (Figure 10.10). Mouratova was the 2nd, Manina 4th, Tanaka (JPN) was 3rd and Bosakova 5th. As a mount Tanaka did squat on and as a dismount, handstand straddle. New elements were backward walkover, backward walkover to handstand, lift to handstand with bent body and straight arms and squat to 'L' hold.

Figure 10.10.

At the 1960 Olympic Games in Rome the best competition was on beam. The winner was E. Bosakova (TCH) (Figure 10.11).

Figure 10.11.

The most difficult routine here was performed by V. Cáslavská (TCH) and took 6th place in the final. She performed a new dismount, layout somersault. The big surprise was the element performed by K. Ikeda, $^1/_1$ pirouette spin. She also did very high jumps in her routine and she took 5th place in the final. As a new mount we saw run and forward roll. New skills included, handspring on 1 arm, flic-flac, forward walkover, backward walkover to front scale, backward walkover to handstand and roll onto the chest.

At the 1962 World Championships in Prague E. Bosakova won again, ahead of L. Latynina. E. Bosakova was at this time 31 years old. She was born on December 18th 1931, and was one of the best gymnasts in Czechoslovakia and the world. She had a silver medal on the beam at the 1954 World Championships and at the 1956 Olympic Games. At the 1958 World Championships she was 5th and won gold at the 1960 Olympic Games and the 1962 World Championships. She was also very good on the floor exercise. She took a gold at the 1958 World Championships and a silver medal at the 1954 World Championships. She was all around Czechoslovakian Champion 10 times. She also was the first coach of the famous V. Cáslavská. She died in 1991 in Prague aged 60. In 1962 the optional routines on average consisted of 20 elements. Compared with the 1958 World Championships when there were 15 elements, this means the routines in 1962 were longer. The gymnasts here performed new mounts, from run jump to handstand, jump to the 'L' hold between arms, lift to handstand with bent body and straight. Other new elements included flic-flac on 1 arm and 1½ pirouettes in the squat position. New dismounts included a salto forward straight.

Routines at the 1964 Olympic Games in Tokyo on average consisted of 23 elements. The winner V. Cáslavská (TCH) performed in the middle of her routine a new element, deep piked sit (Figure 10.12) and ended the routine with round-off salto backward stretched.

Figure 10.12.

At the 1966 World Championships in Dortmund E. Zuchold (GDR) performed a flic-flac or backward handspring. The winner N. Kuchinskaya (USSR) as a mount performed jump to a handstand and turn over forward onto one leg, jump with bent body to handstand, walkover out and as a dismount flic-flac on one arm at the side of the beam.

At the 1968 Olympic Games in Mexico City the routines on average consisted of 22 elements. The new elements here performed by Cáslavská, Zuchold and Janz were handspring forward, and also by Zuchold a double spin.

At the 1970 World Championships in Ljubljana the winner was E. Zuchold who performed a new element again, the triple spin. C. Rigby (USA) took the silver medal.

At the 1972 Olympic Games in Munich the gymnasts performed very difficult routines and in many cases with good stability. Compared with routines from the 1968 Olympic Games routines at the 1972 Olympic Games were most dynamic, with gymnasts performing more dynamic acrobatics elements. The winner was a new face, O. Korbut (USSR), who performed a very difficult routine with new elements, salto backward tucked in the middle of the routine. This element I saw performed by her at the 1970 USSR Championships in Minsk. Also she also did flic-flac with a flight phase and straddle to the sitting position. O. Korbut is shown below in a salto backward (Figure 10.13). Another new connection by Burda (USSR) was the 'Auerbach flic-flac'. As a dismount many gymnasts did round-off salto backward stretched with $^1/_1$ turn or without turn.

Figure 10.13.

Discussions were held by experts at the 1974 World Championships in Varna about O. Korbut. She had exploited her great physical potential and showed an unbelievable connection from handstand, a hyper arched back (Figure 10.14). The Women's Technical Committee of the F.I.G. suggested to forbid this element for a time.

Figure 10.14.

Acrobatic tumbling elements performed on the beam forced the manufacturers to produce more quality apparatus which was the demand of the majority of F.I.G. experts and representatives. "Women's gymnastics development has made unbelievable progress during recent years," said the F.I.G. president, A. Gander, at the meeting of the Women's Technical Committee of the F.I.G.. "The gymnasts are now performing such elements on the beam that a few years ago, could not be predicted, even by experts.". Then he pointed out that the apparatus should be of higher quality to reduce the possibility of injuries and its solidity should be improved. Instead of two posts, there is a need for four, two of which are placed on both ends of the beam and the others 75 cm from ends to provide maximal stability. Free space under the beam should be lined with mats to avoid injuries. The new beam was officially accepted in Stuttgart in 1973. From 1974 on, the covering would be firmly connected to the beam, 8 mm sponge, 5 mm wood and firm cover which allows a certain gliding of feet mainly in jumps. The width of the beam still remains 10 cm in spite of the progress in exercise content. In addition, from 1970 they spoke about the minimal deviation of 5 mm at the loaded place.

At the 1976 Olympic Games in Montreal the routines on average consisted of 18 elements. A perfect routine was performed by the winner N. Comaneci (ROM) (Figure 10.15):

Jump to straddle 'L' in the middle of the beam and press to handstand, ¼ pirouette and step down, skips and steps, kick in to flic-flac step out, aerial forward, side aerial to flic-flac with step out, leap, valdez through walkover to handstand in split position, two flic-flacs, split leap, round-off, double twisting somersault off the end.

Figure 10.15.

As a new dismount here we saw salto forward tucked with $^1/_1$ turn. As a new mount, cartwheel by Dombeck (GDR), in the middle of routines, salto backward piked by Dombeck (GDR) and a 'Butterfly' by Gerschau (GDR).

At the 1977 World Cup the gymnasts performed many new elements which are still in content of routines at the present time. For example press to handstand with bent body and straight arms and slowly lower to free support scale by Shaposhnikova (USSR) (Figure 10.16). As dismounts double salto piked backward by Filatova (USSR), double salto backward tucked by Mukhina (USSR) and Shaposhnkiova. In the middle of routine salto forward tucked by Shalk (GDR).

Figure 10.16.

At the 1978 World Championships in Strasbourg N.Comaneci (ROM) won, but without any new elements. In this final V. Cerna (TCH) competed and took 5th place. At the next World Championships in 1979 at Fort Worth she won the gold medal with this routine:

Jump and press legs together to handstand, lower to planche, to straddle 'L', stag leap, full spin on one foot, free back salto, flic-flac, half turn, split leap, one arm front walkover, press to handstand, double stag handstand, stoop through to high 'V' support, fall to back lying position, inverted needle, standing back salto, split leap, flic-flac, layout.

The finalists at the 1979 World Championships did as dismounts double twist by Grabolle and Gnauck, gainer back by N. Kim piked double backward salto by E. Eberle, full twist by Mareckova, running front salto by Ruhn and layout salto by Filatova.

At the Spartakiada of Soviets nations in 1979 in Moscow N. Yurchenko (USSR) performed a new and very difficult element, flic-flac from the side standing position and backward hip circle (Figure 10.17). This element was also performed in the 1980 Olympic Games final by Zemanova (TCH).

Figure 10.17.

At the 1980 Olympic Games in Moscow many teams did not participate for political reasons. It was a great pity. The final routines on average consisted of 15 elements. The winner was again N. Comaneci. At this Olympic Games Shaposhnikova performed a new handstand (Figure 10.18). As new elements we saw, flic-flac to salto backward stretched, two flic-flacs to salto backward stretched, salto forward tucked with ½ turn by Grigoras (ROM). As mounts from run round-off and flic-flac onto the beam and from run salto forward tucked onto the beam.

Figure 10.18.

At the 1981 World Championships in Moscow the winner was M. Gnauck (GDR) as she said, "I am so happy that I won especially on beam, because I had not expected it.". Her routine was:

Arabian spring on the take-off board, flic-flac to the beam, somersault backward, flic-flac, piked somersault to one leg, flic-flac, full turn on one leg, Arabian spring to back somersault with $2/_1$ twist.

At this World Championships we saw as new elements, handspring backward with full turn to the straddle seat by Rulfova (TCH), (Figure 10.19), Thomas Flair in side support by Talavera (USA), (Figure 10.20).

Figure 10.19.

Figure 10.20.

At the beginning of the 1980s we saw more and more difficulties in routines on beam, especially more acrobatic elements and connections. You can see this tendency from the analysis by the Women's Technical Committee of the F.I.G. when they compared the difficulty of routines and most frequently used elements in the 1981 World Championships with the 1983 World Championships.

Mount:
Round-off, flic-flac.
Salto forward tucked.

Dismount:

Double salto backward.

Double salto backward with $^1/_1$ turn.

Elements:

Flic-flac sidewards.

Handspring with turn or handsprings with flight phase.

As a new mount here we saw, round-off salto backward piked by Eerkhoorn (HOL). New dismounts included salto backward straight with $^3/_1$ turns by Cervenkova (TCH). In the middle of the routine we saw salto backward tucked with $^1/_1$ turn by Shishova (USSR).

At the 1984 Olympic Games in Los Angeles the gold medal was shared by two gymnasts from Romania. S. Pauca with:

Front headspring mount, back handspring to layout to immediate layout, back handspring to piked backward somersault, two back handsprings to $^2/_1$ twist dismount.

E. Szabo performed:

Press handstand mount, straddle planche down, four back handsprings, high scale, back handspring to layout, round-off double salto backward.

At the international competition in Olomouc in 1984 we saw as a new element the 'helicopter' performed at the end of the beam by F. Voight (GDR).

At the 1985 World Championships in Montreal was a big fight for gold on the beam. It was between E. Szabo and D. Silivas, both from Romania. In the end D. Silivas was the better, who stood only 4' 5½" tall (Figure 10.21). This was her routine:

Straddle 'L' press walkover mount, front aerial, flic-flac, layout to two feet, flic-flac layout layout, round-off, flic-flac, tucked double back dismount.

Figure 10.21.

Second was E. Szabo and the 3rd Shushunova (USSR) with:

Planche mount, flic-flac, layout, layout, back dive to straddle swing through, round-off double backward salto dismount.

Here we saw a new mount, round-off and salto backward stretched with $^1/_1$ turn performed by K. Garrison (USA).

At the 1987 World Championships in Rotterdam again the best was the "Romanian school" with the gold medal won by a new star, A. Dobre with this routine:

English press mount to front walkover, side aerial, flic-flac layout step-out flic-flac layout step out, Korbut, flic-flac step-out, two footed flic-flac double tuck.

Second was Shushunova and in 3rd place Szabo and Boginskaya. At this World Championships we saw new elements, swung two circles to a Flair by Baitova (USSR), round-off, flic-flac mount diagonally by Casteckova (TCH) and standing tucked full by Priakhina (USSR).

At the 1987 European Championships in Moscow one of the world's best gymnasts D. Silivas (ROM) performed a new mount, jump to shoulderstand and $^1/_1$ turn on shoulder. She won a gold medal at the 1988 Olympic Games in Seoul with this routine:

Jump to the shoulderstand with $^1/_1$ turn, handspring forward, flic-flac, layout, layout flic-flac, layout, flic-flac, flic-flac, double salto backward piked.

D. Silivas also took the gold medal at the 1989 World Championships in Stuttgart in front of O. Dudnik (URS), who performed a very nice round-off full twist in the middle of her routine.

At the 1990 World Cup in Brussels came a surprise from a 15 year old gymnast from China, L. Li when she performed a new element, 450° back spin to arched hang.

Very interesting and very difficult new elements were performed by the gymnasts at the 1991 World Championships in Indianapolis. Here are some of them:

Round-off onto the board and three layouts by T. Lisenko (URS).

Flic-flac ¼ turn to side handstand by S. Miller (USA).

Standing full by T. Gutsu (URS).

One arm flic-flac to two layouts by Y. Bo (CHN).

Double leg circles on the end of the beam by K. Oka (CAN).

Triple turn by B. Okino (USA).

Three standing layouts by M. Kosuge (JPN).

Flic-flac, layout, flic-flac, layout by S. Umeh (CAN).

Round-off onto the board, tuck-open Korbut mount by L. Milosovici (ROM).

The winner at 1991 was Boginskaya (USSR) ahead of Gutsu and 3rd was Okino and Milosovici.

At the 1992 World Championships in Paris the best was K. Zmeskal (USA). T. Lisenko (UKR) won at the 1992 Olympic Games in Barcelona with 9.975. She performed:

From side, single leg cut to sit, cartwheel off knee to handstand, one-arm handstand, flic-flac to three layout backs, round-off double tuck.

At the 1993 World Championships in Birmingham we also saw great progress, especially in the acrobatics level. It is unbelievable what the gymnasts can do on this apparatus. The most difficult elements and connections were:

Round-off layout full by He (CHN).

Front tuck immediate back tuck by Chusovitina (UZB).

Flic-flac 3 layouts and flic-flac, flic-flac, tucked full-in by Dawes (USA).

Round-off 2½ twist dismount by Valle (ESP).

The gold was won by L. Milosovici (ROM) with:

Round-off onto the board, Chen, flic-flac layout, flic-flac, fish jump, back dive ¼ turn to handstand, side somersault, back dive ¼ turn to handstand, round-off double back tucked. Her routine consist of 5 Bs, 2 Cs and 5 Ds and score 9.850.

The final competition on this apparatus was terrific because three of the top gymnasts, Miller, Li and Fabrichnova made costly errors. So in second place was D. Dawes (USA) with:

Jump to side split, 2 straddle jumps, flic-flac layout layout layout, front somersault, switch leap ¼ turn, straddle jump ½ turn, flic-flac flic-flac tucked full-in.

Elements of E difficulty were only performed by Dawes, Li, Fabrichnova, Mo and Miller.

At the 1994 World Championships in Brisbane the gold medal was won by S. Miller (USA) with a score of 9.875 and with this routine:

Salto forward tucked, flic-flac with ¼ turn to the handstand, flic-flac two layouts, flic-flac with ¼ turn to handstand and Tsukahara tucked.

The silver medal, L. Podkopayeva (UKR) with these excellent parts, salto forward tucked, piked somersault into Korbut roll, salto forward tucked, and a surprise, in headstand spin and Tsukahara tucked. The bronze, Fabrichnova (URS). She had the best flight series of flic layout to layout to layout and she also had an unusual element on beam, flic to shoulderstand, a half flic. In the all around competition we saw a unique combination performed by H. Mo (CHN). She started with one arm handstand lowered down to one arm straddle half lever and a shoulder roll gripped with one arm. Also Kotchetkova (URS) showed a nice element of full twisting back flip on beam.

The Winners on Beam

1938	Dekanova	(TCH)
1950	Rakoczy	(POL)
1952	Bosharova	(URS)
1954	Tanaka	(JAP)
1956	Keleti	(HUN)
1958	Latynina	(URS)
1960	Bosakova	(TCH)
1962	Bosakova	(TCH)
1964	Cáslavská	(TCH)
1966	Kutchinskaya	(URS)
1968	Kutchinskaya	(URS)
1970	Zuchold	(GDR)
1972	Korbut	(URS)
1974	Tourischeva	(URS)
1976	Comaneci	(ROM)
1978	Comaneci	(ROM)
1979	Cerna	(TCH)
1980	Comaneci	(ROM)
1981	Gnauck	(GDR)
1983	Mostepanova	(URS)
1984	Pauca & Szabo	(ROM) & (ROM)
1985	Silivas	(ROM)
1987	Dobre	(ROM)
1988	Silivas	(ROM)
1989	Silivas	(ROM)
1991	Boginskaya	(URS)
1992	Zmeskal (World Championships)	(USA)
1992	Lisenko (Olympic Games)	(URS)
1993	Milosovici	(ROM)
1994	Miller	(USA)
1995	Mo	(CHN)
1996	Miller	(USA)

The Development of Difficulty in Women's Floor Exercise

At the beginning floor exercises consisted mainly of simple elementary static elements. Pioneers of the floor exercise were gymnastic experts of the second half of the 18th century, J. H. Pestalozzi (1746-1827) and E. Eiselen (1792-1846). Adolf Spiess (1810-1848), teacher of physical education in Burgdorf and Basle was especially interested in the utilization of the physical education lessons. He started then with group exercises during which everybody was moving, but they were arranged without any psychological or artistic effect.

The Swedish expert, P. H. Ling (1776-1839), selected for floor exercises those movements aimed at the anatomical or physiological effect. He stressed most of all a hygienic point of view and the correct posture. Floor exercises became part of physical education in Tschechei-Bohemia after establishing the Prague Sport Club in 1862. At the beginning, exercises for women were under the influence of men's exercises, they consisted of static elements. The floor exercise performed at the 6th Sokol Rallye in 1912 is shown below (Figure 11.1).

Figure 11.1.

In the course of time, different pieces of apparatus were used in floor exercises such as big and small balls, hoops, flags and ropes. There we see the influence of Demeny and Herbert from France whose opinion was that the movement in floor exercises must be fluent. They did not suggest long hold positions but the development of strength, flexibility and endurance. At the 7th Sokol Rallye in 1920 routines were performed by whole groups of gymnasts and judges evaluated the team work as well as individual performances. The first competition of individual floor exercises was held in Tschechei-Bohemia in 1928, the content was the same as that of group performance, and compulsory exercises were prescribed two years later.

Floor exercises were not included into the programme of the 1934 World Championships in Budapest, but there were the so called 'variable exercises', handstand without any support and handspring forward over a gymnast in front rest kneeling position. The programme of the 1936 Olympic Games in Berlin included the group floor exercises.

The turning point of the development was the year 1949, when along with variable exercises the term of skill exercises on the floor began to be used. Routines consisted of following skill exercises, backward roll to handstand, handstand and forward roll, and cartwheels. The pioneer of the new conception in Czechoslovakia was E. Bosakova, later World and Olympic Games Champion, who included in her routine, forward and backward handsprings. However in 1949 the judges of those times evaluated these original elements in most cases with a points deduction for unsuitable elements.

The Soviet gymnasts presented themselves for the first time internationally in 1949 in Budapest where they performed all compulsory as well as optional routines with musical accompaniment. Acrobatic elements such as front and side splits, forward and backward walkover were joined into one routine with dance elements. Here in this competition the Hungarian Szarkanyi, later Keleti, was the first of all to perform round-off backward salto tucked.

At the 1950 World Championships in Basle the first compulsory floor exercise was prescribed. What was the content? The content is shown below (Figure 11.2). The best at this World Championships was Rakoczy (POL) then Kocis (YUG) and Reindlowa (POL). After the 1950 World Championships the gymnasts started performing more difficult acrobatic elements in routines.

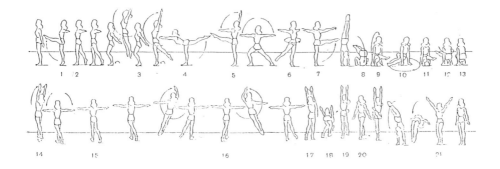

Figure 11.2.

At the 1952 Olympic Games in Helsinki the most difficult acrobatic connection was round-off salto backward tucked, which was performed by four gymnasts. Czechoslovakian gymnasts also included some dynamic acrobatic elements into their routines, such as backward handsprings by Chadimova, and round-off backward handspring by Vancurova. The best here was A. Keleti (HUN) ahead of Gorokhovskaya (USSR) and Korondi (HUN).

At the 1954 World Championships in Rome the compulsory exercises also included acrobatic elements. E. Bosakova (TCH) performed a very nice routine here with a new dance conception and she took a silver medal. The gold went to T. Manina (USSR). At this World Championships the backward salto stretched was performed for the first time. Gorochovskaya (USSR), who was 3rd, performed at the beginning of her routine round-off two backward handsprings and at the end of the routine round-off backward salto tucked.

The gymnast from GDR, Michaelis, was the first to perform three quick backward handsprings combined with backward salto tucked at the 1st Spartakiade in 1955 in Prague. Also E. Bosakova (TCH) presented a new element, the aerial cartwheel.

The Japanese stood out with their acrobatic connections at the 1956 Olympic Games in Melbourne. The gold medal was won by Keleti (HUN) and Latynina (USSR) who started, round-off backward salto tucked and ended round-off backward handspring. However the most difficult routine with a new element in was round-off backward salto stretched with ½ turn on one leg and round-off two backward handsprings and backward salto tucked to splits performed by Yegorova (USSR).

At the 1958 World Championships in Moscow a compulsory musical accompaniment was used for the first time. The winner was E. Bosakova with these acrobatic elements, round-off backward salto stretched onto one leg, two backward handsprings, backward roll to handstand and free walkover. A very difficult connection was done by Tanaka (JAP): round-off, two backward handsprings and salto backward layout.

At the 1960 Olympic Games in Rome the gymnasts performed more difficult elements. On average routines consisted of 20 elements. The most difficult and original element connection came from two Americans, backward salto stretched with full turn. L. Latynina (USSR) won gold in front of P. Astakhova (USSR), (Figure 11.3), who performed at the beginning of routine, round-off two backward handsprings backward salto stretched and ended with a free walkover. In 3rd place was again a gymnast from the Soviet Union, T. Ljukina, who started with salto forward stretched round-off salto backward stretched with ½ a turn and ended with round-off two backward flic-flacs backward salto stretched. In 4th place was E. Bosakova (TCH).

Figure 11.3.

The music accompaniment underwent a fast development after 1958. At the beginning, gymnasts chose some sequences from well known classical compositions. But often the movement content came to be inconsistent with the style of music, with is social importance and aesthetics. A successful combination of music and motion, total gymnastic routines, were the routines of Cáslavská (TCH) and Pervuschian (USSR) at the 1962 World Championships in Prague. E. Bosakova surprised us in collaboration with musician J. Sehak, choosing the accompaniment of electronic music. A clever pianist was always a good support of the best gymnastic performances. One of the best pianists was in Czechoslovakia, Rudolf Kyznar, who remembers his collaboration with top women gymnasts as follows, "Once, V. Cáslavská came to me with a project to do her routine with the music of B. Smetana's Vltava. At the beginning I was terrified because the great Bedrich would turn in his grave, but when I thought about it I came to the conclusion that it was not a bad idea. How we did it? I racked my brains for a long time until once on the way from Vysocany, part of Prague, to the gym I got an inspiration. I called Vera and we did it.". It was gymnastics greatest floor creation.

At the 1962 World Championships in Prague the most difficult routines were performed by gymnasts from GDR, Fost and Radochla, but they took only 13th and 25th place. On the other hand L. Latynina (USSR), the winner on the floor exercise, had according to analysis of the difficulty of routines ranked between the 20th and 48th places. The most common connection was round-off two flic-flacs. The salto forward tucked was performed only 5 times. I. Pervuschina (USSR), who took silver medal, started with round-off two flic-flacs salto backward stretched and ended with cartwheel and two aerial cartwheels. V. Cáslavská (TCH), who took a bronze medal, started with round-off salto backward stretched onto one leg, round-off, flic-flac and salto backward to splits and ended round-off salto backward stretched.

V. Cáslavská (Figure 11.4) remembers about the delivery of her new floor exercise during the preparation for the 1964 Olympic Games in Tokyo as follows, "I wanted to express something through the music to the spectators in Tokyo but I could not show it in dance. I always feel the sporting character of my routine and my classic dance preparation helped me, too. After some consultations with my coach V. Prorok, it was necessary to find suitable musical accompaniment. Many gymnasts perform their routines to the same music and their performance is only average. Chopin's Revolutionary Etude attracted me because it satisfied my dynamic character. I was absorbed in it and it evoked my image of routine which finally had a great success on the Olympic platform." V. Cáslavská at the 1964 Olympic Games took 6th place.

Figure 11.4.

Connections performed by finalists on floor exercises at the 1964 Olympic Games include:

Round-off, two flic-flacs, salto backward stretched at the beginning.

Round-off, salto backward tucked at the end of routine by L. Latynina (Gold).

Round-off, salto backward stretched at the beginning.

Round-off, two flic-flacs salto backward tucked at the end by Astakhova (Silver).

Round-off, flic-flac at the beginning and ending by Janosi (Bronze).

Round-off, two flic-flacs salto backward tucked at the beginning.

Round-off, flic-flac with jump straddle at the end by Radokhla (4th place).

Round-off, salto backward stretched with $^1/_1$ turn at the beginning (which was one of the most difficult elements at this time).

Round-off, salto backward stretched to split at the end by V. Cáslavská.

At the 1966 World Championships in Dortmund there was a big fight in the team competition between the Soviet Union and Czechoslovakia. The Czechoslovakian team, after a long period, won the World Championships again and V. Cáslavská was the all around winner. This big fight was also on the floor exercises especially between V. Cáslavská and N. Kuchinskaya. In the end the winner was N. Kuchinskaya, (Figure 11.5), with these acrobatic connections:

Round-off salto backward stretched with $^1/_1$ turn, free walkover, round-off, flic-flac salto backward stretched with ½ turn on one leg, round-off, flic-flac, salto backward stretched on one leg.

Figure 11.5.

V. Cáslavská did as a beginning:

Round-off, two flic-flacs, salto backward stretched and jump to split and as an end round-off, salto backward stretched on one leg.

In 3rd place was Z. Drouginina (USSR) with:

Round-off, flic-flac, salto backward stretched with $^1/_1$ turn as a start and round-off, flic-flac, salto backward stretched on one leg.

At the 1968 Olympic Games in Mexico City new rules were used. A new evaluation of difficulties was used and according to these rules the gymnasts had to perform two Cs and four Bs. On the floor exercise there was a requirement of performing three acrobatic lines. A huge success came from V. Cáslavská, who was the all-round winner, and took the gold medal on the vault, beam and equal with L. Petrik on the floor. The routine of V. Cáslavská was the climax of the final competition, when she performed her routine with the accompaniment of Mexican music. V. Cáslavská's routine contained round-off, salto backward stretched with $^1/_1$ turn-jump to splits and round-off, salto backward stretched on one leg to end.

L. Petrik was equal winner and did handspring walkover round-off, flic-flac, salto backward stretched with $^1/_1$ turn at the beginning and round-off, flic-flac, salto backward stretched on one leg.

N. Kuchinskaya, who was 3rd, did round-off, 3 flic-flacs salto backward stretched with ½ turn on one leg, round-off, flic-flac, salto backward stretched with $^1/_1$ turn, round-off, salto backward stretched on one leg.

Z. Voronina in 4th place did round-off, flic-flac, salto backward stretched, flic-flac, flic-flac on one leg, round-off, flic-flac, salto backward stretched with $^1/_1$ turn, round-off, flic-flac, salto backward stretched.

However the most difficult element in the 1968 Olympic Games was performed by a gymnast from the U.S.A. salto forward stretched with $^1/_1$ turn.

At the 1970 World Championships in Ljubljana the best on floor were gymnasts from the Soviet Union. The best was L. Tourischeva with round-off jump with ½ turn salto forward piked, round-off salto backward stretched with $^1/_1$ turn. Silver medal was won by O. Karaseva with round-off three flic-flacs backward stretched with $^1/_1$ turn. The bronze medal went to Z. Voronina.

At the 1972 Olympic Games in Munich we saw more difficult routines. The gymnasts performed more and more acrobatic elements in one line series. The longest series consisted of 6 elements, round-off, flic-flac, salto backward stretched with ½ turn on one leg, round-off flic-flac and salto backward tucked. For the first time on women's floor we saw a new element, the salto backward stretched with $^2/_1$ turns, or 720°, performed by Tourischeva (USSR), Moor (USA) and Bujnackova (TCH). The winner was a new star O. Korbut (USSR) with a interesting series round-off, flic-flac, flic-flac salto backward stretched to lie position.

At the 1974 World Championships in Varna the winner was L. Tourischeva who surprised us with two different, very nice routines. On floor the best were the Soviets, all 4 gymnasts from the USSR Korbut, Siharulidze, Saadi, and Dronova.

At the 1976 Olympic Games in Montreal the final was again the 'Soviet Gymnastic School'. The routines on average consisted of 21 elements. Here we saw a new element, performed by N. Kim (USSR): double backward salto tucked.

N. Kim won with this exercise and she received a 10.00:

Round-off, flic-flac, double back, jump out, ¾ twisting stag leap aerial, front handspring to pike front step out, round-off, flic-flac, layout, round-off, flic-flac, full twist.

The silver medal went to L. Tourischeva with:

Split leap towards the corner, into round-off, flic-flac, layout, side aerial, round-off, flic-flac, full twist, free walkover, dive cartwheel, round-off, flic-flac, back salto.

Third was N. Comaneci with:

Round-off, flic-flac, flic-flac, double twist and ended with round-off, flic-flac, layout.

At the 1978 World Championships in Strasbourg we saw a new gymnastic star, E. Mukhina (USSR), who won the all around gold medal equal with N. Kim and silver medal on the beam and uneven bars (Figure 11.6).

Figure 11.6.

After the competitions she said, "I am very happy. Winning the gold was my dream, but I never thought it was possible.". As we know E. Mukhina in preparation for the 1980 Olympic Games in Moscow had a terrible accident on floor, while doing the jump backward with 1½ turn and salto forward tucked to roll forward, (Thomas). At this time E.Mukhina was 153 cm height and weighed 42 kg. Her difficult routine was to the music of "Milord". Here is her routine:

Round-off, flic-flac, ½-in ½-out, aerial walkover, round-off, flic-flac, layout with ½ turn, walkover, round-off, flic-flac, double back.

The gold medal was shared with N. Kim who did this routine:

Round-off, flic-flac, pike double back salto, round-off, flic-flac, pike open salto back, round-off, flic-flac, double full.

Third place was taken by K. Johnson (USA) and E. Eberle (ROM).

At the 1979 World Championships in Fort Worth E. Eberle (ROM) won with a routine of folk music and with these acrobatic elements, double back pike as a beginning and round-off flic-flac Arabian and round-off, salto backward stretched.

At this World Championships we saw at first time in routine: salto backward stretched with $^3/_1$ turn, or 1080°, which was performed by M. Gnauck (GDR) and by N. Shaposhikova (USSR).

At the 1980 Olympic Games in Moscow before the final competition four gymnasts had the same score. In the final the judges evaluated two gymnasts, N. Kim and N. Comaneci, with 9.950 and they took the gold medals. Bronze went to N. Shaposhikova, equal with M.Gnauck (GDR).

In her routine N. Kim performed round-off, double back, round-off, flic-flac, salto layout with $^2/_1$ turn, double back tucked.

N. Comaneci performed round-off, double back piked, round-off, flic-flac 1½ twists to one leg, round-off, high flic-flac with $^1/_1$ turn, round-off, flic-flac, salto backward with $^2/_1$ turns.

M.Gnauck did round-off, double back with $^1/_1$ turn in first salto, round-off, flic-flac, salto backward $^3/_1$ turns, round-off, flic-flac salto backward stretched with ½ turn on one leg, round-off, flic-flac salto backward stretched with $^2/_1$ turns.

At the 1981 World Championships in Moscow we saw very nice and very well composed routines. There were more feminine and more artistic routines. The most beautiful routine was performed by the winner, N. Ilienko (USSR). This 15 years old gymnast, only 145 cm tall, 34 kg in weight and from Alma-Ata, performed her routine to the music of Rossini and she received 9.95.

Her routine was:

Round-off, whip flic-flac double somersault, Arabian spring flic-flac, back somersault stretched with $^2/_1$ turns, Arabian spring flic-flac, double piked somersault.

The gymnasts in Moscow performed very difficult elements, connections and series, for example:

Round-off, salto backward stretched with 1½ turn on one leg, round-off, salto stretched backward with $^2/_1$ turns (Figure 11.7). Salto backward stretched with 2½ turn, or 900° (Figure 11.8). Salto forward stretched from one leg with $^1/_1$ turn (Figure 11.9).

Figure 11.7.

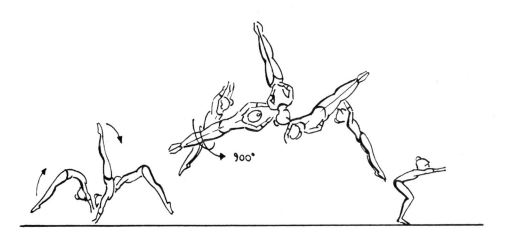

Figure 11.8.

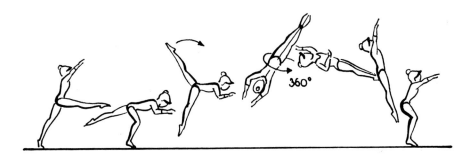

Figure 11.9.

Round-off, flic-flac, salto backward stretched with 1½ turn, salto forward tucked (Figure 11.10). Round-off Arabian 1½ salto forward tucked (Figure 11.11).

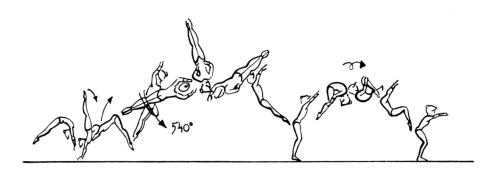

Figure 11.10.

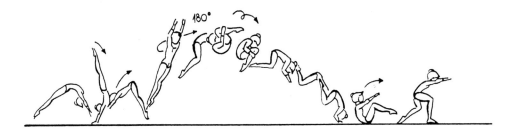

Figure 11.11.

Jump pirouette with $^2/_1$ turns, or 720° (Figure 11.12).

Figure 11.12.

At the beginning of the 1980s the routines of gymnasts had become more and more difficult. The following analysis, made by the women's Technical Committee of the F.I.G., shows this increasing tendency.

Elements	1981	1983
Double salto backward	77	154
in the closing series	9	43
Half in half-out	6	10
in the closing series	0	1
Salto backward with a $^3/_1$ twists	4	11
in the closing series	0	1
Salto backward with a 2½ twists	5	4
Double salto backward stretched	0	1
1½ twisting salto forward	3	16

The most frequent C elements were as follows:

Salto backward with a $^2/_1$ twists	63	121
Salto backward with a 1½ twists	5	9

The most frequent B elements were:

Saltos backwards with a $^1/_1$ twist	95
Tempo saltos (usually saltos forward in a series of two)	35

At the 1983 World Championships in Budapest Szabo (ROM) won in front of Mostepanova (USSR) and Stojanova (BUL). On floor here we saw double salto backward stretched perfomed by Dudeva (BUL). Also O. Mostepanova showed a new original element, jump from both feet with $^1/_1$ turn in flight to a handspring forward and Frolova (USSR) performed a new original leap, a split leap with leg change to a forward scale.

At the 1984 Olympic Games in Los Angeles E. Szabo collected her third gold medal on the floor exercise. For her superb routine she received 10.00. Second was J. McNamara (USA).

E. Szabo performed:

Round-off, flic-flac, full-in back-out, layout-pike, jump full turn straddle, round-off straddle jump, round-off, flic-flic, 1½ twist, punch front, round-off Arabian step-out, round-off, flic-flac, tucked full-in back-out.

McNamara started with round-off, flic-flac, tucked full-in back-out and ended round-off, flic-flac, double twist.

M. L. Retton (USA) took the bronze medal and she was the all around winner. On floor she performed round-off, flic-flac, double layout, switch leg split leap, round-off, flic-flac, tucked full-in back-out, front salto, round-off, flic-flac, double back tuck.

After the 1983 World Championships the world gymnasts did not compete again together until the 1985 World Championships 1985 in Montreal, because many gymnasts did not compete at the 1984 Olympic Games for political reasons. So, it was a very interesting competition also on floor. The winner was O. Omeliantchik, a 15 year old gymnast from Kiev in the USSR. She performed a very nice routine with chirpy music and received 10.00. Her main acrobatic elements were round-off, flic-flac, full-in back-out, layout-pike, round-off flic-flac double twist, punch front step-out, round-off, flic-flac, piked double back, flic-flac layout.

The silver medal went to E. Shushunova (USSR) with:

Round-off, flic-flac, double layout, Round-off, flic-flac, 1¾ side somersault, round-off, flic-flac, full-twisting flic-flac, round-off, flic-flac, tucked double back.

U. Klotz (GDR) took the bronze medal took with a middle series of salto backward stretched with $^3/_1$ turns.

At the 1987 World Championships in Rotterdam the winner was E. Shushunova (USSR) equal with D. Silivas (ROM). Both gymnasts performed very difficult and perfect routines. Shushunova performed:

Round-off, whip, flic-flac, flic-flac, piked full-in, round-off full-twisting back handspring, round-off, flic-flac, 1¾ side somersault, round-off, flic-flac, straddle jump to prone fall, round-off, flic-flac, double tuck.

D. Silivas performed:

Round-off, whip, flic-flac, flic-flac, piked full-in, round-off, flic-flac, double twist, punch front step-out, round-off, flic-flac, flic-flac, double twist, punch front, round-off flic-flac, piked full-in.

In third place was A. Dobre (ROM) who was also all around Champion. Her coach A. Goreac after the competition said, "Nadia Comaneci was our star of gymnastics, and at this time, Aurelia already has better results than Nadia.". Her routine was:

Round-off, whip, flic-flac, flic-flac, piked full-in, round-off, flic-flac, double twist, punch front, round-off, flic-flac, double twist, punch ¾ front to hands and one foot sitting position, round-off, flic-flac, double tuck.

A very difficult series here was performed by Chen Cuiting (CHN), flic-flac whip flic-flac, flic-flac full-in whip-back through to double tuck and a quick high double tuck. She took a 6th place.

At this World Championships 4% of all participants performed double salto backward stretched, 0.7% double salto backward stretched with $1/_1$ turn and 22% of gymnasts finished routines with double salto backward tucked. But nobody finished with salto backward stretched with $3/_1$ twists. For the first time we saw here 'long series' such as double twist punch front through to flic-flac double twist salto, performed by D. Silivas. E. Szabo performed round-off, flic-flac, 1½ twist punch front-half twist (punch front full twist in training).

At the 1988 Olympic Games in Seoul and at the 1989 World Championships in Stuttgart the best on floor was D. Silivas (ROM) and Boginskaya (USSR). At the 1989 World Championships both won with a perfect 10.00. Boginskaya performed her routine as theatre or ballet. Silivas performed her 'old' routine but with new music.

At the 1991 World Championships in Indianpolis the gold medal was shared by C. Bontas (ROM) with round-off, flic-flac, layout full-in, round-off, flic-flac, full flic-flac, round-off, flic-flac, tucked full-in, and Cusovitina (USSR) with, round-off, layout, full-out, round-off, flic-flac, tucked half-in half-out, round-off, flic-flac, double pike.

The all around winner K. Zmeskal (USA) was 3rd on floor and she performed a very difficult series of three whips, flic-flac double tuck. Many others gymnasts performed very difficult and interesting elements and connections:

> Whip, whip, immediate double tuck by Hristova (BUL).
>
> Triple twist punch front by Polokova (TCH).
>
> Double layout dismount by Gutsu (URS).
>
> Front handspring layout front, punch front by Ruud (NOR).

Before the 1992 Olympic Games was the 1992 World Championships in Paris. The gymnasts performed here a difficult routine and its was a very good test for the Olympic Games in Barcelona. On floor K. Zmeskal took gold in front of H. Onodi (HUN), M. Neculita (ROM) and T. Lizenko (CEI). This competition also gave a gold medal for K. Zmeskal on beam, very good especially for coach Bela Karoly because Kim's success proved that is was not an error by the judges to give her higher marks in Indianapolis because it was in the USA.

At the 1992 Olympic Games in Barcelona L. Milosovici (ROM) took the gold with a perfect 10.00 and she performed round-off, flic-flac, whip, flic-flac, tucked full-in punch front, round-off, flic-flac 1½ twist, step-out, round-off, flic-flac, 1½ twist punch barani stag jump, round-off, flic-flac, tucked full-in.

Three gymnasts shared the silver medal. Gutsu (UKR) with a beginning of round-off flic-flac split leg double layout, Bontas (ROM) with a beginning of round-off, flic-flac, double layout and Miller (USA) with round-off, whip, flic-flac, flic-flac, tucked full-in.

From January 1st 1993 new rules applied. According to these new rules at the 1993 World Championships in Birmingham the only gymnast whose start value was a full 10.00 points was N. Bobrova (URS). On average at these World Championships the finalists performed 2.9 Bs, 2.4 Cs, 2.4 Ds and 0.9 E elements or connections. In the competition IB the average was 4.0 Bs, 2.6 Cs, 1.2 Ds and 0.5 E elements.

The gold medal was won by S. Miller (USA) whose start value was 9.90. She performed round-off, whip-back, flic-flac, flic-flac, piked full-in, round-off, whip-back, whip-back, flic-flac, double twist, round-off, flic-flac, tucked full-in, round-off, full twisting back handspring.

> Other very interesting passes were:
>
> Running front full, punch front by Umeh (CAN).
>
> Front handspring, flyspring, double front, front handspring, flyspring, front layout, front layout full by Podkopayeva (UKR).
>
> Running front full step out, round-off, flic-flac, full by Weller (GER).
>
> Front handspring, flyspring, front layout-half, back layout step out by Selivanova (EST).
>
> Whip-back through to 2½ twists, punch front by Milosovici (ROM).

At the last World Championships in 1994 in Brisbane D. Kochetkova (RUS), coached by L. Arkaev, took the gold medal with a very nice double straight back and full twisting front somersault and Tsukahara as a dismount, scoring 9.95.

L.Milosovici took silver medal with double layout, whip through to 2½ twist to punch front, triple twist. In 3rd place was another gymnast from Romania, G. Gogean, with a Tsukahara tucked at the beginning and the end, scoring 9.762.

The Winners on Women's Floor

1950	Rakoczy	(POL)
1952	Keleti	(HUN)
1954	Manina	(URS)
1956	Keleti & Latynina	(HUN) & (URS)
1958	Bosakova	(TCH)
1960	Latynina	(URS)
1962	Latynina	(URS)
1964	Latynina	(URS)
1966	Kutchinskaya	(URS)
1968	Petrik & Cáslavská	(URS) & (TCH)
1970	Tourischeva	(URS)
1972	Korbut	(URS)
1974	Tourischeva	(URS)
1976	Kim	(URS)
1978	Kim & Mukhina	(URS)
1979	Eberle	(ROM)
1980	Kim & Comaneci	(URS) & (ROM)
1981	Ilienko	(URS)
1983	Szabo	(ROM)
1984	Szabo	(ROM)
1985	Omeliantchik	(URS)
1987	Shuschunova & Silivas	(URS) & (ROM)
1988	Silivas	(ROM)
1989	Boginskaya & Silivas	(URS) & (ROM)
1991	Bontas & Cusovitina	(ROM) & (URS)
1992	Zmeskal (World Championships)	(USA)
1992	Milosovici (Olympic Games)	(ROM)
1993	Miller	(USA)
1994	Kochetkova	(RUS)
1995	Gogean	(ROM)
1996	Podkopayeva	(UKR)

The World Championships Merry-go-round: 1994-1996

The Birmingham World Championships heralded a new format of World Championships which was established by the F.I.G., very much the pioneering venture of F.I.G. President, Yuri Titov. Team, Individual and Apparatus World's were split up so that there would be annual opportunities to take part in a World manifestation of gymnastics. The advantages were real. New World Champions every year; more media coverage (especially television); extended careers for older gymnasts or specialists in the apparatus only; a more specific World Circuit for the best gymnasts with exposure and sponsor benefits (money); a continuous measure of World standings; more opportunities for for national hosting of world events. The disadvantages appeared as the venture progressed. Too costly for Federations; the Organisation of two World Championships in a single year and some additional Championships due to national and media requirements for added importance; lack of preparation time for young talent under pressure to compete for their federations. In fact though top, mature gymnasts favoured the system, the Federations and the coaches were not so enthusiastic. I think that the system had many advantages and only required some simple pruning to work well. It brought to our sport four fabulous years of events from which many new gymnasts were propelled to stardom.

The Individual Apparatus World Championships, Brisbane, 1994

Australia featured an Apparatus World Championships and an additional Individual World Championships with interestingly no qualifying round. It would be a world ranking from a single all around tournament.

Vitaly Scherbo took floor, parallel bars and high bar with a confidence and enthusiasm that was totally infectious. This was a gymnast still to 'peak' and well on his way into the history book of legends. Competing for his native Belarus he led the ex-Soviet charge on the media with a following that was to become a bandwagon. And yet within this circus Vitaly remained always his own man, accountable to no one but himself. Marius Urzica of Romania topped out on pommels with a long and complex routine in a finals which was to be played out many times, Urzica, Poujadze (France), Donghua (Switzerland). Also Yuri Chechi opened the tale of the greatest rings gymnast ever, a reign that was to bring him four World titles and the Olympic title.

This new format did not however, throw up any specialists into the medals other than possibly Paul O'Neil of the USA with a silver on rings.

Men's Results

Floor

Position	Name		
1	Vitaly Scherbo	BLR	9.725
2	Ioannis Melissanidis	GRE	9.687
2	Neil Thomas	GBR	9.687
4	Grigori Misutin	UKR	9.650
5	Igor Korobchinski	UKR	9.612
5	Li Dashuang	CHN	9.612
7	Ivan Ivanov	BUL	9.337
8	Masanori Suzuki	JPN	8.700

Pommels

Position	Name		
1	Marius Urzica	ROM	9.712
2	Eric Poujade	FRA	9.700
3	Donghua Li	SUI	9.662
3	Vitaly Marinich	UKR	9.662
5	Huadong Huang	CHN	9.650
6	Mark Sohn	USA	9.625
7	Valeri Belenki	GER	9.600
8	Igor Korobchinski	UKR	8.912

Rings

Position	Name		
1	Yuri Chechi	ITA	9.787
2	Paul O'Neil	USA	9.725
3	Dan Burinca	ROM	9.700
3	Valeri Belenki	GER	9.700
5	Andreas Wecker	GER	9.637
6	Rustam Sharipov	UKR	9.600
7	Szilveszter Csollany	HUN	9.587
8	Jordan Jovtchev	BUL	9.400

Vault

Position	Name		
1	Vitaly Scherbo	BLR	9.674
2	Xiaoshuang Li	CHN	9.618
3	Hong-Chul Yeo	KOR	9.600
4	Ivan Ivankov	BLR	9.481
5	Ok-Ryul Yoo	KOR	9.356
6	Masanori Suzuki	JPN	9.275
7	Murat Canbas	TUR	9.225
8	Grigori Misutin	UKR	9.187

Parallel Bars

Position	Name		
1	Liping Huang	CHN	9.775
2	Rustam Sharipov	UKR	9.612
3	Alexei Nemov	RUS	9.575
4	Evgeni Chabaev	RUS	9.550
4	Ivan Ivanov	BUL	9.550
6	Vitaly Scherbo	BLR	9.525
7	Jin-Soo Jung	KOR	9.487
8	Joo-Hyung Lee	KOR	9.450

High Bar

Position	Name		
1	Vitaly Scherbo	BLR	9.687
2	Zoltan Supola	HUN	9.537
3	Ivan Ivankov	BLR	9.500
4	Albert Umphery	USA	9.487
5	Csaba Fajkusz	HUN	9.450
6	Aijaz Pegan	SLO	9.275
7	Boris Preti	ITA	9.225
8	Jari Mokkonen	FIN	8.950

For the women the hold on the medals remained with the world's top all around girls. China took bars with Li Lou and Gina Gogean vault for Romania. The USA's Shannon Miller was superb on beam. With double straight and full twisting front step out Dina Kochetkova won floor for Russia. Russia had a World Champion.

Women's Results

Vault

Position	Name		
1	Gina Gogean	ROM	9.812
2	Svetlana Chorkina	RUS	9.800
3	Lavinia Milosovici	ROM	9.787
4	Titiana Lyssenko	UKR	9.737
5	Yelena Piskun	BLR	9.725
6	Dina Kochetkova	RUS	9.699
7	Shannon Miller	USA	9.543
8	Lilia Podkopayeva	UKR	9.424

Asymmetric Bars

Position	Name		
1	Lou Li	CHN	9.912
2	Svetlana Chorkina	RUS	9.875
3	Dina Kochetkova	RUS	9.850
4	Dominique Dawes	USA	9.775
5	Lilia Podkopayeva	UKR	9.350
6	Livinia Milosovici	ROM	9.250
7	Nadia Hategan	ROM	9.137
8	Amanda Borden	USA	9.050

Beam

Position	Name		
1	Shannon Miller	USA	9.875
2	Lilia Podkopaeva	UKR	9.737
3	Oxana Fabrichnova	RUS	9.712
4	Nadia Hategan	ROM	9.687
5	Lavinia Milosovici	ROM	9.675
6	Dominique Dawes	USA	9.650
7	Ya Qiao	CHN	9.212
8	Julia Stratmann	GER	8.650

Floor

Position	Name		
1	Dina Kochetkova	RUS	9.850
2	Lavinia Milosovici	ROM	9.837
3	Gina Gogean	ROM	9.762
4	Shannon Miller	USA	9.687
5	Yelena Piskun	BLR	9.675
6	Dominique Dawes	USA	9.662
7	Huilan Mo	CHN	9.462
8	Svetlana Chorkina	RUS	8.487

The Men's All Around World Championships, Brisbane, 1994

The drawing of lots for national places in each round is fair, the next step is to make the draw specific to an individual gymnast. The new computerised scoring system can keep the competition alive throughout the day and throughout each of the three subdivisions, but there is still the expectation that the scores will rise (or that at least the judges will save enough room to manoeuvre) and that the media hype is always for the last round. Everyone in the arena at 10 a.m. knew that they were watching Ivan Ivankov doing something very special, winning. Alas the world was not watching. There were a lot of lost bets on this Championships. Ivan's efforts included double layout on floor, the hollow bounding series and double pike to close on floor. Pommels with Magyar and spindles and 2 inverted crosses to ½ in and ½ out straight from rings maintained a high score line. Vault is one of his best events and he nailed a double twisting Yurchenko dead. Only one weak link lies in his parallel bars routine with double back in the bars to front uprise, but what else do you do from this flesh tearing trick! A Kovacs, neat but not amazing, and a straight Tkatchev make his high bar with a double double straight dismount an easy mid nine score. 57.012 in the early shift was very high but what followed was one of the most error full Championships that I have watched. Possibly the trauma of the apparatus qualifying round had taken its toll or possibly the need to shoot the rapids in bizarre combinations lead to the start stop drop performance that followed.

Vladimir Shamenko, UKR on floor tumbled well enough but with three times step turn into the corner showed the way that floor is going, tumble, tumble, tumble, balance, tumble. And I thought repetitive movements of no value were deductible? 9.225? Alexei Nemov, RUS, Kovacs to Gienger, nice but those naughty bent legs. Li Xiaoshuang, China, who had everything in high bar and nothing right, battled with the pommels and dropped to 10th place overall, well below his real ability. The Korean, Lee Joo Hyung, included in high bar a Kovacs, then a one arm Tkatchev to immediate Tkatchev. My favourite swing combination of the Championships came from Evgeni Chabaev of Russia, parallel bars, Healy to Healy to hop pirouette, what a beautiful swing time rhythm and line. Valeri Belenki had four great events, an unmemorable high bar and a forgetable vault which all but leapt off the podium. Yuri Chechi blew it on pommels as did Lee Joo Hyung and Korobchinski. The latter may be in the twilight of his career but what a great career it still is, two finals and 6th place over all. Alexei Voropaev was medal hunting. Another exciting Russian out of the white knuckle school, half in half out straight on floor, two Maltese crosses and half lever cross press out on rings and double twisting Tzukahara on vault. Parallel bars was a little stinted with flying back half in combination. But on high bar he gives it fair welly with Kovacs to hop twist in back giants, another Kovacs, double double dismount and then his banana crazy leaping around act which was given 9.587. Did he think it was better than that?

Vitaly Scherbo won it, lost it, won it, lost it dropped out of sight and then hit the floor just as everyone was packing their bags to go home and came up with 9.55 to be exalted from 11th to 3rd. His delight was what made the day. The greatest gymnast in the world was happy with 3rd place. He had lost five tenths in combination on rings with a missing strength hold. He dismounted parallel bars to double pike back slipping off the heel of his hand and rolling backwards. He had to be happy with bronze.

For Neil Thomas an incredible 16th place, Paul Bowler 36th and Marvin Campbell 40th. These men have brought British Gymnastics to its best ever result. What a pity the British press reported so little of it.

Results (top 10)

Position	Name	Country	Floor	Pommels	Rings	Vault	P. Bars	H. Bar	Total
1	Ivan Ivankov	BLR	9.450	9.562	9.525	9.500	9.525	9.450	57.012
2	Alexei Voropaev	RUS	9.487	9.450	9.525	9.500	9.375	9.587	56.924
3	Vitaly Scherbo	BLR	9.550	9.675	8.950	9.650	8.925	9.600	56.350
4	Valerei Belenki	GER	9.300	9.600	9.612	9.000	9.525	9.275	56.312
5	Evgeni Chabaev	RUS	9.375	9.275	9.350	9.375	9.550	9.350	56.275
6	Igor Korobchinski	UKR	9.450	9.505	9.200	9.300	9.512	9.300	55.812
7	Joo-Hyung Lee	KOR	9.325	8.800	9.050	9.650	9.400	9.575	55.800
8	Yuri Chechi	ITA	9.200	8.850	9.687	9.350	9.325	9.350	55.762
9	Zoltan Supola	HUN	8.775	9.462	9.350	9.375	9.350	9.350	55.662
10	Xiaonoshuang Li	CHN	9.450	8.775	9.475	9.650	9.350	8.950	55.650

The Women's All Around World Championships, Brisbane, 1994

What a pity that Dominique Dawes has not made her weakness her strength. Vault. She might well have spent the last year working hard with it but she is three tenths adrift of the leader when it counts. Those three tenths (9.506 against Miller's and Milosovici's 9.812) would have given her silver. Some of her acrobatic shapes are none too classic but she has an attraction and a distinctive style which is good to see. Her centre piece in floor, whip whip through to double twist punch front step out round-off round-off flic to 2½ twisting back is a crowd winner and a bonus picker upper. Svetlana Chorkina, RUS, has also a distinctive style. Using a one leg 'gainer' action she lifts straight back full twisting back and double twist dismount from beam really well. We saw in Geneva last year that her ability to pick up landings was suspect and since then she has improved well enough to be an excellent all around gymnast.

Alena Polozkova, BLR, has the highest of flight instincts. Her vaults and her Gienger on bars are dreams of techniques. Hulian Mo of China nearly got it all right, 9.9 bars and 9.612 at beam which started with a one arm handstand lowered down to one arm straddle half lever and a shoulder roll gripped with one arm, a unique combination. Unlucky I thought to not be in the medals but possibly a little jagged on floor. But certainly no less jagged than Nadia Hatagan who with 9.675 paid no attention to the music at all.

Dina Kotchetkova was in the mood to succeed. Russian to the core, a full twisting back flip on beam that was total perfection. Lavinia (have a rest in the corner dear) Milosovici of Romania has everything she needs to be World Champion, but she does not sparkle. I always feel that if she gave it a bit more bubble then she would beat everyone in sight. And she has worked on her weaknesses, that Gienger can now keep the feet together and is only one of 5 women with all her events with 10 value starts. The deviousness of the code, however, makes 23 women start with 10 on floor, 18 of those in the top twenty. There are too many bonus links from odd skills on floor and I think that we have lost some of the class on floor as a result.

Kotchetkova made a strong second half to her day with 9.75 on floor for double straight, handspring full twisting front to punch front, handspring full twisting front to straight front (see what I mean about the code) and full in back out. Her 9.812 for handspring front piked half at vault was enough to keep Gogean and Dawes at bay.

Shannon Miller was much more awake in the all around than she had been in the preliminaries. A safe vault start, Yurchenko half off straight front, for 9.812 and a brighter bars with less leg faults, a good Gienger and Tkatchev, but possibly that slack shape at the knee in the dismount. No matter what Steve Nunno seems to be telling her about setting up the dismount she nods her head in agreement and then throws her head back and belly through. But it is a double straight and spots. At beam she really does look to be in the class league. Solid, choreographed and full of difficulty. Flip quarter turn, the Miller, flip layout, layout and full in back out tucked. The score board was the only way of splitting Milosovici and Miller. In the last round it was Milosovici on beam and Miller on vault. Anything could happen. Lavinia bobbed after her usual solid side somersault, Shannon stepped off her first vault and even more on her second. Lavinia, a flip quarter turn to drop into handstand and double pike back dismount, 9.775. Over scored? Maybe not. Miller 9.812, over scored? Maybe so. But the best contest for a women's overall that we had seen for a long time. The 1994 World Champion is Shannon Miller of the USA.

For Karin Symko, 38th place with 36.142. She did very well to come back from her fall on vault. 44th for Annika with 36.806 with a lot still to come from her great talent. For Zeta, with an 8.050 on beam she still made 35.518 for 47th place. Had beam been held she would have been in the top 30 places. But then the world is made of 'ifs'. Qualifying for the Dortmund World's through the team Europeans is now the target.

Results (top 10)

Position	Name	Country	Vault	A.Bars	Beam	Floor	Total
1	Shannon Miller	USA	9.812	9.850	9.862	9.750	39.274
2	Lavinia Milosovici	ROM	9.812	9.775	9.837	9.812	39.236
3	Dina Kochetkova	RUS	9.725	9.825	9.775	9.800	39.125
4	Gina Gogean	ROM	9.737	9.775	9.762	9.787	39.061
5	Dominique Dawes	USA	9.506	9.850	9.812	9.800	38.968
6	Lilia Podkopayeva	UKR	9.718	9.612	9.837	9.775	38.942
7	Hulian Mo	CHN	9.687	9.900	9.612	9.725	38.924
8	Nadia Hategan	ROM	9.699	9.700	9.762	9.675	38.836
9	Svetlana Chorkina	RUS	9.693	9.825	9.612	9.675	38.805
10	Yelena Piskun	BLR	9.693	9.662	9.762	9.650	38.767

Men's and Women's World Team Championships, Dortmund, 1994

The winter of 1994 saw the year's second World Championships, this time a team event only. But there was to be a qualifying competition to find the top 6 teams for the actual final placings.

The Men

Germany led after the set exercises, then dropped to second after the first round of voluntary routines. Russia, 4th after sets climbed to the top of the qualifying rounds after superb voluntary exercises. China jumped from a nail biting 6th after sets to qualify in 3rd place. So, Russia, Germany, China, Ukraine, Belarus and Japan went through for a gymnastics match as complex as a chess game.

The Women

There were few surprises in the women's competition giving qualifying team places to Romania, USA, China, Russia, Ukraine and Belarus. The score drop between Russia in 4th on 385.515 points and 7th non qualifiers France on 370.017 was enormous and shows the immense differences in team ability and personal skill in what has become a very difficult sport to perform.

The Men's Team Finals

Two competitions and two changes of lead so far. This was to be an even score start and the stadium was packed. German Federation optimism of a place in the top six could not be contained by the fanatical audience who saw no reason why their team should not be number one at least. By the end of the first round they had a few good reasons why not. Mario Franke and Andreas Wecker were both pommels. Ukraine's Stepanchenko went down on Yurchenko 1½ twist, but Grigori Mitsutin brought the first madness to the day with handspring double front on vault. What a corker. Yoshiaki Hatakeda of Japan had a high bar more in flight than on the bar: Stalder out to Tkatchev, Tkatchev to Tkatchev, stoop in and out to Gienger roll and triple off. The Russian floor exercises were unbeatable. They were on a roll with Alexei Voropaev nailing double straight full twist so easily. At the end of round one it was Russia, China, Germany, Ukraine, Belarus and then Japan.

Russian resolve cracked a little at pommel with Dimitri Karbonenko almost losing his triple wende swing. I think he said something when he walked off, in Russian of course. Hikaru Maeda of Japan on floor, an interesting Arab spring piked roll out. Vitaly Scherbo on bar with a massive hand adjustment bent the metal like no other can with one arm combinations into Gienger somersault. He still looks good. At the end of round two Chinese vault, so long a weakness, had lifted them to 1st place, next Russia, Germany hanging in third and then Belarus, Ukraine and Japan.

It was to be a Russia-China conflict. The gap was opening between them and the rest of the world. Germany on parallel bars had an uninspiring time. The Russian vaulters were excellent again with good team variety. Alexei Nemov used Yurchenko half turn to piked front off. Chinese high bar was fantastic. Linyao Guo, Tkatchev to Gienger, double double straight dismount. Xiaoshuang Li, hop pirouette to one arm Tkatchev and another one arm Tkatchev and double double dismount. Liping Huang twice a one arm Tkatchev and double straight full twist dismount. Now it was Russia 1st, China, Belarus, Ukraine, Germany and Japan.

The Chinese floor has much improved in mid body tension and certain landings along with Russian bodges at parallel bars made for an interesting change. Now China 1st, Russia 2nd, Ukraine, Belarus, Germany (with three triples from bar and two double doubles) then Japan. With this round 5 I think that we lost a lot of the excitement atmosphere as German television went live. Television went live and the competition went dead. For the benefit of those sitting at home with a Deutschmark's worth of licence, those sitting in the stadium with a 60 Deutschmark ticket had to wait until each exercise, slow motion replay and score had been broadcast before the next routine could begin. After 20 minutes they dropped waiting for the scores to ensure that the event would finish before Atlanta.

In the final round the German team that so recently beat the Ukraine looked ordinary on floor. Maybe they were over hyped or maybe they were just doing their best. But they beat Japan into 6th place and Wecker was hero worshipped for the hero that he is. Ukraine held off Belarus even with Scherbo and Ivankov vaulting at their best. Russia, already ruffled at parallel bars, let the high bar go. Their best event! Karbonenko cut a section out, Troush made Gaylord on to the floor and Voropaev made Kovacs twice to the floor. He would have had a third shot but he could only see five of the ten fingers the Arkaev was holding up. Leonid, a wise man, said no more. He must have known in his heart of hearts that it was all over. As China completed their demonstration of pommel horse technique the new order was clear. Linyao Guo worked four stoklis on each handle in a full Magyar and Dashuang Li Flair spindles above one handle. But from Huadong Haung, not 'simply' but 'complexly' the best, Magyar with four stoklis on each handle, Flairs to handstand pirouettes down to Flair spindles and forward march again along the horse. Applaud these men, their like on a horse has never been equalled. The new World Champions pounded high fives as they marched past Li Ning to take their title, Champions of the World. For Russia silver and for the Ukraine bronze. The only Marxist country in the finals at the top. I wonder. I lied, I stop wondering.

Results

Position	Country		Floor	Pommels	Rings	Vault	P. Bars	H. Bar	Total
1	China	Total	46.837	48.149	46.537	47.598	47.100	47.112	283.333
2	Russia	Total	47.250	46.925	46.849	48.136	45.812	47.186	282.158
3	Ukraine	Total	47.462	47.012	47.050	46.812	46.625	46.125	281.086
4	Belarus	Total	46.537	47.275	46.712	47.187	46.612	46.650	280.973
5	Germany	Total	46.537	45.700	47.795	46.475	46.425	47.049	280.161
6	Japan	Total	45.825	46.800	46.325	46.612	46.462	46.675	278.699

The Women's Team Finals

With six teams working and only four in a round the picture was bound to be fuzzy until at least half way through when the teams had all completed two pieces of apparatus.

Oxana Fabrichnova made super tumbling in a 'custy wootsy' 'Can Can' floor exercise with full in back out piked and layout front full twist to punch front. Chorkina's triple twist was complete and sailed to the floor: just perfect. Elena Grosheva used a blues piano which gave way to rock very effectively choreographed. Svetlana Tarasevich dismounted beam double front to stick. The US battle of the bars was very efficient and they topped the leader board before Romania marched in.

It was a nice touch to see the team members of each country take a turn at carrying their own flag to a real swaggering yabadabadaba, zoog zoog zoog tune that took quite a hold once the shock had passed. Romania and China joined the competition, Russia and USA went off for a quick sandwich and a training session. The teams marched very nicely out of the arena but I bet they didn't half run to the training hall once they were out of the tunnel. Better than Harrod's sale.

It was Romania's privilege to start on vault and they were making no mistakes. From China a line on beam that was evangelical for the cause of gymnastics. From Linlin Ye a reverse one and a quarter spin, not so easy. Olga Yurkina danced to Strauss, also not easy to choreograph or to pull off convincingly, waltz and polka time is very demanding. With round three Russia, Romania, the USA and China were in it together at last and the pace was hotting up. Russia dumped two vaults whilst the Romanian bars went through and through and through, but just short of the USA total for this apparatus. At the half way stage it was Romania by less than three tenths, Russia, USA, China, Ukraine and Belarus.

Round 4 was kick started by Dominique Dawes on floor, with double twist punch front step out and return tumble of back half punch front. Yelena Piskun jumped double twisting Yurchenko on vault and Eugenia Rochina closed Russia's challenge dropping her Marinitch to the ground. China, Russia and the USA were a tenth or so apart, Romania was climbing away. In round 5 Julia Yurkina was kick started with a Mercer cowboyed to her shoulder blades which would not rotate. She bounced very nicely. Yelena Shapornaya was choreographed to Bolero, spliced together with a dead chewy wrapper. Oksana Knizhnik had a church organ Phantom theme which gave way to a cello ghost. Christmas came early for Claudia Predescan, 9.8 on beam. Flic straight back feet glued together she was all but off! What's Romanian for 'the shoe is on the other foot now'?

Results

Position	Country		Vault	A.Bars	Beam	Floor	Total
1	Romania	Total	49.050	48.374	49.049	49.374	195.847
2	USA	Total	48.861	48.512	48.461	48.811	194.645
3	Russia	Total	48.674	48.925	48.561	48.386	195.546
4	China	Total	48.261	48.924	48.099	48.848	194.132
5	Ukraine	Total	47.974	48.087	47.899	47.774	191.734
6	Belarus	Total	47.561	47.212	46.286	47.962	189.021

Men's and Women's World Championships, Sabae, 1995

For the last time setwork was to be used to complete a World Championships. For many gymnastics buffs this was to be the last real World Championships, the complete format, IA, IB, II and III. In the men's competition the shock result was the poor showing of Russia in the set exercises leaving them an impossible job to climb into the team medals. The Romanian men, possibly in their last 'old guard stand' were superb, 3rd in competition IA and a fantastic showing in IB gave them a surprise and well deserved team bronze. The new young Japanese team were amazing, very modern and exciting to watch, their team silver was no fluke and returned Japan to the position they held in gymnastics many years ago, at the top. Where Russia had dropped on the sets, Ukraine dropped on the voluntary routines. With Belarus just short of a full team of stable performers, 4th, 5th and 6th for Russia, Ukraine and Belarus was the greatest upset of the Championships.

With the women's competition came the head to head, Romania verses USA. Strangely Russia simply lacked a 'superstar' to turn on the judges and never looked like threatening for gold. Their eventual 4th was a shock. The USA, so close to Romania in the sets, could not take the heat in the voluntary competition and watched as China sailed past them for silver. For Romania and for Octavian Belu The World Title, no team worked harder for it.

Not only in Japan did we see many new nations but we also saw the start of the ex-Eastern European block exodus making its mark. Germany had already absorbed its Eastern half and many Soviet names were spread across the globe.

Men's Team Results

Position	Country		Floor	Pommels	Rings	Vault	P. Bars	H. Bar	Total
1	China	Total IA	46.575	47.100	46.712	46.800	47.462	47.399	
		Total IB	46.775	47.874	46.862	47.237	47.912	47.911	566.619
2	Japan	Total IA	47.087	46.475	46.675	47.225	46.712	47.886	
		Total IB	46.000	47.462	47.062	46.425	47.662	46.887	563.558
3	Romania	Total IA	46.775	46.475	46.125	47.075	46.100	47.424	
		Total IB	47.062	47.687	46.612	46.700	46.725	47.187	561.947
4	Russia	Total IA	46.400	45.600	45.850	47.362	46.150	45.175	
		Total IB	47.749	47.900	46.762	47.474	47.712	46.837	560.971
5	Ukraine	Total IA	46.812	45.550	46.200	47.350	46.325	47.037	
		Total IB	46.612	46.800	46.937	46.550	47.737	47.024	560.934
6	Belarussia	Total IA	45.975	45.825	46.075	47.362	46.437	46.387	
		Total IB	47.137	46.712	46.637	46.787	47.674	47.150	560.158

Women's Team Results

Position	Country		Vault	A.Bars	Beam	Floor	Total
1	Romania	Total IA	48.199	48.048	47.374	48.949	
		Total IB	48.323	49.174	48.649	49.149	387.865
2	China	Total IA	46.673	47.649	48.224	48.273	
		Total IB	49.023	49.023	48.874	48.737	386.476
3	USA	Total IA	47.450	48.462	47.612	48.198	
		Total IB	47.985	48.525	48.336	48.137	384.705
4	Russia	Total IA	47.624	48.087	47.561	48.136	
		Total IB	48.149	48.998	48.098	48.036	384.689
5	Ukraine	Total IA	47.261	46.824	46.636	48.312	
		Total IB	47.449	48.762	48.236	48.524	382.004
6	France	Total IA	46.361	46.512	46.586	48.024	
		Total IB	46.698	48.299	47.712	48.011	378.203

The Men's All Around World Championships, Sabae, 1995

Li Xiaoshuang set a standard that was hard to beat. Perhaps if Alexei Nemov had made the finals it would added a bit of spice but really Vitaly Scherbo was only able to snap at Li's heels all the way around. Chabaev and Voropaev scrapped with Belenki for bronze. Dimitri Karbonenko dropped pommels yet again and Yuri Chechi was fitting into 7th place by virtue of a mighty rings. There were a lot of falls in total: the search for a combination bonus and an upgrading demands risk taking.

Results (top 10)

Position	Name	Frederation	Floor	Pommels	Rings	Vault	P. Bars	H. Bar	Total
1	Xaioshuang Li	CHN	9.612	9.700	9.662	9.675	9.712	9.637	57.998
2	Vitaly Scherbo	BLR	9.650	9.500	9.375	9.562	9.700	9.712	57.499
3	Evgeni Chabaev	RUS	9.562	9.600	9.437	9.425	9.587	9.637	57.248
4	Alexei Voropaev	RUS	9.487	9.425	9.625	9.625	9.550	9.500	57.212
5	Valeri Belenki	GER	9.487	9.612	9.587	9.562	9.600	9.350	57.198
6	Yoshiaki Hatakeda	JPN	9.537	9.675	9.375	9.100	9.662	9.650	56.999
7	Yuri Chechi	ITA	9.250	9.450	9.837	9.100	9.587	9.637	56.861
8	Jinjing Zhang	CHN	9.425	9.125	9.425	9.587	9.650	9.587	56.799
9	Yoon-Soo Han	KOR	9.125	9.612	9.425	9.325	9.625	9.650	56.762
10	Andreas Wecker	GER	9.150	9.450	9.675	9.225	9.450	9.662	56.612

The Women's All Around World Championships, Sabae, 1995

Mighty Mo, no go. First round, beam. A pencil line straight back to two feet, so good but the double tuck dismount had enough for three somersaults and it was roly poly 9.312. Say no Mo! Sad. Lilia Podkopayeva is the technical wizard on bars with two hop pirouettes from back giants into immediate Gienger. With half in half out and 9.812 she was already on her way. Another good bars came from Anna Mirogorodskaia of the Ukraine, 2 Steineman giants to Tkatchev (back straddle style) 9.712, by far her best routine. France, Spain and Greece had three finalists with even Brazil taking 36.292 out of the competition.

The USA tried very hard, Moceanu was not as sharp as in the team event and Miller was not so sharp at all but still showed an amazing quality that eludes so many others of her class. Svetlana Boginskaya was enjoying herself and lent credibility to the theory of second life gymnastics. Still a world beater and now a real character with a personality that shines through.

Podkopayeva kept up the pressure by hitting again and again. Handspring double front half out to open on floor fitted like the last piece of jigsaw into that awkward corner. Podkopayeva, Chorkina, Milosovici and Amanar could each have taken the honours with the last routine and here was the recipe for the best showdown since the OK Corral. Simona Amanar and Milosovici had beam to finish on. Simona with 9.637 was just short. Chorkina hit bars for 39.130, Podkopayeva stuck Yurchenko half to piked front half off for 9.799 and it was all down to Milosovici to do the business. The last competitor of the finals up on beam, the overall title that she wanted so badly ... 9.737. No uneasy wait these days as the computer show in a fraction of a second the Milosovici is 0.188 short of the overall World Title. Lilia Podkopayeva is the 1995 Champion of the World.

Results (top 10)

Position	Name	Frederation	Vault	A.Bars	Beam	Floor	Total
1	Lilia Podkopayeva	UKR	9.799	9.812	9.787	9.850	39.248
2	Svetlana Chorkina	RUS	9.756	9.912	9.775	9.687	39.130
3	Lavinia Milosovici	ROM	9.662	9.862	9.737	9.825	39.086
4	Simona Amanar	ROM	9.862	9.775	9.637	9.775	39.049
5	Dominique Moceanu	USA	9.737	9.800	9.637	9.712	38.886
6	Hulian Mo	CHN	9.818	9.862	9.312	9.762	38.754
7	Kerri Strug	USA	9.600	9.762	9.612	9.775	38.749
8	Dina Kochetkova	RUS	9.449	9.775	9.750	9.712	38.686
9	Yanling Mao	CHN	9.306	9.787	9.812	9.725	38.630
10	Yelena Piskun	BLR	9.656	9.825	9.262	9.787	38.530

The Men's Apparatus Finals, Sabae, 1995

Men's floor came and went without Neil Thomas, not the same really is it. Eugeni Podgorni of Russia made the only triple tuck of the Games but touched down. The excitement in the men's floor was all but over as the double straight and bounding hollow front sequences are not so easy to separate. Li Xiaoshuang made the best of the double straights with with a lot of energy in the rotations.

Pommel horse was all Chinese. Even the Swiss was Chinese as Li Donghua took the gold back to Toblerone land. Màrius Urzica was left out in 4th place, Eric Poujade in 7th, the best pommel horse workers in the world without a medal. Rings was an interesting matter of tastes and styles. Dan Burnica a little more accurate in the strength holds and a little less free in the swings. Yuri Chechi more positive in the holds and a millimetre more accurate in the landing. Chechi has the reputation and the eye of the judges and I am inclined to agree this time, gold for Yuri.

Vault this time did not reward the monster vaults of Grigori Mitsutin. How could handspring double front and handspring hollow front Rudi out be compared to Yurchenko ½ on piked Birani out and Yurchenko straight. But it was compared and found to be equal and so Mitsutin had to share with Nemov. At parallel bars Huang made double back tucked in the bars and then double back piked in the bars for 9.750, but it was the sure fire attack of Vitaly Scherbo that netted the gold with so little cause for deduction in a high start value routine. And to the high bar, a thousand curses from Dimitri Karbonenko, with legs that long it's odds on the he will hit something when he straddles in the Stalder, the upright in Birmingham and the crossbar in Sabae. At least it was the other leg this time, Krasimir Dounev of Bulgaria, 6 consecutive releases for 9.75, it's a hard life. Wecker made Kovacs to giants Kovacs to giants, Tkatchev to giant, 9.812. Good according to the code but not historic. But no one in Germany reads history books so it was Wecker World Champion T-shirt time by the soonest commercial break on DSF TV. A gold rush indeed at 26 Deutschmarks each.

Results

Floor

Position	Name		
1	Vitaly Scherbo	BLR	9.812
2	Xaioshuang Li	CHN	9.775
2	Grigori Misutin	UKR	9.762
4	Ivan Ivankov	BLR	9.662
5	Ivan Ivanov	BUL	9.625
6	Jardan Jovtchev	BUL	9.575
7	Alexei Nemov	RUS	9.500
8	Evgeni Podgorni	RUS	9.400

Pommels

Position	Name		
1	Donghua Li	SUI	9.762
2	Huadong Huang	CHN	9.737
2	Yoshiaki Hatakeda	JPN	9.737
4	Marius Urzica	ROM	9.725
5	Hiraka Tanaka	JPN	9.650
5	Mihai Bagiu	USA	9.650
7	Eric Poujade	FRA	9.575
8	Bin Fan	CHN	9.125

Rings

Position	Name		
1	Yuri Chechi	ITA	9.850
2	Dan Burinca	ROM	9.762
3	Jordan Jovtchev	BUL	9.750
4	Marius Toba	GER	9.700
5	Andreas Wecker	GER	9.687
6	Xiaoshuang Li	CHN	9.650
7	Hikaru Tanaka	JPN	9.562
8	John Roethlisberger	USA	9.550

Vault

Position	Name		
1	Alexei Nemov	RUS	9.756
1	Grigori Misutin	UKR	9.756
3	Vitaly Scherbo	BLR	9.662
4	Alexei Voropaev	RUS	9.637
5	Cristian Leric	ROM	9.606
6	Hong-Chul Yeo	KOR	9.550
7	Xiaoshuang Li	CHN	9.412
8	Adrian Ianculescu	ROM	9.312

Parallel Bars

Position	Name		
1	Vitaly Scherbo	BLR	9.525
2	Liping Huang	CHN	9.750
3	Hikaru Tanaka	JPN	9.725
4	Rustam Sharipov	UKR	9.700
5	Ivan Ivankov	BLR	9.687
6	Xaioshuang Li	CHN	9.675
7	Yoshiaki Hatakeda	JPN	9.600
8	Jin-Soo Jung	KOR	7.850

High Bar

Position	Name		
1	Andreas Wecker	GER	9.812
2	Yoshiaki Hatakeda	JPN	9.775
3	Krasimir Dounev	BUL	9.750
3	Jinjing Zhang	CHN	9.750
5	Vitaly Scherbo	BLR	9.725
6	Nistor Sandro	ROM	9.687
7	Boris Preti	ITA	9.650
8	Dimitri Karbonenko	RUS	8.925

The Women's Apparatus Finals, Sabae, 1995

Chorkina had already attracted attention in the warm up by bouncing on her head and was heartily cheered on to make two spots on vault for 9.618. Fei Meng of China was ruled out of order with a piked Tzukahara for zero. Just how the set vault piked can be done almost straight and still be piked and a straight Tzukahara be slightly piked and be the set vault escapes me for the moment. There is some asylogical thought at work here. When Grosheva did the same thing moments later her straight Tzukahara done with a pike was not the set vault and was awarded 9.293. Strange.

On bars Mo and Podkopayeva shared 9.837, Mo with a small step back. This apparatus more than any other has changed over the years and we must recognise with these two gymnasts the daring of Mo in contrast with the technical perfection of Podkopayeva. The missing ingredient came with Svetlana Chorkina, sheer artistry. An exercise designed and created for a particular talent. Each skill is built into the swing, Markelov, Korbut between the bars and back in full out dismount are all inside the swing. Other mortals tack their skills together with swing. Morceanu at last came up with the goods on beam. Three shoulder rolls, flip to three layout backs, front somersault and dismount to double tuck, 9.837. Lilia Podkopayeva was faultless, 9.837 again. Bela Korolyi was wetting himself with excitement. Only Mo left and probably her last realistic chance of a title. Round-off straight back down the timber and round-off flip (two feet) double tuck off were just part of a perfect exhibition, 9.9. Mo took the gold and Bela Korolyi carried on wetting himself.

Floor would have been Lilia Podkopayeva's but that double front half went right out of the area. Mo was slick but over bounced her tumbles with extra steps: double layout, whip to 2½ twisting back somersault, full twisting front to punch front and full in back out tucked. Moceanu left Bela Korolyi to mop up with full twisting front to punch hollow front, then 2½ twist out of the area for 9.087. Ludivide Furnon came in as a reserve to replace Miller and ended up with bronze for a nice little routine with double straight and choreography that worked with the 'Hall of the Mountain King'. Ji Liya from China did some serious tumbling and full in double straight but a stepped landing was deadly, 9.675. Gina Gogean knew what to do. Tumble here, tumble there, wave an arm here flap an arm there and finish at the same time as the background noise, 9.825. Live by the rules, win by the rules. Romania and Octovian Belu had a fantastic Games, only Milosovici worries me, will she take that elusive title one day?

Women's Results

Vault

Position	Name		
1	Simona Amanar	ROM	9.781
2	Lilia Podkopayeva	UKR	9.871
3	Gina Gogean	ROM	9.706
4	Huilan Mo	CHN	9.643
5	Svetlana Chorkina	RUS	9.618
6	Oxana Chousovitina	UZB	9.612
7	Elena Grosheva	RUS	9.293
8	Meng Fei	CHN	4.831

Asymmetric bars

Position	Name		
1	Svetlana Chorkina	RUS	9.900
2	Huilan Mo	CHN	9.837
3	Lilia Podkopayeva	UKR	9.837
4	Alexandra Marinescu	ROM	9.800
5	Lavinia Milosovici	ROM	9.775
6	Dina Kochetkova	RUS	9.737
7	Shannon Miller	USA	9.712
8	Jaycie Phelps	USA	9.687

Beam

Position	Name		
1	Huilan Mo	CHN	9.900
2	Lilia Pokopaeva	UKR	9.837
2	Dominique Moceanu	USA	9.837
4	Alexandra Marinescu	ROM	9.737
4	Shannon Miller	USA	9.737
6	Dina Kochetkova	RUS	9.725
7	Ya Qiao	CHN	9.625
8	Elena Grosheva	RUS	9.562

Floor

Position	Name		
1	Gina Gogean	ROM	9.825
2	Lavinia Milosovici	ROM	9.837
3	Ludivine Furnon	FRA	9.625
4	Huilan Mo	CHN	9.600
5	Joana Juarez	ESP	9.462
6	Simona Amanar	ROM	9.437
7	Dominique Moceanu	USA	9.087
7	Lilia Podkopaeva	UKR	9.087

World Apparatus Championships, Peurto Rico, 1996

At the Apparatus World Championships held in Puerto Rico there were as many gymnasts not attending as were attending. In the same year as a European Championships and an Olympic Games it was hard, tiring and expensive. The greatest result of the competition came from Yuri Chechi, a record 4th World Title on rings, a feat which may never be bettered. By this time the F.I.G. had already reconsidered its programme of world events and a return to less crowded schedule was inevitable.

For the women Gina Gogean took two golds for Romania and Kotchtkova and Chorkina took beam and bars for Russia. The men's titles were spread across the world much more the way that the F.I.G. had hoped for, Belarus, Korea, Italy, Russia, Ukraine and Spain, the latter on high bar with Jesus Carballo who risked new elements to win all.

With this World Championships the merry-go-round stopped and the Gymnastics Federations of the world sighed with relief. The public, the media and the gymnasts were quite disappointed.

Men's Results

Floor

Position	Name		
1	Vitaly Scherbo	BLR	9.787
2	Alexei Voropaev	RUS	9.700
3	Grigori Misutin	UKR	9.625
4	Sergei Fedorchenko	KAZ	9.562
5	Ivan Ivanov	BUL	9.550
6	Thierry Aymes	FRA	9.525
7	Ivan Ivankov	BLR	9.450
8	Eugeni Podgorni	RUS	9.125

Pommels

Position	Name		
1	Gil Su Pae	PRK	9.825
2	Donghua Li	SUI	9.812
3	Alexei Nemov	RUS	9.787
4	Hyon Kim	PRK	9.762
5	Patrice Casimir	FRA	9.725
6	Eric Poujade	FRA	9.700
7	Ivan Ivankov	BLR	9.650
8	Grigori Misutin	UKR	8.200

Rings

Position	Name		
1	Yuri Chechi	ITA	9.825
2	Jordan Jovtchev	BUL	9.737
2	Szilveszter Csollany	HUN	9.737
4	Dan Burinca	ROM	9.712
5	Ivan Ivankov	BLR	9.675
5	Damian Merino	CUB	9.675
7	Chris Lamorte	USA	9.537
7	Alexei Voropaev	RUS	9.537

Vault

Position	Name		
1	Alexei Nemov	RUS	9.756
2	Hong-Chul Yeo	KOR	9.743
2	Andrea Massucchi	ITA	9.743
4	Sergei Fedorchenko	KAZ	9.643
4	Vitaly Scherbo	BLR	9.643
6	Dieter Rehm	SUI	9.556
7	Valeri Belenki	GER	9.437
8	Alexei Voropaev	RUS	9.637
9	Zoltan Supola	HUN	9.400

Parallel Bars

Position	Name		
1	Rustam Sharipov	UKR	9.750
2	Vitaly Scherbo	BLR	9.737
2	Alexei Nemov	RUS	9.737
4	Ivan Ivankov	BLR	9.725
4	Jin-Soo Jung	KOR	9.725
6	Ivan Ivanov	BUL	9.650
7	Gil Su Pae	PRK	9.625
8	Valeri Belenki	GER	9.587

High Bar

Position	Name		
1	Jesus Carballo	ESP	9.800
2	Krasimir Dounev	BUL	9.775
3	Vitaly Scherbo	BLR	9.762
4	Aijaz Pegan	SLO	9.750
5	Chainey Umphrey	USA	9.712
6	Sergei Fedorchenko	KAZ	9.475
7	Zoltan Supola	HUN	9.375
8	Richard Ikeda	CAN	8.075

Women's Results

Vault

Position	Name		
1	Gina Gogean	ROM	9.800
2	Simona Amanar	ROM	9.787
3	Annia Portuondo	CUB	9.756
4	Elizabeth Valle	ESP	9.668
5	Svetlana Chorkina	RUS	9.637
6	Joana Juarez	ESP	9.537
7	Vasiliki Tsavdaridou	GRE	9.518
8	Yureisis Bermudes	CUB	9.456

Asymmetric bars

Position	Name		
1	Svetlana Chorkina	RUS	9.787
1	Huilan Mo	CHN	9.837
3	Isabelle Severino	FRA	9.775
4	Elivre Teza	FRA	9.750
4	Lioubov Seremeta	UKR	9.750
6	Kathleen Stark	GER	9.725
6	Anna Migorodskaia	UKR	9.725
8	Jaycie Phelps	USA	9.712
9	Xuan Liu	CHN	9.700
10	Livinia Milosovici	ROM	9.687
11	Dominique Dawes	USA	8.787

Beam

Position	Name		
1	Dina Kochetkova	RUS	9.887
2	Alexandra Marinescu	ROM	9.812
3	Xuan Liu	CHN	9.800
3	Dominique Dawes	USA	9.800
5	Vaskiliki Tsavdaridou	GRE	9.675
6	Mercedes Pacheco	ESP	9.637
7	Jaycie Phelps	USA	9.187
8	Gina Gogean	ROM	9.075

Floor

Position	Name		
1	Gina Gogean	ROM	9.850
2	Yuanyuan Kui	CHN	9.850
3	Lioubov Sheremeta	UKR	9.800
3	Lavinia Milosovici	ROM	9.800
5	Gemma Paz	ESP	9.775
5	Vaskiliki Tsavdaridou	GRE	9.775
7	Ludivine Furnon	FRA	9.712
8	Rocaliya Galiyeva	RUS	9.637

Bibliography

Barrul, Raymond: Les étapes de la gymnastique au sol et aux agres en France et dans le Monde. Fédération Française de Gymnastique, Paris, 1984.

Frederick, A. B: Gymnastics: Then, now and what next? International Gymnast, 25, 1983, No. 9, pp. 61-63.

Frederick, A. B: Gymnastics: Then, now and what next? Uneven Parallel Bars. International Gymnast, 26, 1984, No. 1, pp. 82-84.

Frederick, A. B: Gymnastics: Then, now and what next? Balance beam. International Gymnast, 26, 1984, No. 2, pp. 55-57.

Frederick, A. B: Gymnastics: Then, now and what next? Pommel horse. International Gymnast, 26, 1984, No. 5, pp. 54-55.

Frederick, A. B: Gymnastics: Gymnastics: Then, now and what next? High bar. International Gymnast, 25, 1983, No. 10, pp. 61-63.

Fédération Internationale de Gymnastique (F.I.G.) Code of Points for Men and Women. Editions from World War II until 1993.

Gajdos, Anton: Préparation et entrainement à la gymnastique sportive. Amphora, Paris, 1983.

Gajdos, Anton and Jasek, Zdeno: Sportová gymnastika. História a súcasnost. Sport, Bratislava, 1988.

Gajdos, Anton and Göhler, Josef: Die Entwicklung der Turnübungen am Stufenbarren. Leistungsport, 1986, No. 4, pp. 23-26.

Gajdos, Anton and Göhler, Josef: Die Entwicklung der Turnkunst am Reck. Leistungsport, 1987, No. 5, pp. 46-50.

Gajdos, Anton: Development and Prognosis of Elite Routines. Technique (USA), No. 1, pp. 29-32.

Gajdos, Anton: Entwicklung der Schwierigkeit am Pauschenpferd bei den Weltmeisterschaften. Olympisches Turnen Aktuel, 1992, No. 6, pp. 19-22.

Gajdos, Anton: Entwicklung der Schwierigkeit am Pauschenpferd bei den WM. Olympisches Turnen Aktuell, 1993, No. 1, pp. 21-24.

Gajdos, Anton: Entwicklung und Prognose an den Ringen. Olympisches Turnen Aktuell, 1993, No. 6, p. 22.

Gajdos, Anton: Entwicklung und Prognose der Turnubungen am Boden. Turnen und Gymnastik in Osterreich, 1994, No. l, pp. 18-21.

Goddbody, John: The Illustrated History of Gymnastics. Hutchinson Publishing Group, London, 1982.

Göhler, Josef: Japanische Turnkunst. Wilhem Limpert Verlag, Frankfurt am main - Wien, 1962.

Göhler, Josef & Spieth Rudolf: Geschichte der Trungerate, p. 137, 1989, F.I.G.

Göhler, Josef & Spieth Rudolf: Geschichte der Trungerate. 1989, W. Germany

Göhler, Josef: Die Längsachsendrehung (LAD) Ein Kapitel der Turnkunst. Olympisches Turnen Aktuell, 1993, No. 2, p. 24.

Göhler, Josef: Der freie Flug am Reck. Olympisches Turnen Aktuell, 1994, No. 2, pp. 32-33.

Götze, Andreas and Zeume, Hans-Jürgen: Flic-flac. Sportverlag, Berlin, 1986.

Götze, Andreas, Uhr Jurgen: Mond Salto. Die grossen Erfinder. p. 292, 1994, Druckerei Verlag Steinmeier, Nordlingen.

Huguenin, Andre: 100 Years of the International Gymnastics Federation.1881-1981.

International Gymnast. Vol. 1 to Present Vol. (1997).

Jordanov, Dimo: Analiz na XXII. svetovne prvenstvo po gimnastika-muze. Budapesta 83. Voprosy na fiziceskata kultura, 1984, No. 1, pp. 20-30.

Kaneko, Akitomo: Exercises on parallel bars. Fumaido, Tokyo, 1970.

Kaneko, Akitomo: Exercises on pommel horse. Fumaido, Tokyo, 1970.

Kaneko, Akitomo: Exercises on rings. Fumaido, Tokyo, 1971.

Kaneko, Akitomo: Exercises on high bar. Fumaido, Tokyo, 1971.

Krsak, Pavol: Novoveké Olympiady, Sport, Bratislava, p. 446, 1979.

Krsak, Pavol: Novoveké Olympiady, Sport, Bratislava, p. 446, 1982.

Magakian, Arthur: La Gymnastique artistique et sportive contemporaine masculine et féminine. Chiron-Sports, Paris, 1978.

Pahncke, Wolfgang: Gerätturnen einst und jetzt. Sportverlag, Berlin, 1983.

Shaklin, Boris: Moja gimnastika.Fiskultura i sport, Moscow, 1973.

Titov, Yuri: Voschozdenije (Gimnastika na olimpijadach). Sovetskaja Rossija, Moscow, 1978.

Titov, Yuri: Zapiski presidenta. Sovetskaya Rossija, Moscow, 1983.